The Blood of Abel

The Blood of Abel

The Violent Plot in the Hebrew Bible

by

Mark McEntire

MERCER UNIVERSITY PRESS

1979   1999

TWENTY YEARS OF PUBLISHING EXCELLENCE

ISBN
0-86554-628-2 Hardback edition
0-86554-629-0 Paperback edition
MUP: H488//P183

© 1999 Mercer University Press
6316 Peake Road
Macon, Georgia 31210-3960

∞The paper used in this publication meets the minimum requirements of
American National Standard for Information Sciences—Permanence of Paper
for Printed Library Materials, ANSI Z39.48-1984.

Library of Congress Cataloging-in-Publication Data

McEntire, Mark Harold, 1960 —
The blood of Abel : violence in the Hebrew Bible / Mark McEntire.
p. 15x23 cm.
Includes bibliographical references and index.
ISBN 0-86554-628-2 (alk. paper).
ISBN 0086554-629-0 (pbk.: alk. paper)
1. Violence in the Bible. 2. Bible. O.T.—Theology. I. Title.
BS1199.V56M37   1999
221.8'3036—dc21
98033339
CIP

TABLE OF CONTENTS

To Marie

PREFACE

This book was originally conceived as the first of a two volume project. The first volume was to deal exclusively with what I see as the narrative framework of the Hebrew Bible, essentially what is in Part I. The second volume would have addressed the remainder of the Hebrew Bible, the predominantly poetic middle of the canon (Prophets, Psalms, and Wisdom). In various ways, I understand these latter portions of the Bible as a response to the narrative framework. For a number of reasons, the decision was made by myself and Mercer Press that the prophetic response needed to be addressed immediately in this volume. Part II therefore is my attempt, in limited format, to examine representative texts from the prophetic books that are frequently understood to offer an alternative vision of the world. Readers will discover that I do not concur with this evaluation of the prophetic material.

The narrative framework of the Hebrew Bible, the Primary History (Genesis-2 Kings) and the Secondary History (Ezra-2 Chronicles), tells the violent story of the people of Israel. Like Abel, the first wandering herdsman in the Bible, they are caught up in the drama of city and empire building and they suffer a violent end. Even their own advances in status are won only when they play the dangerous games of monarchy and sustained state-of-the-art warfare. Even the greatest of the prophetic visions are ultimately unable to escape the basic assumption that a peaceful space can only be carved out by violent means.

One last question persists. What about the Psalms and Wisdom material? The history of biblical theology attests that this material is the most difficult to fit into any scheme. The lack of cohesion within individual books like Psalms and Proverbs and the tension between books like Proverbs and Job make unified patterns and trajectories difficult to establish. Representative texts are difficult, if not impossible, to identify. In its final form, the present work examines the problem of violence as it develops in the narrative tradition of Israel and one particular response to this development, the prophetic one. Examination of the issue of violence in Psalms and the wisdom literature awaits considerable further thought and a separate treatment. My only defense is that not being prepared to fit the latter into the scheme of my work at this point puts me in better company than I deserve.

I would like to thank a number of people who have helped me along the way during the writing of this book. Most of the writing was done while I was on the faculty of the Mekane Yesus Theological Seminary in Addis Ababa, and later the Ethiopian Graduate School of Theology. The support, encouragement, and interaction of my colleagues in both institutions were always a stimulating source of energy. I would also like to thank my students who helped me to formulate the exegeses in this book by listening to, questioning, and challenging me when I presented some of them in various classes. A number of individuals helped along the way by acquiring research materials for me and reading parts of the manuscript. These include Paul McEntire, John Hiott, and Marie Hiott McEntire. I owe a great debt of gratitude to Marc Jolley of Mercer University Press for his patience and persistence in working with me and with this manuscript.

Mark McEntire
Raleigh, North Carolina
October 26, 1998

INTRODUCTION

During recent years, biblical scholarship has been moving along a variety of different vectors. Three of them are crucial to this study. First, because of our increasing awareness of the brutality of the world in which we live, tremendous attention has been given to the issue of violence in the Bible. Second, literary approaches are beginning to dominate the practice of biblical exegesis. Third, while biblical theology is still in a state of flux, one clearly discernible note within the discipline is the need to focus on texts and to allow them to determine the theological agenda. The confluence of these three movements, along with other factors, has led me to this present work. These three emphases will provide this study with: (A) a hermeneutic, critical reflection on the theme of violence; (B) a method, rhetorical criticism; and (C) a purpose, the production of text-centered biblical theology.

Violence in the Bible

Concern about the degree of violence in the Bible has existed for some time. It dates back at least to the Marcionite heresy of the fourth century C. E. This concern has intensified, however, during the past two or three decades. The work of René Girard has probably been the most potent force behind this new emphasis. He began applying his work to the Bible in *La Violence et la sacré*, which was published in 1972, followed by the English edition, *Violence and the Sacred*,[1] five years later. A brief explanation of Girard's system is in order here. His theory of violence begins with the observation that mimetic desire pervades human relations. Human beings live in a state of continual conflict and rivalry because they desire the same things.

This observation does not sound terribly innovative, except that Girard insists it is not the desirability of the object itself so much as the desire to imitate the other who has it which fuels mimetic rivalry. Rivalry eventually leads to violence, but such pervasive violence would

---

[1]René Girard, *Violence and the Sacred*, trans. Patrick Gregory (Baltimore: Johns Hopkins University Press, 1977).

completely disrupt the functioning of human societies. To establish a sense of order, societies must control such violence. They accomplish this through a mechanism of surrogate victimization. Parties in conflict agree upon a surrogate victim, the killing of which becomes the outlet for their violent energies. This is, for example, the mechanism operating behind the practice of sacrifice and it explains why sacrifice is such a common element of religion. The example of sacrifice reveals a key element of the victimage mechanism. In order to work it must be misunderstood. People believe they are offering sacrifices as gifts to a deity or to appease an angry spirit. The truth about the mechanism must be hidden in order to be effective. Girard's conclusions appear to fit the workings of human societies quite accurately, and his system has produced stunning hermeneutical results. He is on less certain ground when he extrapolates backward into the history of human culture to define a generative anthropology. Girard has proposed that the emergence of the victimage mechanism gave birth to the first human society. The killing of a surrogate victim produced order out of chaos and human culture was created. One need not accept his theory of origins, however, in order to use his system as an interpretive key to the behavior of human societies observed both in literature and in the real world.

One competing theory of human origins is offered by Walter Burkert. Burkert has also developed a generative anthropology based on collective violence. His conclusions are based largely on observations of ritual and myth in the literature of Ancient Greece. Burkert differs from Girard, however, in attributing the original organization of human culture to the practice of hunting rather than the need to deflect mimetic rivalry. Human beings initially joined together into societies for the purpose of cooperative hunting. Rituals, such as sacrifice, arose to order hunting behavior, to focus aggression on the object of the hunt, and to alleviate the guilt of killing.[2] Burkert's system has been less influential than Girard's in part because it is more dependent upon the correctness of its theory of origins.

Even if the first human society did not form around a collective victim in order to deflect mimetic rivalry, Girard's system still exposes

---

[2]See Walter Burkert, *Homo Necans: The Anthropology of Ancient Greek Sacrificial Ritual and Myth*, trans. Peter Bing (Berkeley: University of California Press, 1983) 1-40. See also the interpretation of Burkert's system by Burton Mack in "Introduction: Religion and Ritual," in *Violent Origins: Walter Burkert, René Girard, and Jonathan Z. Smith on Ritual Killing and Cultural Formation*, ed. Robert G. Hamerton-Kelly (Stanford: Stanford University Press, 1987) 24-32.

contemporary human behavior in a highly coherent manner. On the other hand, if the original human society did not form itself on the basis of collective hunting behavior, then Burkert's anthropology seems to lose much of its coherence. Among biblical interpreters, Girard has received a tremendous amount of attention because his explanation of human violence has provided a very effective hermeneutic. Burkert's explanation has not. Girard himself has given biblical interpreters an important starting point by applying his ideas extensively to biblical texts, while Burkert's focus remained on ancient Greek literature.

Girard, of course, is a literary critic and not a biblical scholar. A number of biblical scholars have built upon Girard's seminal work with their own related studies which are more strictly biblical.[3] This concern about violence, as it relates to the Hebrew Bible,[4] has been most strikingly expressed by Raymond Schwager:

---

[3]Most notable among these are Raymond Schwager, Robert Hamerton-Kelly, and James G. Williams. Schwager's *Brauchen Wir Einen Sündenbock?* was published in 1978 and appeared in English (1987) as *Must There Be Scapegoats?* Hamerton-Kelly has published a number of studies applying Girard's model of redemptive violence to the New Testament, including the recent *Sacred Violence: Paul's Hermeneutic of the Cross* (Minneapolis: Fortress, 1992). Williams published *The Bible, Violence, and the Sacred: Liberation from the Myth of Redemptive Violence* in 1991. In addition, Walter Wink has produced a trilogy (*Naming the Powers: The Language of Power in the New Testament*, 1984; *Unmasking the Powers: The Invisible Forces that Determine Human Existence*, 1986; and *Engaging the Powers: Discernment and Resistance in a World of Domination*, 1992 [all from Fortress]) which is not a direct application of Girard's work, but has a multitude of points of contact with it. Girard, himself, has followed his earlier work with *Des choses cachées depuis la foundation du monde* in 1978 (published in English as *Things Hidden Since the Foundation of the World* in 1987) and *Le Bouc émissaire* in 1982 (published in English as *The Scapegoat* in 1986).

[4]R. W. L. Moberly has argued effectively for the retention of the term "Old Testament" by Christian interpreters. See Moberly, *The Old Testament of the Old Testament: Patriarchal Narratives and Mosaic Yahwism* (Minneapolis: Fortress, 1992) 155-166. In the case of this study, however, the focus is upon the Hebrew scriptures as a self-contained narrative. Therefore, I have chosen to avoid the term "Old Testament" which emphasizes the relatedness of the Hebrew scriptures to the New Testament and, thus, their incompleteness. The theology I propose in these pages is also dependent upon the order of the books in the Hebrew Bible.

Approximately one thousand passages speak of Yahweh's blazing anger, of his punishment by death and destruction, and how like a consuming fire he passes judgement, takes revenge, and threatens annihilation. He manifests his might and glory through warfare and holds court like a wrathful avenger. No other topic is more often mentioned as God's bloody works. A theology of Old Testament revelation that does not specifically deal with this grave and somber fact misses from the very start one of the most central questions and thus will hardly find the right perspective for a profound understanding of the revelation event."[5]

This study will attempt to take Schwager's warning seriously. The problem of violence, particularly God's involvement in it, will always be the lens through which I will endeavor to bring the biblical text into focus.

Still others have raised this issue more in terms of the results of violence—pain, suffering, and death. For Walter Brueggemann, "The question of pain is the main question of Old Testament faith."[6] Brueggemann's recent proposals for Old Testament theology begin with the tension between "structure legitimation" and "the embrace of pain."[7] The message of the Old Testament moves between these two poles. At times it accepts, supports, and promotes the religious, political, and social establishment of ancient Israel. Fewer, but not less significant, passages cry out in pain and protest against this same establishment.[8] The question for Israel is on which side can God be found. There is a considerable body of interpretation which stresses the solidarity of God with the innocent victims of violence and oppression.[9] Whether this

---

[5]Raymond Schwager, *Must There Be Scapegoats: Violence and Redemption in the Bible*, trans. Maria L. Assad (New York: Harper & Row, 1987) 55.

[6]Walter Brueggemann, *Old Testament Theology: Essays on Structure, Theme, and Text* (Minneapolis: Fortress, 1992) 18.

[7]Ibid., 1-44.

[8]Ibid., 26.

[9]This is evident in Girard and his followers. See James G. Williams, *The Bible, Violence, and the Sacred Liberation from the Myth of Sanctioned Violence* (San Francisco: HarperCollins, 1991) 185-212. A separate stream is present within liberation theology. See Robert McAfee Brown, *Unexpected News: Reading the Bible with Third World Eyes* (Philadelphia: Westminster, 1984) 13. A significant convergence between these two lines of interpretation may be observed in the monographs on the book of Job by Girard (*Job: The Victim of His*

assertion holds up to exegetical scrutiny will be a significant question throughout this study.

For Tom Milazzo, "The moment of death always stands before us. That moment shapes our existence and colors our world."[10] This is true not only for contemporary human beings, but for the people of ancient Israel whose existence produced the Hebrew Bible.

The choice of texts for detailed exegesis in this study requires some explanation. One way of understanding the Hebrew Bible is to view it as the story of Israel.[11] As a story, it has a plot. A plot here is understood as a series of events which gives a story its shape. To put it in the simplest of terms, the plot of the Hebrew Bible is as follows: A people emerges from the larger human community, becomes enslaved, escapes to freedom, acquires land, becomes a nation, divides into two nations, is destroyed, and is partially reconstructed. This entire story is governed by an omnipotent God who has chosen this people. The plot of the Hebrew Bible, as it will be treated in this study, is slightly different because I will be following the order of the Hebrew canon, which ends with 2 Chronicles and the destruction of Judah. The Restoration, as recorded in the books of Ezra and Nehemiah, is thus subordinated from the main lines of the plot. Of course, following the story of Israel within the text of the Bible combines the two large blocks of historical material, namely the Pentateuch/Deuteronomistic History (or Primary History) and the Chronistic History.[12] The placement of these books within the Hebrew canon, however, argues for seeing these two blocks of historical

---

People, trans. Yvonne Freccero [Stanford: Stanford University Press, 1987]) and Gustavo Gutierrez (*On Job: God-Talk and the Suffering of the Innocent* [Maryknoll, N. Y.: Orbis, 1989]).

[10]G. Tom Milazzo, *The Protest and the Silence: Suffering, Death, and Biblical Theology* (Minneapolis: Fortress, 1992) 138.

[11]The use of this starting point entails no judgment, either positive or negative, of the Hebrew Bible as the "history" of Israel.

[12]David J. A. Clines has offered several provocative alternatives for understanding these two histories and their relationship to each other. His primary thesis is that the two histories offer competing views , one pessimistic (the Pentateuch/Deuteronomistic History) and one more optimistic (the Chronistic History). See *What Does Eve Do to Help? And Other Readerly Questions to the Old Testament* (Sheffield: JSOT Press, 1990) 85-105. While Clines's individual assessments of the two histories seems to the point, their existence within a single canon reshapes each of them. They may have very different viewpoints, but this does not preclude them complementing each other in the telling of the same story.

of material as complementary, rather than simply parallel or competing.

The texts I have chosen to read closely in Part I mark what I believe to be the most significant turns in the plot of the Hebrew Bible. The texts were not specifically chosen because they depict violent events, nevertheless this is no mere accident. That the plot of the Hebrew Bible pivots on acts of violence illustrates that violence is a central, if not the central, issue for the entire text. I will deal with the remainder of the biblical story briefly in a series of interludes. These will stand between the detailed exegeses of the texts which I have identified as significant turning points in the plot of this story. The observations within these interludes will be based not so much on close reading as on the broader literary developments of the biblical story.

Part II contains exegeses of three texts from the middle of the Hebrew Bible, the prophetic literature. The purpose of Part II is to test these prophetic ideas and images as a response to the violent plot portrayed in Part I. The texts in Part II are not chosen in a systematic way. They are simply representatives of the themes of compassion, restoration, and peace, three possible alternatives to a violent end.

A variety of explanations have been offered as to why violence so pervades the Hebrew Bible. Two of these require special mentioning. One places the blame on the inherent nature of human beings, while the other focuses on the belief in mythic conflict which permeated the ancient Near East. First, Terrence Fretheim has asserted that "force and violence are associated with God's work in the world, because, to a greater or lesser degree, they are characteristic of the means of those in and through whom the work is carried out."[13] There is a troubling sense of resignation in this statement. If God's work is accomplished through means we consider inconsistent with the character of God, then can we still consider it to be God's work? Fretheim's statement begs the question as to whether violence is such an essential element of human nature that human beings are incapable of living without it. Walter Wink has offered a resounding "no" to this question and has attempted to document a period of human existence when violence was absent, or at least rare.[14] Wink has also contrasted the worldview of Ancient

---

[13]Terrence Fretheim, *The Suffering of God: An Old Testament Perspective* (Minneapolis: Fortress, 1984) 76.

[14]Walter Wink, *Engaging the Powers: Discernment and Resistance in a World of Domination* (Minneapolis: Fortress, 1992) 33-43. Wink typically uses the term "Domination System" to describe a world characterized by violence. He has

Babylon with that of the New Testament. The former epitomizes the Domination System, while the latter offers a "Domination-free Order."[15] Unfortunately, Wink gives primary attention to the relationship between this Domination-free Order and the New Testament, and leaves the relationship between the ancient Near Eastern conflict myth and the Hebrew Bible in question.[16]

This leads to a second explanation for the prevalence of violence in the Hebrew Bible. Jon D. Levenson has presented a thorough analysis of the role played by the continuing existence of the forces of chaos in the Hebrew Bible and the portrayal of God's combat with these forces. In examining passages which speak of such conflict, Levenson points to "a necessary and generally overlooked tension in the underlying theology of these passages."[17] The contemporary world and the world of the Hebrew Bible are filled with evidence of the continuing survival of chaos and evil. The reality of these negative forces presented, and still presents a challenge to faith communities of both eras. The acknowledgment of continuing conflict in the biblical text amounts to a refusal to silence a realistic evaluation of human existence. For Levenson, "The cognitive pressure of faith and realism to fly apart from each other is, in every generation, so intense that the conjunction of the two in these texts continues to astound."[18] The texts examined in this study will not be about direct divine conflict, but the conflict between human beings, as agents of good and evil, follows similar principles.

---

argued that this Domination System arose in Mesopotamia sometime during the fourth millennium B. C. E. (p. 36).

[15]Ibid., 43-49.

[16]Ibid., 28, 90, 334. Wink's book does make some mention of this problem, but does not treat most of the major texts about divine conflict in the Hebrew Bible. It does make reference to the way in which Yahweh's battle with Marduk in Psalm 74 casts Yahweh in the role of Marduk, however, it describes this divine conflict imagery as something which "penetrated" the Bible. This description does not take account of the extent of the conflict myth within the Hebrew Bible and may overemphasize the sense of discontinuity between the Hebrew Bible and its ancient Near Eastern context.

[17]Jon D. Levenson, *Creation and the Persistence of Evil: The Jewish Drama of Divine Omnipotence* (San Francisco: Harper & Row, 1988) 17. Among the passages that Levenson used in presenting this argument are Psalm 74:10-11 and 18-20, Psalm 104:6-9, Job 38:8-11, and Job 40:25-32. It should be noted that these are all poetic texts. Combat myth is almost entirely absent from the narrative portions of the Hebrew Bible. Therefore, the role of combat myth in the plot of the Hebrew Bible, as it is presented in this study, will remain ambiguous.

[18]Ibid., 25.

In treating these violent and troubling texts, it is necessary to remember Phyllis Trible's admonition at the beginning of her study of texts about violence against women: "To account for these stories as relics of distant, primitive and inferior past is invalid...to contrast an Old Testament God of wrath with a New Testament God of love is fallacious...to seek redemption of these stories in the resurrection is perverse."[19]

Rhetorical Criticism

A discussion of method is in order here, for it has been Trible, following in the tradition of James Muilenburg, who has become the most significant proponent and practitioner of rhetorical criticism. The emerging world of the literary study of the Bible is a vast and confusing one, often dominated by a preoccupation with method and laced with cumbersome jargon. Indeed, even the term "rhetorical criticism" defies definition. I repeat here two definitions, offered by Muilenburg and Trible, followed by a brief discussion of my own intentions in using this method. First, Muilenburg asserted that "responsible and proper artic-ulation of the words in their linguistic patterns and in their precise formulations will reveal to us the texture and fabric of the writer's thought."[20] One reason why rhetorical reading of the Bible has only recently become a widespread phenomenon is that the more traditional views of inspiration have mitigated against an emphasis on how the biblical writers use language.[21] If the Bible was dictated directly by God, then the words do not represent the deliberate, meticulous choices of brilliantly artistic human writers. The words are, therefore, not an appropriate object for such human scrutiny. Only the message matters.[22] In Muilenburg's view, the words chosen by the biblical authors are an inseparable component of the message they intended to convey.

---

[19]Phyllis Trible, *Texts of Terror: Literary-Feminist Readings of Biblical Narra-tives* (Philadelphia: Fortress, 1984) 2.

[20]James Muilenburg, "Form Criticism and Beyond," *JBL* 88 (1969): 7.

[21]This has not always been so. Ancient rabbinical and medieval Christian interpreters often analyzed language quite closely, but this was typically done in service of allegorical and typological methods, ways of understanding the hidden meaning in texts. The emphasis of rhetorical criticism is on the literal meaning of the text.

[22]Robert Alter expressed an understanding of the workings of biblical narrative that focuses on the literary artistry of the authors, their "pleasures of invention and expression," without denying divine inspiration. See Robert Alter, *The Art of Biblical Narrative* (New York: Basic Books, 1981) 156.

Second, in Trible's words, "Critics may trace overall design and plot movement, follow the unfolding of a single stylistic device or motif, analyze selected portions, or pursue close reading of the parts and the whole. The last approach describes full rhetorical analysis; the others present facets."[23] This study will attempt to accomplish at least three of these tasks in succession. Each chapter will begin with a close reading of the selected text, followed by a discussion of theological conclusions, specifically concerning how the theme of violence operates within the text. The interludes will present a broader view of the development of the plot. Each interlude will also illustrate the manner in which the text in the preceding chapter establishes a pattern of violence for the continuing story.

The study as a whole will examine how the biblical plot develops through a series of violent events. The reader will notice that I make frequent reference throughout this study to the works of authors who describe their method as "narrative criticism" or some other similar term. The relationship between narrative criticism and rhetorical criticism is difficult to describe. There is certainly considerable overlap between the two. Narrative criticism is concerned with the components of a story such as plot, characters, settings, and the use of time. In studying these components, narrative critics must pay careful attention to how the writer employs language to tell the story.[24] Rhetorical criticism, with its goal of articulating how the form of the story and its content are related can certainly not ignore these components of narrative literature,[25] and I will make no attempt to do so.

Hans W. Frei has described the confusion in methods of interpretation brought about by changes in the eighteenth and nineteenth centuries. Though interpreters in this era typically noticed the realistic nature of biblical narrative, they often ignored this feature because of their ideas about how biblical narrative related to history. As a result, they often separated the meaning of the stories from the stories

---

[23]Phyllis Trible, *Rhetorical Criticism: Context, Method, and the Book of Jonah* (Minneapolis: Fortress, 1994) 93.

[24]This dependence is perhaps best illustrated by Shimon Bar-Efrat's fifth chapter on "Style" in his brilliant work, *Narrative Art in the Bible* (Sheffield: Almond, 1984).

[25]One important difference is that rhetorical criticism would not be limited to texts which are narrative in form. An obvious illustration of this is Muilenburg's commentary on Isaiah 40-66, almost all of which is poetry, in the *Interpreter's Bible*.

themselves.[26] Frei's statement that "Meaning and narrative shape bear significantly on each other"[27] is a sound rationale for rhetorical criticism in itself. It must be stressed, however, that rhetorical criticism is not a pre-critical reading of the text, but is characterized by what Paul Ricouer has called a "second naïveté."[28] Further, Louis S. Mudge, in his own analysis of the work of Ricouer, has noted that "we have no alternative today to working through criticism toward a second naïveté because the first naïveté available to us in our culture is so deeply idolatrous."[29] No one has so poignantly demonstrated this idolatry, particularly in regard to gender, as Trible has in her groundbreaking work *God and the Rhetoric of Sexuality*.

Significant questions have been raised concerning the scope of rhetorical criticism. Michael V. Fox, among others, has attacked the tendency to ignore the issue of "persuasion." This critique is half correct. Some contemporary rhetorical studies do "... seem to assume that once the details of the construction of a text are laid out, its rhetoric has been discovered."[30] The pursuit of theological conclusions in this study is intended to avoid such shortcomings. On the other hand, I am reluctant to assume that I can somehow measure the persuasive appeal of a text. In the interpretations which follow, I attempt to examine and describe what I think texts are trying to communicate and how the structure of these texts relates to their meanings. Gauging the degree to which they succeed in persuading audiences, both past and present, is beyond my

---

[26]Hans W. Frei, *The Eclipse of Biblical Narrative: A Study in Eighteenth and Nineteenth Century Hermeneutics* (New Haven: Yale University Press, 1974) 10-11. For an excellent discussion of how biblical stories create an "image" of reality, see Jacob Licht, *Storytelling in the Bible*, 2nd ed. (Jerusalem: Magnes, 1978) 9-12. Licht calls this image of reality "mimesis," though he draws a distinction between his analysis of biblical literature and Erich Auerbach's study of European literature. The remainder of Licht's work is filled with examples of how biblical writers have produced a mimetic quality to their work.

[27]Ibid., 11.

[28]Paul Ricouer, *The Symbolism of Evil*, trans. Emerson Buchanan (Boston: Beacon, 1969) 351.

[29]Lewis S. Mudge, "Paul Ricouer on Biblical Interpretation," in *Essays on Biblical Interpretation*, ed. Lewis S. Mudge (Philadelphia: Fortress, 1980) 23.

[30]Michael V. Fox, "The Rhetoric of Ezekiel's Vision of the Valley of the Bones," *HUCA*, 51 (1980): 2. See also the critique of Wilhelm Wuellner, "Where Is Rhetorical Criticism Taking Us?," *CBQ* 49(1987): 448-463. Trible has responded to Fox, Wuellner, and others. See *Rhetorical Criticism*, 48-52.

competence.[31] Fox is also technically correct that "One can study the rhetoric of any stage of development he believes he can distinguish in the text...." Hence, rhetorical criticism need not be restricted to reading the final form of the text.[32] The problem with any text other than the final form is that it is hypothetical. The final form is often not the original form, but we do know that real audiences have heard and read the final form.

Biblical Theology

The most important questions I will be attempting to answer are: What view of the world and how it works emerges from the biblical text? and, In what way do we apply this worldview to our own world?[33] Muilenburg said that "The cultural mentality of a people is reflected not only in its rhetoric but in the literary types and patterns of speech in which it expresses itself most congenially and naturally."[34] Muilenburg went on to call narrative "the most representative and characteristic mode of biblical speech."[35] As such, biblical narrative needs to be the beginning point of biblical theology.

---

[31]Persuasive appeal would depend in large part on the manner in which a message is delivered. Only in the last few centuries has individual, silent reading become common. Thus, for any biblical text, the vast majority of the history of its use is characterized by other modes of delivery. Fox placed much emphasis on the persuasive nature of prophecy. See Fox, "The Rhetoric of Ezekiel's Vision of the Valley of the Bones," 4. His contention that both positive and negative responses to a message constitute evidence of the force of its rhetoric, however, confuses definitions. If the persuasive quality of rhetoric is to be measured or estimated, surely the criterion for measurement must be its ability to generate its intended effect, not just any response at all. If the Hebrew Bible gives any indication, it is that the people of Israel consistently failed to respond to the prophets' call to repentance.

[32]Ibid., 1.

[33]In his analysis of the theological work of Walter Brueggemann, Patrick D. Miller has aptly described literary and rhetorical analysis as "a tool for a theological reading of the text and not a replacement for it." See Miller, "Introduction," in *Old Testament Theology: Essays on Structure, Theme, and Text* (Minneapolis: Fortress, 1992) xiv. I intend for this observation to serve as a rule throughout this study.

[34]James Muilenburg, *The Way of Israel: Biblical Faith and Ethics* (New York: Harper, 1961) 24.

[35]Ibid.

The importance of interpreting biblical stories theologically has been argued effectively by Moberly.[36] It is commonly understood that stories are an expression of a worldview and that, in a sense, they create a world of their own.[37] Whether or not the Hebrew Bible is an accurate report of Israel's history, it creates a world which the contemporary reader may enter. Ricouer refers to this as "the world the text unfolds before itself."[38] What, then, is our response to this world when we encounter it through reading? The traditional response of faith has been profoundly expressed by Robert McAfee Brown: "Christians make the initially bizarre gamble that the strange new world within the Bible is a more accurate view of the world than our own and that we have to modify our views as a result."[39] A somewhat different response is the realization that the world created in the biblical text is a striking reflection of our own experience. Margaret Farley has described this reaction as a "responding recognition" and has argued that such recognition of the connection between a narrated or described world and our own personal experience is what gives communication power.[40] I judge this to be closely related to Ricoeur's more general statement about revelation, that "the signs of the absolute's self disclosure are at the same time signs in which consciousness recognizes itself."[41] The most stunning example of this phenomenon is the realization that the world portrayed by the Bible is as violent as our own.

The practice of theology of the Hebrew Bible requires one additional question. In what way is God involved in this violent plot? Violent

---

[36]Moberly, *At the Mountain of God: Story and Theology in Exodus 32-34*, JSOTS 22 (Sheffield: Sheffield, 1983) 18-27.

[37]For representative discussions of this understanding of biblical narrative, see Leo G. Perdue, *The Collapse of History: Reconstructing Old Testament Theology* (Minneapolis: Fortress, 1994) 232-233; Amos N. Wilder, *The Bible and the Literary Critic* (Minneapolis: Fortress, 1991) 134; and Robert McAfee Brown, *Unexpected News*, 13.

[38]Paul Ricouer, "Toward a Hermeneutic of the Idea of Revelation," in *Essays on Biblical Interpretation*, ed. Lewis S. Mudge (Philadelphia: Fortress, 1980) 100.

[39]Brown, *Unexpected News*, 13.

[40]Margaret Farley, "Feminist Consciousness and the Interpretation of Scripture," in *Feminist Interpretation of the Bible*, ed. Letty Russell (Philadelphia: Westminster, 1985) 42. Farley has discussed this phenomenon specifically in reference to feminist readers (p. 46), but I believe it applies, to some extent, to all readers. For a more general expression, see Wilder, *The Bible and the Literary Critic*, 134-144.

[41]Ricoeur, "The Hermeneutics of Testimony," in *Essays on Biblical Interpretation*, ed. Lewis S. Mudge (Philadelphia: Fortress, 1980) 143.

stories in the Bible always contain at least three characters — perpetrator, victim, and God.[42] Though God may not be mentioned by name in every episode, God's presence is implicitly assumed. The theological conclusions of this study will focus on God's people as both perpetrator and victim of violence, and will persistently question God's role in the narrative.

---

[42]There are a few exceptions to this statement, where God acts directly as perpetrator rather than using a human intermediary, but these are few. Exodus 4:24-26 is a clear example of direct divine violence. Numbers 11:1-3 is a more debatable illustration, where the text may describe a fire caused by a lightning strike. In this case, nature may be the intermediary. In many other texts, such as Exodus 14-15 and Numbers 16:31-33, nature is clearly the intermediary, though God is the ultimate cause.

Part I

The Narrative Framework
of the Biblical Story

1

VIOLENCE ENTERS THE HUMAN COMMUNITY

GENESIS 4:1-16

Surface readings of this narrative have led to such bizarre and erroneous theological conclusions as the assertion that the "sign" of Cain's curse was black skin and that he was the origin of the African race. This text is vital to the understanding of violence in the Bible because it is the initial occurrence. It follows immediately the cursing of the ground and the serpent and the casting out of Adam and Eve from the garden. It is perhaps ironic that the primary result of the cursings for Eve, according to Genesis 3:16, would be bringing forth children in pain. The curse text fails to foresee the infinitely greater pain with which she would lose her first two children to violence. This first act of violence foreshadows the wickedness and evil of all humanity that would cause God to blot it out with the flood (Genesis 6:5-7). A critical reading yields legitimate theological conclusions concerning the issue of violence.

The Text

The story of Cain and Abel begins and ends with the presence of God. In spite of being cast out (גרשׁ)of the garden in 3:24,[1] Eve still claims the presence of God with her statement in 4:1, "I have acquired a man with

---

[1] It should be noted that Eve is not explicitly mentioned in Genesis 3:25. God casts out "the man" (האדם). In 4:1 Adam is again not mentioned by name, but is merely "the man" (האדם). Eve is called by her name in 4:1. For a thorough discussion of the connections between Genesis 4 and Genesis 2-3, see Alan J. Hauser, "Linguistic and Thematic Links between Genesis 4:1-16 and Genesis 2-3," *JETS* 23(1980): 297-305.

the LORD."[2] The result of Cain's being cast out (גרש) in 4:14 is that he goes away from the presence of (literally, "the face of" — פני) God (4:16).[3] Thus, the boundaries of this particular story are also signaled by Cain's entrance into and exit from God's presence. Licht has described this kind of beginning and ending of biblical stories as one of their basic structural features. These boundary points distinguish independent stories from their larger contexts.[4] Throughout this study, the first task in examining each text will be the attempt to locate such boundaries. Between the introductory verse in 4:1-2 and the conclusion in 4:16, the narrative takes place in four scenes:[5] The offerings of Cain and Abel (4:3-5), Yahweh's first conversation with Cain (4:6-7), the murder of Abel (4:8), and the second conversation between Yahweh and Cain (4:9-15).[6]

---

[2] There is no philological connection between the name of Cain (קין) and the verb "acquire" (קנה), but virtually all commentators note the alliterative connection. The translation of the verb, and the subsequent effect on the meaning of Eve's statement, is a more difficult issue. I have chosen the most literal, straightforward translation. For a full discussion of the alternatives, see Gordon Wenham, *Genesis 1-15*, WBC (Waco: Word, 1987) 101-102.

[3] George W. Coats, *Genesis: With an Introduction to Narrative Literature*, FOTL (Grand Rapids: Eerdmans, 1983) 64. Ellen van Wolde, "The Story of Cain and Able: A Narrative Study," *JSOT* 52 (1991): 28.

[4] Licht, *Storytelling in the Bible*, 27-28. Trible and Muilenburg have also identified the determining of boundaries by locating the proper beginning and end of a text as the first step in rhetorical criticism. This is far from a precise procedure, however, and results may vary. See Trible's discussion in *Rhetorical Criticism*, 102.

[5] Westermann treated 4:1-16 as a narrative unit, but also proposed that vv. 2-16 constitute a narrative inserted into a genealogy composed of vv. 1-2a and vv. 17-26. See Claus Westermann, *Genesis: A Practical Commentary* (Grand Rapids: Eerdmans, 1987) 31. Likewise, Blenkinsopp noted the possibility of reading all of Genesis 4 "as one segmented Adamic genealogy with narrative developments." See Joseph Blenkinsopp, *The Pentateuch: An Introduction to the First Five Books of the Bible* (New York: Doubleday, 1992) 67. Wenham divided the passage into five units of alternating narrative and dialogue. See Wenham, *Genesis 1-15*, 99. This structural arrangement will be discussed in further detail at a later point.

[6] The connections between 4:1-16 and Genesis 3 have been noticed by many commentators. In arguing that 4:1-16 may have originally been a separate fall story, Bruce Vawter noted the parallel elements of temptation, fall, and banishment. See *On Genesis: A New Reading* (London: Geoffrey Chapman, 1977) 93. Claus Westermann also made reference to these parallels, asserting that the Yahwist deliberately wrote 4:1-16 as a parallel to chapter 3. See *Genesis 1-11: A*

Verses 1-2 contain, aside from the affirmation of God's continuing presence, two parallel statements. Verse 1 reports that Eve bore Cain and v. 2 that she bore Abel. Verse 2 also states that Abel was a shepherd and Cain a worker of the ground (אדמה). The importance of the reversal of the names will become apparent in the analysis of the following verses.[7] The introduction of Cain's connection to the ground at the end of these introductory verses signals a theme which will pervade the entire narrative, to the extent that the ground becomes a character in the middle of the story and provides the climax at the end.

The first scene, vv. 3-5, contains two pairs of parallel statements reminiscent of those in vv. 1-2. In v. 3, Cain brings (בוא) "an offering from the fruit of the ground" (אדמה). In v. 4a Abel brings (בוא) "an offering from the firstlings of his flock and the fat portions of animals." Verses 4b-5a report that "The LORD looked (שעה) unto Abel and unto his offering. But unto Cain and his offering, he did not look." These two sets of statements, along with the two sets in vv. 1-2, strike an unmistakable note of balance and symmetry between the two brothers. In each succeeding couplet, the names of Cain and Abel are reversed: Eve bears Cain and Abel, the vocations of Abel and Cain are identified, Cain and Abel bring offerings, and Abel and Cain are evaluated. Does the alternation, at times placing the younger brother uncharacter-istically first, forecast God's favor and at the same time hold onto the possibility that favor might be shown to both?[8] The text goes to great lengths to treat

---

Commentary, trans. John J. Scullion (Minneapolis: Augsburg, 1984) 303. Coats has stressed the structural similarities between the two narratives. See *Genesis,* 63.

[7] These two pairs of statements may be viewed as a chiasm:

A Eve bore Cain
B Eve bore Abel
B' Abel was a shepherd
A' Cain was a worker of the ground

Shimon Bar-Efrat has outlined two such four element chiasms in vv. 1-5. See *Narrative Art in the Bible* (Sheffield: Almond Press, 1984) 112. There may be greater importance, however, in the continuing alternation of the names in the larger unit of vv. 1-6. See below.

[8] Francis I. Anderson described the effect of this alternation in slightly different, but not contradictory terms. "What is achieved throughout it [vv. 2-5] is an emphasis on the similarity and contemporaneity of the pairs of actions. Neither Cain nor Abel occupies the centre of the stage." See *The Sentence in Biblical Hebrew* (The Hague: Mouton) 123.

the brothers with equality until the complication of Cain's rejection arises at the end of v. 5. The reason for the rejection of Cain has been the object of a great amount of speculation. Notice that the text seems to offer no explanation at all. The traditional view is that appropriate sacrifice to God must involve blood.[9] The most helpful proposal is that of Westermann, who contended that the offering of Cain was not overtly rejected. Rather, Cain did not enjoy the same subsequent success as Abel, which might be interpreted as the absence of God's blessing.[10]

The alternating statements also combine to produce an almost rhythmical pattern which is broken abruptly at the end of v. 5 when only Cain's response is reported.[11] The break in the alternating pattern moves the reader dramatically into the next portion of the story where Cain will be the focus of Yahweh's attention. This treatment of the two brothers begins, in a subtle way, an extensive pattern in the book of Genesis in which the younger brother will take precedence over the older.[12]

Following Cain's reaction to his rejection by Yahweh the story, which has been moving along quickly through a series of actions, pauses for speech.[13] Abel disappears from the story, and Yahweh addresses Cain alone.[14] The first two questions in the divine speech in

---

[9] E.g. Gerhard von Rad, *Genesis*, OTL (Philadelphia: Westminster, 1972) 104.

[10] See Westermann, *Genesis: A Practical Commentary*, pp. 32-33. Frank Anthony Spina has developed a creative argument supporting the position that the cursing of the ground in Genesis 3 led to a condition in which God could not accept the produce of the ground as an offering. See "The "Ground for Cain's Rejection (Gen 4): *ʾadamah* in the context of Gen 1-11," *ZAW* 104 (1992): 327. It is not clear whether the sacrifices and Yahweh's evaluation represent one single occurrence or a repeated set of events, what Robert Alter has referred to as the habitual or iterative sense of the verb. See Alter, *The Art of Biblical Narrative*, 80.

[11] Licht has labeled this kind of repetition "quasi-poetical." See *Storytelling in the Bible*, 93-94.

[12] Meir Sternberg has described the initiation of the pattern in this text, a pattern which "grows in predictive determinacy and ideological force with each new successful application." See *The Poetics of Biblical Narrative: Ideological Literature and the Drama of Reading* (Bloomington: Indiana University Press, 1985) 269.

[13] For a discussion of how the use of narration and dialogue effect the apparent flow of time in a story, see Bar-Efrat, "Some Observations on the Analysis of Structure in Biblical Narrative," *VT* 30 (1980): 159.

[14] Casper J. Laubuschange has developed an elaborate scheme of divine speech formulas in the Pentateuch. Narratives in the Pentateuch tend to contain seven or four speech units in an alternating pattern. Gen. 4:1-16 has four speech

v. 6, "Why does it burn for you, and why has your face (פְנֶי) fallen?,"
reflect the report of Cain's response in v. 5b. These questions, in the
light of the following verse do not indicate ignorance on the part of
Yahweh. On the contrary, they indicate that Yahweh is aware of Cain's
inner motives and feelings. This leads to the troubling conclusion that
Yahweh must also be aware of Cain's murderous intentions. Verse 7
begins as v. 6 ends, with a question from God to Cain, but this question
is extremely difficult to translate. Among the possibilities are: "Will you
not do well to lift up (נְשֹׂא)?," "If you do well will you not be lifted up,"
"If you do well will you not lift up?, "If you do well will you not be
forgiven?," or "If you do well will you not be favored?" The meaning
may not be altered appreciably by the translation decisions in the first
three options, but the difference between active rendering of the Hebrew infinitive, "to lift up," and the passive rendering does seem
significant.[15] The last two options do reveal a significant difference in
the meaning of the verb itself. While "lift up" is by far the most
common meaning for נְשֹׂא, such possibilities as "forgive"[16] or "show
favor"[17] are attested elsewhere. It is crucial, however, that the sense of
lifting up not be lost, as it is in some English translations, since it
counters the falling (נָפַל) of Cain's face in the previous verses.

The second episode ends with three statements by Yahweh in v.
7bc, which counterbalance the three questions in vv. 6-7a.[18] This rapid

---

units, each introduced by the verb אמר, beginning in v. 6, v. 9, v. 10, and v. 15. The
narratives on either side, 3:1-24 and 5:32-9:29, each have seven such units. If
Laubuschange is correct, then the four units of speech in 4:1-16 may be a pattern
forced on this story by the literary structure of the Pentateuch, not just a function
of the internal literary nature of the passage. See Casper J. Labuschange, "The
Pattern of Divine Speech Formulas in the Pentateuch," VT 32 (1982): 269,282.

[15] It is simply impossible to construct a sensible English sentence using an
infinitive form of the verb.

[16] For example, Gen. 50:17; Ex. 10:17, 32:32; Num. 14:18; I Sam. 15:25; Hos.
14:3.

[17]This possibility is discussed at length by Mayer I. Gruber in his article "The
Many Faces of Hebrew פנים נשׂא>lift up the face<," ZAW 95 (1983), pp. 252-260.

[18]The first of these statements presents additional translation difficulties.
Traditionally, the statement is rendered as something like, "And if you do not
do well, sin is crouching at the door." The primary problem is that the subject in
the second clause, sin (חטּאת), is feminine while the verb form, crouching (רבץ), is
a masculine participle. In addition, the third person pronoun in the second
statement, "Its desire is for you," is also masculine. It is fairly common in
biblical Hebrew for feminine subjects to take masculine verbs, but these two
differences in gender taken together present a formidable problem. There have

sequence of divine questions and statements dramatically portrays Cain's position and the options which lay before him. The reader is left hanging in suspense with the choices Yahweh has laid out for Cain as the speech unit ends abruptly, with no verbal response from Cain.

The third scene is remarkable for its brevity. The rapid nature of Cain's three-fold action seems quite intentional. He says (אמר), he rises up (קוּם), and he kills (הרג). The first phrase appears to be the opening of a dialogue between the two brothers. The Hebrew verb אמר (say) typically introduces a direct quotation, but the words between the two brothers are missing. It is as if the dialogue has been ripped out of the story in order to bring on the murderous act of Cain that much more quickly.[19] Licht has described how obvious elements of a story may be omitted in order to "make the narrative concise and dense at its climax."[20] The overall structure of 4:1-16 also highlights v. 8 by placing it alone at the middle of the passage:

> Opening Narrative (vv. 1-5)
> Speech of Yahweh to Cain (vv. 6-7)
> The Murder of Abel (v. 8)
> Dialogue between Yahweh and Cain (vv. 9-15)
> Closing Narrative (v. 16)[21]

Violence stands in bold relief at the center of the text.[22]

---

been numerous attempts to solve this issue. For a thorough discussion see van Wolde, "The Story of Cain and Abel: A Narrative Study," 30-31. Van Wolde also offered her own solution, arguing that רבץ is an additional subject along with חטאת. Her translation reads, "At the door is sin, the sin of lying in wait" (pp. 31-32).

[19] A textual difficulty highlights the dramatic effect of this verse. In the other major versions of the Hebrew Bible, most significantly the Samaritan Pentateuch and the Septuagint, Cain says, "Let us go into the field." This statement shows every sign of being an obvious addition to fill in an apparent gap. Unfortunately, most English translations have chosen to include it, though some add a footnote.

[20]Licht, *Storytelling in the Bible*, 44.

[21]Wenham diagrams the chiastic structure in this way. See Wenham, *Genesis 1-15*, 99.

[22] It is possible to see vv. 8-11 as a unit at the center of the text because of the rapid succession of occurrences of the word "brother." This is proposed by Donald E. Gowan who later confirms, however, that the murder alone forms the center. See Donald E. Gowan, *Genesis 1-11: From Eden to Babel*, ITC (Grand Rapids: Eerdmans, 1988) 64.

One other narrative possibility deserves mention. Verse 8 is narrated in scenic fashion. The intent is to show the reader, verbally, what is happening. It is possible then that the reader is supposed to see, but not hear, Cain's speech. In other words, he whispers. This would further highlight the deceptive nature of Cain's actions. The fact that the reader finds, in the absence of a direct quotation, the unexpected אמר rather than the expected "speak" (דבר) may create this perception.

After the murder, Yahweh again addresses Cain. Yahweh initiates the dialogue in a manner reminiscent of the conversation with Adam and Eve in 3:9-13. Brueggemann's suggestion that 4:9-16 be viewed as a lawsuit is quite helpful.[23] Yahweh asks a question. Cain responds with a statement and a question, both of which are evasive. Alter has suggested that "the initial words spoken by a personage will be revelatory, perhaps more in manner than in matter, constituting an important moment in the exposition of a character."[24] The evasiveness of Cain's first words fit perfectly on the lips of one who is to become "a fugitive and a wanderer on the earth." Yahweh responds with a second question which Cain is not permitted to answer. It has already been answered by "the voice of the blood[25] of Abel," who has been voiceless in the story to this point.

Two additional literary features focus our attention on the center of the story. First, as the story moves away from the murder to Cain's resulting predicament, the words of Cain and Yahweh at the end of the dialogue in vv. 9-15, recall the crime. Cain laments that anyone finding him will kill (הרג) him, just as he killed (הרג) Abel in v. 8. In response, Yahweh pronounces judgement on anyone who kills (הרג) Cain.

Second, the pattern in which Abel's name and his designation as Cain's brother appear takes on a distinct form. The words "Abel" and "brother" (אח) appear seven times each in the story, four times together and three times each alone. Of the resulting ten occurrences, the middle two appear in v. 8, the central verse of the passage.[26] In addition, of the four full identifications of Abel, by both his name and אח, the middle

---

23Brueggemann, *Genesis*, Interpretation (Atlanta: John Knox, 1982) 60.

24Alter, *The Art of Biblical Narrative*, 74.

25 The Mishnah, in Sanhedrin 4:5, comments on the plural form of the word "blood" here and in v. 11. It explains that "the bloods of your brother" indicates that not only Abel was killed, but all of his potential descendants.

26 Wenham has indicated the fourteen occurrences of Cain's name in the passage, if it is expanded to include v. 17. Verse 8 would then contain the middle two, seventh and eighth, occurrences of "Cain." See Wenham, *Genesis 1-15*, 96.

two are in v. 8. These patterns increase the emphasis on v. 8 as the center of the passage.

v. 2a — his brother, Abel
v. 2b — Abel
v. 4a — Abel
v. 4b — Abel
v. 8a — Abel, his brother
v. 8b — Abel, his brother
v. 9a — Abel, your brother
v. 9b — my brother
v. 10 — your brother
v. 11 — your brother

In the introduction (v.2), the designations appear together. During the story of the offerings, Abel is mentioned three times by his name only. During the murder and Yahweh's first question, he is identified by both designations. Beginning with Cain's evasive statement, "Am I my brother's keeper?", Abel's name disappears, and he is merely referred to as "brother." The dual designations at the center of the story increase the impact of the crime by constantly reminding the reader of the relationship between perpetrator and victim, which had been intro- duced at the beginning of the story (v. 2). This is no mere murder, but fratricide. Once Cain responds to Yahweh in v. 9, Abel loses his name and becomes a victim of memory as well as murder.

Beginning in 4:10, the Hebrew word אדמה becomes the most promi- nent feature of the story. The five occurrences of the word in vv. 10- 15 combine with two occurrences in vv. 2-3 to make the important total of seven again. These uses can be obscured in English translations by the various renderings of אדמה as ground, soil, and earth. The ground (אדמה) which provided Cain's livelihood (v. 2) later becomes a character (a co-conspirator?) as it opens its mouth to take the blood of Abel (v. 11).[27] The ground (אדמה) which fails to conceal his crime (v.10) will now fail to sustain him (v. 12). Cain will be estranged from the ground (v. 14). Indeed, this curse upon Cain alters the very nature of the surface beneath his feet. While Yahweh sentences him, in v. 13, to be "a wan- derer and a fugitive upon the earth (ארץ)," Cain further understands

---

[27]Modupe Oduyoye has interpreted the involvement of the ground (אדמה) quite differently, emphasizing its role as the "moral guardian" in African tradition. See *The Sons of the Gods and the Daughters of Men: An Afro-Asiatic Interpretation of Genesis 1-11* (Maryknoll, N.Y.: Orbis, 1984) 17.

that he will become "a wanderer and a fugitive on the earth (אֶרֶץ)" for he is "cast out from the face (פְּנֵי) of the ground (אֲדָמָה)." Cain also understands his punishment to be magnified in another way. God curses Cain from (מִן) the ground (אֲדָמָה)which took Abel's blood from (מִן) Cain's hand, but Cain states that he is cast out from (מִן) the face (פְּנֵי) of the earth (אֶרֶץ) and is hidden from (מִן) Yahweh's face (פְּנֵי). He is separated from both sustaining forces in his life. The only sustenance remaining in Cain's life is the sign Yahweh places on him in response to his complaint. This theme is echoed in v. 16 when Cain goes out from (מִן) the face (פְּנֵי) of Yahweh and dwells in the land (אֶרֶץ) of Nod.

Thus ends the story of the first murder.

Theological Conclusions

The first family on earth, according to Genesis, consists of four persons at the point of Genesis 4:2. By the end of the narrative in Genesis 4:1-16, twenty-five percent of the earth's population has committed homicide, twenty-five percent is the victim of a homicide, and the remaining fifty percent are immediate family members of both a victim and a perpetrator. Though a picture of the intimate life of this first family is not provided, Eve's statement in 4:1 can not be understood in any way such that it does not include pleasure. In this brief passage, the world has changed dramatically because of the entrance of violence.

This text may tell us much about how God is related to violence, how violence affects humanity, and how violence changes creation. It may also raise as many questions as it answers. First, the motive behind this murder is jealousy concerning God's favor.[28] The analysis above reveals the essential balance with which the brothers are treated until v. 5. It is difficult to avoid feelings that Cain receives unfair treatment.

There is not complete agreement among liberation theologians as to who the victim in this story is. Alan A. Boesak interprets this story in

---

[28]René Girard has drawn the connection between Genesis 4:1-16 and the story of Romulus and Remus. In each case, an antagonism arises between two brothers. One brother (Cain, Romulus) then kills the other (Abel, Remus) and founds a city (Enoch, Rome) as the home for a new civilization. See René Girard, *Things Hidden Since the Foundation of the Earth*, trans. Stephen Bann and Michael Metteer (Stanford: Stanford University Press, 1987) 38-39. Oduyoye has placed great emphasis on the beginning of urbanization in 4:17 and Israel's suspicion of settled, urban life. See *The Sons of God and the Daughters of Men*, 17.

the more obvious way, with Abel as the victim and Cain as the oppressor. The primary meaning of the story for Boesak is "that oppressors shall have no place on God's earth."[29] The materialist reading of Itumaleng J. Mosala arrives at the opposite conclusion. The dominant society which produced the text cast itself in the place of Abel, the victim, in justifying its own attempt to disposes peasant farmers, represented by Cain.[30] This is unlikely, however, if attention is kept on the story and what Cain did get, the continuing presence of God in vv. 6-7. Yahweh's question in v. 6b makes it plain that Cain has another option besides jealousy, anger, and dejection. Yahweh's statement in v. 7a indicates to Cain and to the reader that Cain still has the opportunity to do well and find favor. The ominous saying in v. 7b reveals that Cain's reaction up to that point does not constitute sin. Rather, the potential for sin lies in how he responds to the feelings that have come over him. Cain does not respond to Yahweh's presence, though. Instead of speaking unto Yahweh, he speaks unto Abel.

The abruptness of v. 8 discloses how the mechanism of violence operates in its first appearance. It is sudden, it is anti-relational, and it stands at the center of human existence. As observed above, the story is constructed to highlight the suddenness of the murder.[31] The would be conversation with Yahweh lies unfinished. There is no response from Cain. The missing words from Cain to Abel accelerate the action. All relationships are broken for the perpetrator. His parents are absent, he does not respond to his God, and his speech to his brother is secretive and deceptive. Violence is the creature which has been crouching at the door of the human family, and it pounces destructively when the door is left open by disrupted relationships. The presence of God is pushed to the margins of the story, affirmed by the words of Eve in v.2 and

---

[29]See Alan Boesak, *Black and Reformed: Apartheid, Liberation and the Calvinist Tradition* (Johannesberg: Skotaville, 1984) 49.

[30]See *Biblical Hermeneutics and Black Theology in South Africa* (Grand Rapids, Eerdmans, 1989) 35. Mosala's reading is based upon certain socio-historical and related source-critical assumptions, most significantly that Genesis 4:1-16 is a J narrative generated by the Davidic-Solomonic empire. His conclusions, therefore, are not fully compatible with a literary reading. See also the analysis of the interpretations of Boesak and Mosala in Gerald West, *Biblical Hermeneutics of Liberation: Modes of Reading the Bible in the South African Context*, 2nd ed. (Maryknoll, N. Y.: Orbis, 1995) 64-82.

[31]Brueggemann interprets the brevity of the report of the murder as a sign that it is not of primary interest to the story teller. See *Genesis*, 55. The view offered here is quite the opposite. The abruptness of the murder serves to accentuate its importance.

denied by Cain in v. 14. Violence crowds out this presence. Even the divine speech immediately surrounding the murder is nullified by failure to respond in v. 7 and a dishonest response in v. 9. Samuel Terrien has described the presence of God as "unexpected, unwanted, unsettling, and often devastating."[32] Certainly this is true for Cain in this story.

Terrien has also characterized God's presence as "divine disruption."[33] This is more problematic in Genesis 4. While Cain's life is disrupted by Yahweh's curse in v. 11, his act of murder is not disrupted by Yahweh's address in vv. 6-7. Certainly for Abel, the disruption is too little too late. G. Tom Milazzo has pressed this point further by questioning God's responsibility for suffering and death. If God's presence sustains life and God's absence ends it, then what is the extent of God's responsibility?[34] Again, God is present, attempting to sustain Cain, but God's absence from v. 8 raises profound theological questions. The implications of God's presence or absence for the victim will be treated more extensively below.

Not only human and divine relationships are disrupted by acts of violence. Cain also loses his connection to the ground (אדמה), the source of his livelihood. The seven-fold mention of the word אדמה in the story will not allow the reader to miss the significance of this loss. If we infer from vv. 10-11 that Cain buries Abel in the ground, then we see that Cain tries to use his long-time ally to hide his crime. He misuses the ground, making it his accomplice. Thus, Yahweh severs the connection between the two, and the ground fades out of the story as it draws to a close. When Cain repeats and adds to the words of Yahweh's curse (v. 12) saying, "you have driven me from the ground, and I will be hidden from your face, and I will be a fugitive and a wanderer on the earth," the dry land of creation changes character.[35] No longer is it the stuff from which humanity is made (Gen. 2:7), but merely a desolate place for Cain to wander. Violence reorders human existence, destroying all facets of human identity. Cain is no longer a son, a brother, or a farmer. The severing of his connection to the ground (אדמה) even calls into

---

[32] Samuel Terrien, *The Elusive Presence: Toward a New Biblical Theology* (San Francisco: Harper & Row, 1978) 28.

[33] Ibid.

[34] G. Tom Milazzo, *The Protest and the Silence: Suffering, Death, and Biblical Theology* (Minneapolis: Fortress, 1992) 52.

[35] Alter has noted that slight changes in repeated statements are often used to create "the psychological, moral, and dramatic complications of biblical narrative." See Alter, *The Art of Biblical Narrative*, 97.

question his identity as a human being (אדם). This story of Cain and his estrangement from the land and from God inaugurates two themes which will appear many times throughout Genesis. First, brothers are unable to live in the land together. One of them (Cain, Lot, Ishmael, Esau) must always leave. Second, the brothers who depart always move to the east (קדם), away from the land of promise.[36]

The other side of violence is the role of the victim. If the perpetrator's identity is irrevocably altered by the act of murder, the victim's identity is threatened with complete annihilation. Abel's identity is tenuous from the beginning, his name (הבל) meaning "wind" or "breath."[37] As the foregoing analysis shows, his identity ebbs and flows through the course of the narrative. He begins as Abel, son, and brother (v.2), becomes simply Abel (vv. 3-4), disappears altogether (vv. 5-7), reappears as Abel and brother (vv. 8-9a), becomes merely brother (vv. 9b-11), and finally disappears completely.[38] The tendency to forget victims, of course, is a human phenomenon of which most of us are aware. More troubling, theologically, in this story is the definitive lack of God's presence for the victim and what might be interpreted as God's forgetting of the victim. Yahweh talks to Cain, but not to Abel. Yahweh is quick to warn Cain of the dangerous creature "crouching" in wait for him, but there is no such warning for Abel. That Cain "rose up unto Abel" (v. 8) may imply that he was crouching as well. In his study of the characterization of God in the Hebrew Bible, Dale Patrick has correctly asserted that both Yahweh's presence and absence serve to "render him dramatically."[39] Yahweh's absence in v. 8 must reveal something of Yahweh's character. The final two occurrences of the word brother (אח) come from the mouth of Yahweh (vv. 10-11) and are not

---

[36]See the excellent treatment of these two themes in the patriarchal narratives by Devora Steinmetz in *From Father to Son: Kinship, Conflict, and Continuity in Genesis* (Louisville: Westminster/John Knox, 1991) 89-91.

[37] Readers of the English text should be aware that this word, הבל, is the one used in the book of Qoheleth (commonly known as Ecclesiastes), which is traditionally translated "vanity." A better translation might be "meaninglessness," which carries rather dire theological implications for the first murder victim.

[38] After Seth "replaces" Abel in Genesis 4:25, Abel's name is never again mentioned in the Hebrew Bible. Likewise, Cain's name goes unmentioned after this verse. The names of the two brothers do appear in 4 Maccabees 18:11.

[39] Dale Patrick, *The Rendering of God in the Old Testament* (Philadelphia: Fortress, 1981) 21.

accompanied by Abel's name. We are thus left to wonder if Yahweh has also forgotten his name.[40] Milazzo has put it best:

> In the presence of death, then, all aspects of the relationship between the human and the divine are called into question. As long as God remains silent, the death question remains without answer. As long as the death question is without answer, the questions of the reality of God and the meaning of existence remain open and unanswered.[41]

Indeed, the text of Genesis 4 leaves all of these questions unanswered.

A final troubling question in relation to this text has been raised by Girard. The complication in the plot of Genesis 4 arises from the first performance of sacrifice. Girard understands animal sacrifice as a mechanism of victimization whereby human beings find a controlled outlet for violent aggression. The story of Cain and Abel presents two brothers, one with such an outlet (Abel) and one without such an outlet (Cain). Cain's act of murder may then be viewed as his only viable outlet for the violent tendencies which seem basic to human existence.[42] James G. Williams moves one step further, calling Abel "the first sacrifice for the descendants of Cain."[43] Williams points to the command in Leviticus 17:13 that the blood of a sacrificial victim should be poured on the ground (cf. Gen 4:10) as confirmation of this evaluation. Genesis 4 does not state explicitly that Yahweh requires or demands sacrifice, but this idea does seem to be present implicitly. If Yahweh places upon Cain a requirement he cannot fulfill otherwise, is Yahweh responsible for the instigation of the homicide? Such anthropological theories aside, however, Yahweh's response to the murder in the text makes it clear that Yahweh had something else in mind when encouraging Cain to "do well."

In summary, violence alters relationships of all kinds, including those among human beings and those between human beings and

---

[40]Because this is an investigation of violence in the theology of the Hebrew Bible, I am forced into a dead end on this question. For Christians doing biblical theology, the remembrance of Abel's name on the lips of Jesus in Matthew 23:35 and Luke 11:51 may carry profound meaning.

[41]Milazzo, *The Protest and the Silence*, 53.

[42]René Girard, *Violence and the Sacred*, trans. Patrick Gregory (Baltimore: Johns Hopkins University Press, 1977) 4.

[43]James G. Williams, *The Bible, Violence, and the Sacred: Liberation from the Myth of Sanctioned Violence* (San Francisco: Harper Collins, 1991) 27.

God. At the beginning of Genesis 4, Cain is a son, a brother, and a worshipper of Yahweh. At the end of the story, he is none of these. All of his relationships are broken and he and his descendants become an insignificant branch off of the main line of the biblical plot. In addition, violence alters the identity of human beings, both perpetrators and victims. By the end of the story, Abel is no longer called by name, and he is unceremoniously replaced by Seth in Genesis 4:25. Cain began the story as the firstborn child of the human race, causing his mother to rejoice. He became a successful farmer. In the end he is only a fugitive and a wanderer, estranged from the land that had been the partner in his vocation. Finally, violence both affects and is affected by the presence of God. Cain's violent intentions cause God to speak directly to him. His act of violence brings further speech from God.

Mysteriously, the crime itself takes place in God's absence. Genesis 4 raises important issues about God's presence and absence in relation to the victim and, subsequently, God's role in the suffering and death created by violence. Sternberg has argued that the tension created by the alternatives Yahweh gives to Cain in 4:6-7 foreshadow the tension between faith and doubt which characterize Israel's history.[44]

Most of the texts examined in the remainder of this book will concern violence carried out by and against groups rather than indi-viduals. Whether the theological conclusions drawn here from the analysis of the first act of violence, a fratricide, will be consistent with those drawn from large scale acts of violence remains to be seen.

---

[44] Meir Sternberg, *The Poetics of Biblical Narrative: Ideological Literature and the Drama of Reading* (Bloomington: Indiana University Press, 1985) 92-93.

INTERLUDE ONE:
CONFLICT AMONG BROTHERS
LEADS TO CAPTIVITY

As depicted in the preceding chapter, violence enters the human community as soon as the human community enters the real (non-Edenic) world. The story of Cain and Abel is followed by a long and twisted tale of humanity in the remaining forty-six chapters of the book of Genesis. Two patterns established in Genesis 4:1-16 continue to shape the plot as it moves along. First, conflict continues to arise between brothers causing them to be separated and differentiated. The stories of conflict among the sons of Noah, between Abraham and Lot, Isaac and Ishmael, and Jacob and Esau serve to separate out and identify the people of Israel from the surrounding Canaanites, Moabites, Ammonites, Ishmaelites, Edomites, and others. Second, the role of God continues to be the choosing and favoring of one brother. In this role, God becomes the force behind the separation and differentiation of the people groups which populate the ancient world of Genesis.

Certain brotherly conflicts are portrayed more explicitly than others. In the genealogy of Genesis 5, which quickly carries the reader through the eight generations from Adam to Noah, no explicit conflict is mentioned. In each step, however, the text says that the father "had other sons and daughters" aside from the single, named son. Each stage in the genealogy, therefore, subtly indicates a process of choosing, separating, and differentiating.[45] Genesis 6:11 says that "the earth (אֶרֶץ) was filled with violence." In the biblical story of humanity, only nine generations old at the time of the flood, it must certainly be assumed that much of the violence is among close kin.

In the flood story, God chooses and favors one brother among many. Through the medium of nature, God violently destroys all but Noah

---

[45]The reader can not know whether the named sons in the genealogy are eldest, youngest, or something in between. The advanced ages of the fathers (Methuselah was 187 when Lamech was born in 5:28), however, may be a hint that these were not all first-born sons.

and his descendants. Some careful arithmetic indicates that even Noah's grandfather, Methuselah, was killed in the flood.[46] Yahweh promises not to use flood waters as a means of separation and differentiation again, but immediately after the flood the process continues by other means.

In the post-deluvian world, the genealogies take on even greater import. Genesis 10 is not simply speaking of individuals, but of peoples and nations—Canaan, Cush, Egypt, etc. The perceptive reader quickly realizes that this is more than just a genealogy. It is an elaborate ethnography. Israel understood itself as a people arising out of familial conflict, beginning with the conflict among Noah's sons. The world is no different after the flood.

The story of the Tower of Babel offers a stark point of irony. This text defies interpretation as a literary component of the Genesis story. How odd that on the single occasion of global harmony and cooperation in the book of Genesis Yahweh takes offense and determines to undermine this spirit by scattering peoples and confusing languages. The ancient Israelites understood every bit as well as modern people how ethnic rivalry fuels violent conflict. Yet they told stories of a God who punishes violence (Genesis 6:11) and creates the greatest motivation for it (Genesis 11:8-9). The juxtaposition of the flood and Babel stories thus form a poignant echo of the Cain and Abel story.

The patriarchal narratives continue the story making use of the same patterns of choice, brotherly conflict, separation, and ethnic differentiation.

Chosen	Separated	Ethnically differentiated
Abraham	Lot[47]	Moabites and Ammonites
Isaac	Ishmael	Ishmaelites
Jacob	Esau	Edomites

Step by step the children of Israel are chosen out of this ethnic mix of the Ancient Near East. Yet even once they are clearly defined in the twelve sons of Jacob, the pattern of divine favor and conflict continues.

---

[46]I do not know who first noticed this detail, but it was first pointed out to me by my teacher Joel F. Drinkard. 187 (Methuselah's age when Lamech was born) + 182 (Lamech's age when Methuselah was born) + 600 (Noah's age when the flood came) = 969 (Methuselah's age when he died)

[47]Note that at the point of their separation Abraham calls Lot his brother (אח), though most English translations obscure this point. See the discussion of this issue by Devora Steinmetz in *From Father to Son: Kinship*, 81.

Joseph is favored, and the violence which ensues eventually results in the arrival of the whole family in Egypt, thus setting the stage for the next turning point in the plot of Israel's story.

In chapter 1 I identified three important conclusions about human violence which are perpetuated in the remainder of the book of Genesis. First, violence alters human relationships. The conflict between brothers puts an end to brotherhood. Second, violence alters human identity. The brotherly conflict in Genesis gives rise to the ethnic identities of the people of the Middle East. The losers frequently go unmentioned in the genealogies and the winners become nations in perpetual conflict. The final clash between brothers in the Genesis narrative in chapter thirty-seven changes Joseph from favored son to slave. The poem in Genesis 49 forms a fitting conclusion in its expression of identities. In nine of the twelve descriptions of Jacob's sons violence forms a key component to the understanding of the son's (tribe's) identity (vv. 3c, 5b-7b, 8b, 15d, 17, 19, 23-24, and 27). Only three of the briefest descriptions (Zebulun, Asher, and Naphtali) contain no such reference. Is it significant that these non-violent tribes never achieve any degree of prominence in the biblical story of Israel?

Third, the place of God in the violent plot is ambiguous. In the continuing story of Genesis, God punishes violence by violence, establishes the root cause of most violence, and sets brother against brother by showing favor. God can clearly be on the side of the victim (Joseph) or the oppressor (Jacob), or God can be absent from stories of violence (Genesis 34).

2

GOD'S PEOPLE OPPRESSED
BY VIOLENCE

EXODUS 1:8-22

From Genesis to Exodus, the biblical narrative moves from stories primarily about individuals to stories primarily about a people. Exodus 1:8-22 is the first story about violence perpetrated against a group, the group that would become God's chosen people. The story explains how the people of Israel came to be enslaved in the land of Egypt. This text sets the agenda for the rest of the Pentateuch. The purpose of God will become the deliverance of these people from the oppression described here, to a situation wherein they can determine their own destiny. Before the plot can move on, however, their condition as slaves in Egypt must be characterized. This characterization of the condition of slavery reveals much about how violence operates

Text

Exodus 1:8-22 begins and ends with the King of Egypt, or Pharaoh,[1] speaking to his people about the children of Israel. The plot of the story involves Pharaoh's schemes to utilize the children of Israel as slaves and murder their male offspring in order to keep them under control. The structure of the story may be outlined as follows:

vv. 8-10   Speech: King of Egypt to his people
vv. 11-14 Narrative: Oppression of the children of Israel
vv. 15-16 Speech: King of Egypt to midwives
v. 17   Narrative: Midwives disobey king

---

[1]The significance of the fluctuating use of the designations "King of Egypt" and "Pharaoh" will be discussed in detail below.

vv. 18-19 Speech: Dialogue between king and midwives
vv. 20-21 Narrative: God blesses the midwives and the people
vv. 22   Speech: Pharaoh to people

The possibility that these divisions indicate a chiastic structure is readily apparent. S. Bar-Efrat has warned against "an excessive tendency to discover chiastic structure."[2] Nevertheless, the possibility that such a structure exists here should not be excluded. The discussion in the rest of this chapter will proceed on the assumption that this possibility exists. The schemes for the division of this narrative are numerous. The issue is complicated by the long-standing practice of assigning portions of this and other pentateuchal narratives to the traditional sources. The significance of the structure outlined above will be discussed throughout the chapter. For now, a brief discussion of the application of traditional source criticism to this passage is in order.

There is general agreement that vv. 8-12 are from the Yahwist. Verses 13-14 are then assigned to the Priestly source.[3] The assignment of vv. 15-22 is more difficult. Some critics assign this whole section to the Elohist.[4] Others split vv. 15-22 between the Yahwist and the Elohist.[5] The division of the text by Brevard Childs into two episodes, vv. 8-14 and vv. 15-22, is somewhat consistent with the standard source divisions.[6] In spite of the results of source criticism, this narrative stands as a coherent whole, with an interlude between v. 14 and v. 15, during which the King of Egypt apparently determines that his initial plan has been unsuccessful.[7] From a more traditional perspective, U. Cassuto divided Exodus 1 into three sections of seven verses and labeled v. 22 a

---

[2]S. Bar-Efrat, "Some Observations on the Analysis of Structure in Biblical Narrative," *VT* 30 (1980): 170.

[3]For examples of this type of source division see John I. Durham, *Exodus*, WBC (Waco: Word, 1987) 6 and J. P. Hyatt, *Exodus*, NCBC (Grand Rapids: Eerdmans, 1980) 66. These schemes also assign Exodus 1:1-7 to the Priestly source.

[4]Hyatt, *Exodus*, 66.

[5]Durham labeled this section an "EJ amalgam" and provided a thorough discussion of the various suggestions concerning source division. Durham, *Exodus*, 10-11.

[6]Brevard Childs, *The Book of Exodus: A Critical, Theological Commentary*, OTL (Philadelphia: Westminster, 1974) 14-17. It is not clear to what extent Childs's division of the text is influenced by source analysis.

[7]Durham, *Exodus*, 11. Childs noted that it is not obvious how slave labor would prevent population growth, but he offered some proposals and concluded that "the narrative is not bothered by lack of vigorous logic." Childs, *Exodus*, 16.

conclusion. This understanding of the structure of the chapter is attractive, from a literary point of view, and is not inconsistent with my own. Cassuto's division is based on Masoretic punctuation and his understanding of the Bible's predilection for sevens. He argued that the root, רבה (become many) links the paragraphs in Exodus 1, appearing at or near the end of each (vv. 7,12, and 20).[8]

The scheme outlined above further divides the story in 1:8-22 into seven sections by dividing it into speech and narrative units. In the first section (vv. 8-10) the new king is introduced and speaks to his people. This king who rises up (קוּם) over Egypt fears that the children of Israel with rise up (קוּם) from the land.[9] In v. 9, he recognizes that they are many (רב) and mighty (עצוּם). The apparent conflict between this statement and the king's plan in v. 10 to prevent the people from becoming many (רבה) may deliberately point to the futility of his plan. As J. Cheryl Exum has observed, there is considerable irony in the fact that the precise situation which concerns this Pharaoh becomes the central plot of the book of Exodus.[10]

The perpetrator and the victim of violence in this narrative are both mentioned by name seven times. The names by which they are called fluctuate, however.[11] The perpetrator is called:

> King...over Egypt (v. 8)
> Pharaoh (v. 11)
> King of Egypt (v. 15)
> King of Egypt (v. 17)
> King of Egypt (v. 18)
> Pharaoh (v. 19)
> Pharaoh (v. 22)

---

[8]See U. Cassuto, *A Commentary on the Book of Exodus*, trans. Israel Brahams (Jerusalem: Magnes, 1951) 7-16.

[9]Adele Berlin has pointed out that קוּם is often used as a marker indicating passage of time and the beginning of the action in a narrative (e. g. Ruth 1:6 and 1 Samuel 1:9). See *Poetics and Interpretation of Biblical Narrative* (Winona Lake, Ind.: Eisenbrauns, 1983) 104.

[10]J Cheryl Exum, "You Shall Let Every Daughter Live: A Study of Exodus 1:8-2:10," *Semeia* 28 (1983): 68.

[11]The traditional explanation for this is the composite nature of the narratives. For example, the Yahwist uses the singular noun "people of the children of Israel" (v. 9), while the Priestly source uses the plural construction "children of Israel" (v. 13). See Durham, *Exodus*, 6.

The two basic names given to this character, "king" and "Pharaoh," cannot be easily attributed to the composite use of sources. The fluctuation in names appears somewhat random with respect to traditional source divisions of the text. The change in names does seem to fit with the flow of the story, however. In the beginning of the narrative he is "king," a neutral term, and in the end he is the much despised "Pharaoh" of Hebrew tradition.[12] The first transition from king to Pharaoh appropriately takes place as he begins to enslave the Israelites. The change back to king in v. 15 is more difficult to understand. The first plan to control the Israelite population has failed and the king next attempts to work indirectly through the midwives. That he speaks to the midwives as "King of Egypt" holds open the possibility that they will obey rather than oppose him. This reversion back to king is temporary. As the failure of this indirect plan comes to light during the confrontation between the king and the midwives in v. 19, he again becomes the despised Pharaoh.[13] The overall pattern of the appearance of this character is quite revealing. The middle (fourth of seven) occurrence is in the middle section (v. 17) of the narrative. The first reference to God (אלהים) also appears in this verse.[14] That this is the only section in the structure outlined above in which the King/Pharaoh and God appear together represents further evidence for regarding v. 17 as the peak of the story. The King/Pharaoh is absent from only one of the seven sections (vv. 20-21), the one which describes God's activity of blessing towards the midwives and the people. God (אלהים) is mentioned twice in vv. 20-21, making a total of three references in the entire narrative. Just as Pharaoh is absent from vv. 20-21, where God is

---

[12]For a thorough discussion of how changes in designation indicate changes in point-of-view, see Bar-Efrat, *Narrative Art in the Bible*, 36-41.

[13]Donald W. Wicke has proposed that "'Pharaoh' is a more personal title than 'King of Egypt'." He offered no support for this suggestion. See "The Literary Structure of Exodus 1:2-2:10," *JSOT* 24(1982): 102-103. This fails to explain, for example, the preponderance of references to "Pharaoh" in Exodus 14. On the other hand, the proposal that the two names for Egypt's leader reflect whether he is one who is being obeyed (King of Egypt) or is one who is opposing the Israelites (Pharaoh), is illustrated perfectly by the use of both terms side by side in 14:5. Here he is King of Egypt to his own people who are informing him of events, but he instantly transforms into Pharaoh as his mind "changes toward the people" and he decides to pursue them.

[14]It must be acknowledged that standard source criticism would associate the appearance of God at this point in the story with the beginning of the Elohist account in v. 15. See Hyatt, *Exodus*, 66.

the narrative subject, God is absent from vv. 11-14, where Pharaoh's people are the primary narrative subject.

The names by which the victims are called varies to a greater extent. As the narrative progresses, they are identified as:

> The people (עם) of the children of Israel (v. 9)
> The children of Israel (v. 12)
> The children of Israel (v. 13)
> The Hebrews (v. 15)
> The Hebrews (v. 16)
> The Hebrew women (v. 19)
> The people (עם) (v. 20)[15]

Here a striking pattern is apparent. They begin the narrative with the fullest of designations, "the people of the children of Israel." In the course of the account of oppression (vv. 11-14) they are diminished to "children of Israel."[16] After the account of oppression, they become "the Hebrews." The term "Hebrew" is typically used by foreigners while the chosen people tend to refer to themselves as "the children of Israel."[17] The name change, therefore, signals a change in the story

---

[15]LXX, Targums, and Samaritan Pentateuch all read "newborn sons of the Hebrews" in v. 21, which would add one more reference to the chosen people by name in these versions.

[16]As mentioned in note 8 above, the change in name for this group may be attributed to the author's use of sources. In no way am I denying the composite nature of the narrative or this conclusion about the change of names. Rather, I wish to emphasize the artistry of the author responsible for the final form. Such narrative artistry is magnified if achieved in spite of the constraints of existing sources. Vv. 8-12 and vv. 13-14 may represent two originally independent accounts of Egyptian oppression, the Yahwist and Priestly respectively. Nevertheless, they are each woven into the overall story to serve a literary (and theological?) purpose, not simply plopped down into the text side by side. For more thorough discussions of this phenomenon, see Alter, *The Art of Biblical Narrative*, 147-154 and Anthony C. Thiselton, *New Horizons in Hermeneutics* (Grand Rapids: Zondervan, 1992) 481.

[17]The chosen people occasionally referred to themselves as Hebrews, but only in comparison or reference to other nations. For a detailed discussion, see E. Kautzsch and A. E. Cowley, *Gesenius' Hebrew Grammar* (Oxford: Clarendon, 1910) 8-9.

from an Israelite to an Egyptian point-of-view.[18] Only when God's blessings are described in vv. 20-21 do the slaves regain some of their stature, being designated the "people" (עַם).This term is one of great significance in the first half of the book of Exodus, in which the children of Israel strive, with the help of their God, to become a people. The climactic moment comes when they become a people (עַם) acquired by God in Exodus 15:16. So it is not surprising to find the term used in the first and last reference to this chosen people in this text. Likewise the Egyptians are described twice by the word עַם, the first and last times they are mentioned in passage. The two references to the Egyptians as people (עַם) in v. 8 and v. 22 completely enclose the two references to the Israelites using this word, holding them captive in the text just as in history. Only Joseph (v.8) and the "newborn sons" (v.22) stand outside this verbal bracket. To the reader who is aware of the biblical tradition, this is a final word of hope. For just as Joseph was thrown (שׁלך) into a pit to die (Genesis 37:24), but survived to rule over Egypt, a male child who was to have been thrown (שׁלך) into the Nile will lead the Israelites to victory over Egypt.

The experience that changes this group from the children of Israel to Hebrews is the narrative of oppression in vv. 11-14.[19] The transformation of the people into slaves takes place through a series of terms piled onto this narrative like so many heavy bundles piled onto the back of a slave.[20]

> v. 11 They placed over them captains as <u>taskmasters</u> to <u>afflict</u> them in their <u>labor</u>.

> v. 12 But as they <u>oppressed</u> them, they became many (רבה) and spread, and they <u>loathed</u> the presence of the children of Israel.

---

[18]Cassuto noted the diminishing status of the Israelites in v. 15 as they become enslaved, but he did not discuss specifically the issue of literary point of view. See *Commentary of the Book of Exodus*, 13.

[19]Norbert Lohfink has outlined within the Pentateuch a negative view of technology. In Exodus 1:8-22, technological development is dependent on slave labor. God delivers the Israelites from what amounts to "false work." See Lohfink, *"Theology of the Pentateuch: Themes of the Priestly Narrative and Deuteronomy* (Edinburgh: T&T Clark, 1994) 132.

[20]An additional sign of hope in v.22 may be its connection with Abraham's fear (Genesis 12:12) that the Egyptians would kill him and let Sarah live, and the knowledge that God saved Abraham. Ibid., 16.

v. 13 The children of Israel served (עבד) Egypt in <u>harshness</u>.

v. 14 They made their lives <u>bitter</u> with <u>hard service</u> (עבד) in clay and brick and in every kind of <u>service</u> (עבד) in the field. All their <u>service</u> (עבד) which they <u>served</u> (עבד) for them was with <u>harshness</u>.[21]

The reader, in any language, cannot help but feel the weight of these verses.[22] The fivefold appearance of the root עבד is quite significant here. This root appears twice more in 2:23 completing a total of seven occurrences leading up to the time when God hears (שמע) God's people and remembers (זכר) the covenant in 2:24. The same pattern recurs later when the root, עבד, appears seven times in Exodus 5 before God hears (שמע) and remembers (זכר) in 6:5.[23] The enslavement of the Israelites, which forms the crisis which consumes the beginning of the book of Exodus begins here in these verses in a devastating and oppressive manner which the language of the text makes profoundly clear. The use of "bitter" (מרר) in v. 14 links this description with the Passover tradition of the bitter (מרר) herbs in

---

[21]Some commentators have suggested that vv. 13-14 be viewed as a second, separate set of actions from vv. 11-12. Exum has carefully and convincingly demonstrated how the structure of these two pairs of verses fits them together into a coherent whole. See "You Shall Let Every Daughter Live: A Study of Exodus 1:8-2:10," 69.

[22]Durham has indicated an "intensification" of oppression in vv. 13-14 (the Priestly description) compared to vv. 11-12 (the Yahwist description). He has even raised the possibility that vv. 13-14 were written specifically to heighten the effect of vv. 11-12. See Durham, *Exodus*, 6-8. This is a good example of a case where source analysis does not contradict rhetorical analysis. The source critic here would be attempting the additional step of identifying the final composer of the text as the Priestly writer.

[23]The appearance of עבד in groups of seven is one of the many examples of this phenomenon of sevenfold repetition observed by Cassuto. See *A Commentary on the Book of Exodus*, 12. Cassuto also noted a total of seven uses of the roots עבד and פרך combined in vv. 11-14 (p. 12). J. P. Fokkelman has also noticed that עבד occurs seven times in the portion of the Jacob cycle which takes place in the household of Laban. See *Narrative Art in Genesis* (Amsterdam: Van Gorcum, 1975) 130. Once again, this group of seven is followed by God hearing (שמע) and remembering (זכר) Rachel in Genesis 30:22. The link between עבד and זכר/שמע is pointed out by Devorah Steinmetz in *From Father to Son: Kinship, Conflict, and Continuity in Genesis* (Louisville: Westminster/John Knox, 1991) 137-139.

Exodus 12:8.[24] Nevertheless, the chosen people are undaunted. They continue to become many (רבה) before (v. 9), during (v. 12), and after (v. 20) this report of their oppression.

The failure of the King/Pharaoh's first plan gives rise to a second even more diabolical plan in vv. 15-21. He asks the Hebrew midwives to kill all the male children of the Hebrews.[25] As illustrated in the outline at the beginning of this discussion, the account of the midwives takes place in four units alternating between speech and narrative. It is within this account of the midwives that the true conflict of the story lies.[26] The midwives disobey the King of Egypt and fail to do (עשה) as he tells them because they fear God.[27] Verse 17, which forms the high point of the passage reports God's victory through the actions of the midwives. Vv. 20-21 reiterate the midwives' fear of God, confirming that God's favor has overcome the King's second plan, and that God will make (עשה) houses for the midwives. English translations cannot reflect the duplication of the root עשה in reporting what God "will make" for them in v. 21 because of what they do not "do" in v. 17.[28] The people become "many (רבה) and very mighty (עצם)." In addition,

---

[24]Cassuto, *A Commentary on the Book of Exodus*, 11.

[25]The word typically translated "birthing stool" in v. 16 is the most problematic word in the entire passage. Its only other occurrence in the Hebrew Bible is in Jeremiah 18:3, where it refers to some device used by a potter. Because this word is in the Hebrew dual form and derives from the root meaning "stone" (אבן), many interpreters have suggested that it is a euphemism for "testicles." This linguistic argument appears to be quite strong and the subsequent meaning fits the context very well. See the discussion in Durham, *Exodus*, 11-12.

[26]At least two possible chiastic arrangements of vv. 15-22 have been proposed. See Exum, "You Shall Let Every Daughter Live...," 71-72; D. W. Wicke, "The Literary Structure of Exodus 1:-2:10," *JSOT* 24 (1982): 101-102. Exum's proposal is particularly appealing. She pointed to Pharaoh as a source of death on the outside of the passage in v. 15 and v. 22, the midwives as a source of life in the middle of the passage in v. 17b and v. 18, and the fear of God as the factor separating the midwives from Pharaoh in v. 17a and v. 21 (p. 71).

[27]There has been some debate over the ethnicity of the midwives. The phrase in v. 15, "the midwives of the Hebrews," is ambiguous. Their names, on the other hand, are clearly Semitic names from that period. See W. F. Albright, "Northwest-Semitic Names in a List of Egyptian Slaves from the Eighteenth Century B. C.," *JAOS* 74 (1954): 233. It is difficult, however, to understand why Pharaoh would expect Hebrew women to murder the children of their own people. See Childs, *Exodus*, 16.

[28]The repetition of עשה forms part of the chiastic structure in vv. 15-22 proposed by Wicke. See "The Literary Structure of Exodus 1:2-2:10," 101-102.

the midwives are blessed with children of their own.[29] The role of the midwives is further emphasized by the sevenfold appearance of the term in this passage.[30] Drorah O'Donnell Setel has summed up powerfully the significance of the midwives in the story, "As those who aid birth, they are the first to assist in the birth of the Israelite nation."[31]

Pharaoh's third plan (v. 22), to have his people throw the male children into the Nile, completes this narrative and serves at least two other purposes. As mentioned previously, it functions along with the reference to Joseph in v. 8 to remind the reader that Israelite boys thrown (שלך) to their deaths ultimately rise up over Egypt. V. 21 also serves to set up the story of Moses' childhood which follows it. The story ends with an increasingly desperate Pharaoh still trying to destroy a growing people. He offers his first plan (v. 10) to his people using a cohortative form of the Hebrew verb ("come let us deal wisely"). His second plan he simply speaks (אמר) to the Hebrew midwives in a straightforward fashion (v. 15). In his final attempt, he now "commands" (צוה) his people to carry out the third. That the speech beginning in v. 9 is directed to "his people" while the speech in v. 22 is to "all his people" may indicate that the first plan is made privately among royal officials while the third is announced publicly.[32] Again, this would highlight a growing sense of desperation. Thus, the story ends on a frightening but hopeful note.

Theological Conclusions

The violence described in Exodus 1:8-22 does not involve explicit murder, but is primarily about the oppression of one group of people by another. To be sure, murder is not absent from the story. Forced labor can lead to the death of some individuals (see Exod. 21:20-21). The plot involving the midwives is a conspiracy to commit murder. The final verse of this text leaves open the possibility that some infants were killed. Nevertheless, this story should be a reminder that violence can take on more subtle forms. Such continuous violence has a cumulative effect, just as the heavy words in the sequence in vv. 11-14 weigh down the reader one by one.

---

[29]The possibility that barren women were used as midwives would magnify the miraculous power of God's provision. See Hyatt, *Exodus*, 61.

[30]Cassuto, *A Commentary on the Book of Exodus*, 15.

[31]Setel, "Exodus," in *The Women's Bible Commentary*, ed. Carol A. Newsom and Sharon H. Ringe (London: SPCK, 1992) 30.

[32]Cassuto, *A Commentary on the Book of Exodus*, 16.

The focus of this account of violence, because of its context in the biblical plot, is on the victim. A free people becomes an enslaved people, subject to the whims, fears, and desires of a tyrannical ruler. Violence alters the victim. The change in the status of the victim is reflected in the change of the victim's name in the text. The children of Israel, a group with the freedom to name itself, become the Hebrews, a group named by their oppressors. The account of oppression in vv. 11-14, which brings about the gradual change in identity, leaves the reader wondering about the presence of God in the midst of brutality. The divine appearance is delayed in this story, but it does finally arrive. At the moment when it appears the King of Egypt might prevail, God appears in v. 17 to foil the first plan to kill the male children. The daring belief that God is on the side of the victim rather than the side of the powerful and successful, which first surfaces in the stories of Joseph's rise from slavery, becomes clearer. This notion of God is the direct opposite of that which dominated the ancient Near East. The gods all around the people of Israel were gods which inaugurated and upheld the structures of the wealthy and powerful.[33] Such a notion was so original and radical that even the Israelites themselves were unable to maintain a society based on the ethic of a group of former slaves and their God.[34] Through two courageous midwives, God confronts the oppressor, and God's blessings spoil the plans of the despot. Yet, if the violence of this text is somewhat subtle, then the presence of God is subtler still. There is no theophany here, as in the later stories in the Book of Exodus. There is no direct speech from God to these victims. Only successful procreation, as a sign of God's blessing, serves as a promise of God's presence and deliverance.

The oppressor in this story is motivated by a fear of being displaced. The King of Egypt is afraid he will lose his position of power over others (v. 9). The reaction to such fear is a plan of oppression proposed in a rather cordial manner, "Come let us deal wisely..." (v. 10). When this first attempt fails, another is secretly promoted in a more urgent manner (v. 15). Encountering failure again, the king publicly "commands" a final, desperate scheme. Violence is conceived and carried out in a progressively vigorous and open manner. What begins as a discretely planned attempt to maintain the status quo becomes a publicly announced attempt at genocide. The identity of the perpetrator again is altered by violent activity. He is "King of Egypt" only to those who

---

[33]Paul D. Hanson, *The People Called: The Growth of Community in the Bible* (San Francisco: Harper & Row, 1986) 21-22.

[34]Ibid., 23.

acknowledge and obey his authority. To those whom he oppresses and who defy his authority because of this oppression, he becomes "Pharaoh."

Girard has proposed that a dominating principle which functions in certain societies is the need for "cultural distinctions." He has stated further that "it is not these distinctions but the loss of them that gives birth to fierce rivalries."[35] This principle is clearly in operation in Exodus 1:8-22. As long as the Egyptians and their king can differentiate themselves as "many and mighty" compared to the other groups within their society, there is no need for oppression. It is the threat that others are becoming like them that creates the crisis in this text. Williams, following Girard's theory, characterized this story as a "rivalry between Israel and Egypt." This rivalry is the result of "undifferentiation." The subsequent disorder in the society portrayed in this text is revealed by typical signs, such as the murder of infants.[36]

Though this story is dominated by conspiracies of violence, there is also prevention of violence. What gives rise to such hopeful activity? The courageous actions of the midwives are grounded in their fear of God (v. 17). The blessing of children comes to them because of this same fear (v. 21). From the biblical perspective, "The fear of the LORD is the beginning of knowledge" (Proverbs 1:7). The King of Egypt lacks knowledge (v. 8) because his fear is misplaced. Those like the midwives who fear God have the knowledge which provides hope even in the midst of oppression.

In summary, violence results from the fear of losing power and being displaced. The emotions that drive violence become more intense when it fails to accomplish its purpose. As violence intensifies it emerges from secrecy and begins to consume an entire society. The effects of oppression on the victims are also progressive and eventually alter their identity, making them unable to act freely and to name themselves. The reader glimpses God's solidarity with victims, which is enacted through faithful and courageous human individuals.[37] Thus, questions about God's presence with the victim are answered here only in part. Schwager's view of violence stands as a challenge: "In a world no longer illumined by [God's] face, work and pregnancy become

---

[35]Girard, *Violence and the Sacred*, 49.

[36]Williams, *The Bible, Violence, and the Sacred*, 73.

[37]Brown has noted the importance of recognizing that the individuals in this story are women, who receive too little attention from scripture and its interpretation, both of which tend to be male-dominated. Brown, *Unexpected News*, 38.

burdensome, and one feels the urge to kill another...People punish one another and hide from God's face. He is hidden because violent human beings crawl away from him."[38] But what about the victim? Liberation perspectives find hope in the Exodus story. It affirms that God is on the side of the oppressed. [39] This hint of hope in Exodus 1:8-22 will come into clear view as the biblical plot progresses.

---

[38]Schwager, *Must There Be Scapegoats*, 70.
[39]Brown, *Unexpected News*, 34-39.

3

GOD'S PEOPLE LIBERATED
BY VIOLENCE

EXODUS 11:1-12:39

The people who are oppressed in Exodus 1:8-22 have found a source of hope for liberation. In 2:24, God hears their groaning and raises up a leader to deliver them from bondage. Moses meets God in the wilderness. In 3:15, Moses is given God's personal name, Yahweh, and is commanded to return to Egypt to free the children of Israel. A series of nine relatively minor plagues fails to convince Pharaoh to let the people go. His refusals lead to the climax of the Exodus story.[1] Exodus 11-12 reports the killing of the firstborn in Egypt, the violent act which makes it possible for the children of Israel to escape from slavery. This story of violence is fundamentally different from the texts examined so far. Because God becomes the perpetrator of violence, profound theological questions should arise from the reading of this text.

The Text

The Passover complex in Exodus 11-12 provides a tremendous challenge to anyone attempting a rhetorical analysis.[2] The first task is to

---

[1]It may seem that the deliverance at the sea could be the climax of the Exodus story, but George W. Coats has shown that Exodus 14-15 properly belongs with the Wilderness tradition and serves to connect Exodus to Wilderness. See "The Traditio-historical Character of the Reed Sea Motif," *VT* 17 (1967): 265.

[2]This difficulty is due primarily to the obvious composite nature of the text. Traditional source analysis of these two chapters is quite complicated and is in dispute at a few points. The results of such analysis will be referred to occasionally below. For a detailed summary of the results of source criticism on this passage, see Durham, *Exodus*, 146-173.

determine the boundaries of the unit to be treated. The Passover complex provides no clear signals. At the same time, there are several ambiguous alternatives. The actual episode of violence is reported in 12:29-36. While these eight verses are, to some extent, a self-contained unit, they are too intimately associated with the material around them to be analyzed in isolation. Because nearly all of the material in these two chapters is reported twice, it is possible to see 12:21-42 as a complete report of the inauguration of the Passover celebration, the enactment of the final plague, and the escape from Egypt. This realization, however, points to the decisive factor. The final decision here, to establish the text as 11:1–12:39, is based on this very repetition. The text may be organized as follows:

> 11:1-3   Yahweh foretells the departure from Egypt to Moses
> 11:4-8   Moses announces the final plague to Pharaoh
> 11:9-10   Pharaoh refuses to obey Yahweh
> 12:1-20   Yahweh instructs Moses and Aaron about the Passover
> 12:21-27a   Moses instructs the elders about the Passover
> 12:27a-28   The Israelites obey Yahweh's command
> 12:29-32   Yahweh carries out the final plague
> 12:33-39   The Israelites depart from Egypt[3]

---

[3]Both the selection of boundaries for this text and the division into smaller units cuts across the traditional divisions of both source critics and other commentators, such as Childs, who see Exodus 11 as the completion of the plague narrative in 7:8 through 11:10. See Childs, *Exodus*, 160-162. Cassuto likewise places a major division between chapters eleven and twelve. See *A Commentary on the Book of Exodus*, 131-136. Coats extended the plague narrative from 7:8 to 12:36, but he understood the Passover complex as and "appendix" (p. 108) that was only added later in the development of the tradition (*Moses: Heroic Man, Man of God*, JSOTS 57 [Sheffield: Sheffield, 1988] 89-108). Moshe Greenberg argued for a structure which divides the plague narratives into three sets of three plagues based on introductory formulas. The Passover is not included in this sequence. See "The Thematic Unity of Exodus iii-xi," *Fourth World Congress of Jewish Studies* (Jerusalem: World Union of Jewish Studies, 1967) 153. Dennis J. McCarthy developed an elaborate chiastic pattern of ten plagues, but this included the changing of the rod into a snake as the first plague and excluded the Passover. See "Moses' Dealings with Pharaoh: Ex. 7, 8-10, 27," *CBQ* 27 (1965): 336-345. These arguments become somewhat entangled in source critical and traditio-critical attempts to determine stages of development in the plague traditions. Licht's argument, based on literary factors, that the final plague forms an entirely separate story from the first nine is quite convincing. His separation of the two is based largely on the distinct literary patterns found

I have not divided the text in terms of narration and discourse, as with previous passages. Thus, some of the sections are a mixture of the two modes of storytelling. The more important organizing factor is repetition. Once again, there is the temptation to see a chiastic structure within the unit.[4] Certainly, the sections match, to some degree, in a concentric pattern. I will leave open the possibility of such a structure, without insisting upon it. In light of the possibility of a chiastic structure, however, two observations are necessary at the outset. First, the center of the passage is the two sets of instructions concerning the Passover celebration. This arguably makes these instructions the focal point of the story. They certainly dominate the account in terms of length. Second, the episode of violence (12:29-32) and its prior announcement (11:4-8) are not central. A key issue for the evaluation of this text will be the effect of the decentralization of violence.

In 11:1-3, Yahweh announces to Moses that a final plague will bring about the departure of the people from Egypt. In 12:33-39, the fulfillment of this announcement is described.[5] There are four important elements which are repeated in each of these passages. First, the Israelites are driven out (גרש) of the land of Egypt (11:16 and 12:34). As mentioned in chapter two, Adam and Eve were driven out (גרש) of the garden in 3:24 and Cain is driven away (גרש) from the ground in Genesis 4:15. The word carries with it a dramatic sense of an altered state of existence. Second, the Israelites ask their Egyptian neighbors for objects (כלי) of silver and gold.[6] In 12:35, the Israelites also ask the

---

in the first nine plagues, which do not extend into Exodus 11-12 (*Storytelling in the Bible*, 66).

[4]See Bar-Efrat's warning against the ubiquity of chiastic analysis in "Some Observations of Structure in Biblical Narrative," 170.

[5]The relationship between these two sections is further complicated by the fact that they both repeat much of Exodus 3:20-22. These relationships, of course, provide the material for extensive source critical debate. For a thorough discussion of the interpretative and theological problems created by the "despoiling" of the Egyptians, see Childs, *Exodus*, 175-177.

[6]The change in translation to "jewelry of" in the NRSV at 12:35 does not reflect any difference in the Hebrew of 11:2 and 12:35. The NRSV also renders כלי as "jewelry of" at 3:22. This likely points to a desire on the part of translators to connect these objects with the gold earrings (נזמי הזהב) which Aaron uses to make the golden calf in Exodus 32:2-4. See Hyatt, *Exodus*, 139. Lying behind the desire to make this connection is perhaps the wish to demonstrate a theological link between the corrupting influence of Egyptian wealth and Israelite idol worship in the wilderness.

Egyptians for clothing (שׂמלה). This additional item is not included in 11:2 but is in 3:22. Third, Yahweh gives the Israelites favor (חן) in the sight of the Egyptians (11:3 and 12:36). The narration in 12:35-36 states more clearly that this favor caused the Egyptians to give the Israelites the articles of value for which they asked. The word חן, which can also be translated as "grace," is too common in the Hebrew Bible for a full catalogue of its use here. Aside from the three references to Israelites finding favor with the Egyptians (3:21, 11:3, and 12:36), the other six uses in Exodus (33:12,13[2],16, 17, and 34:9) all refer to Moses finding favor with Yahweh. The most significant use of this term, theologically, in the Hebrew Bible is probably Noah's finding favor in the eyes of Yahweh (Gen. 6:8). All of this goes to demonstrate that חן carries a very positive meaning, a meaning which adds a note of puzzlement to the present narrative. One would expect the Egyptians to fear and despise the Israelites at this point, but not to look on them with favor.

Indeed, the odd nature of this third point of repetition points to the most significant of the differences between 11:1-3 and 12:33-39.[7] The troubling statement at the end of 12:36, that the Israelites plundered (נצל) the Egyptians, is not reflected in 11:3 but is present in 3:22.[8] Contrary to what the outline of the Passover complex presented above might indicate, the violence of the text is not fully contained within 11:4-8 and 12:29-32. It spills out into the rest of the passage at important points. The verb נצל occurs most frequently in the *niphal* and *hiphil* stems and can clearly carry a meaning such as "deliver." The occurrences in 12:36 and 3:22 are in the *piel* stem which is relatively rare. While נצל can still mean "deliver" or "save" in the *piel* stem (see Ezekiel 14:14), the use in Exodus 12:36 seems to fit much more naturally with the sense of taking spoil after victory in war (see 2 Chronicles 20:25). Thus, the translation, "plunder," with all of its negative connotations seems appropriate. Such connotations clash with the impression created by the finding of favor (חן) and asking (שׁאל) for the objects. The tension here cannot, and should not, be removed from the

---

[7]See Alter's assertion that the differences present in primarily repeated material are the result of a technique used to create "dramatic complications" in *The Art of Biblical Narrative*, 97.

[8]If there is a linguistic connection between the articles taken from the Egyptians and the golden calf episode in Exodus 32-34, it lies in this verb. After the calf is destroyed and the worshippers punished, the people stripped (נצל-plundered?) themselves of their ornaments, presumably to remove the temptation of slipping into idol worship again.

text.[9] The appearance of this new and startling element of plundering in 12:36 heightens the impression that a war has taken place.

In 11:4-8, Moses announces to Pharaoh the coming of the final plague. Much of the language of this section is repeated in the narration of the actual event in 12:29-32. Again, it will be important to examine several repetitions within the two sections and a few revealing differences. Both 11:4-8 and 12:29-32 report the time of the plague as the middle of the night. Both describe the death of the firstborn, followed by a "great cry" in Egypt. Finally, both contain the command from Pharaoh for the people to leave. The first telling difference between the announcement of the event and the event itself is in the corresponding statements of the extent of the plague. In 11:5, death is predicted for all of the firstborn from Pharaoh to "the female slave" (השפחה).[10] The account in 12:29 describes the death of the firstborn from Pharaoh to "the prisoner" (השבי) in the house of the pit.[11] "While the purpose of both statements appears to be the same, to assert that the plague affected Egyptian society from top to bottom, the change is compelling. The story of the Exodus is about the liberation of slaves. It is, therefore,

---

[9]This understanding is in conflict with the influential interpretation of Coats, which may be summarized as follows: (1) God gave the Israelites favor in the sight of the Egyptians, (2) because of this favor the Israelites were able to ask to borrow the objects, (3) the Israelites were able to escape having thus obtained the objects by deception, and (4) this deception amounts to a plundering. See "Despoiling the Egyptians," *VT* 18 (1968): 452-57. Coats's interpretation resolves the tension between asking/receiving favor and plundering, but it does so by assuming that ask (שאל) "suggests borrowing" (p. 453) and that "there is no indication that the Israelites won her spoils as the result of a battle" (p. 453). The former assumption is part of a circular argument—i. e. שאל must mean borrowing so that the Israelites can plunder by deception, and the Israelites plundered by deception because שאל implies borrowing. To the latter assumption I must respond that there are no indications of a battle except that a conflict between the Israelites and the Egyptians which has been raging for nearly five chapters has just ended with a dead body in every Egyptian house. For further arguments against Coats see Durham, *Exodus*, 148.

[10]Cassuto noted that this phrase of inclusion is common in Egyptian literature. See *A Commentary on the Book of Exodus*, 133.

[11]The translation of בית הבור as "dungeon" (NRSV) is unsatisfactory, as it implies a place under the palace. While this translation does provide top-to-bottom imagery, it does not match the statement in 12:30 that "there was no house which was not a place of death." The literal rendering of בית הבור, "house of the pit," paired with the reference to Pharaoh's throne, provides a fuller picture of destruction from the top house to the bottom house.

surprising to find a slave as a potential victim of Yahweh's liberating activity in 11:5. It is not surprising to find that in the actual record of the event the slave is not mentioned as a victim. This word for female slave, שׁפחה, does not appear again in the book of Exodus. No Hebrew slave is so designated, however, שׁפחות is frequently paired with עבדם (male slaves) elsewhere in the Bible to create the phrase "male slaves and female slaves.[12] עבדם is used to describe the condition of the Israelites in Egypt (see Exodus 13:3). Therefore, the slave in 11:5 could be seen, along with Israel, as a victim of Egyptian oppression, and her inclusion among those who would be stricken by the final plague adds a troubling note to the plague narrative. This element is removed from the report of the actual event.[13]

While the replacement of the female slave (11:5) with the prisoner (12:29) may mitigate the effects of violence for some, the overall impact of the final plague is intensified from 11:4-8 to 12:29-32. The phrase "for there was no house which was not a place of death" is added to the report in 12:30.[14] In addition, the speech of Pharaoh in 12:31-32 is a great deal more desperate than the one foretold in 11:8. Not only does he ask a blessing for himself, but he calls the people by name, "children of Israel" (בני ישראל), for the first time in the book of Exodus since 1:8.[15]

Exodus 11:9-10 tells of Pharaoh's refusal to heed Moses' warning about the final plague. This brief section of the text does not have a matching repetition. A connection to 12:27b-28 will be developed momentarily, however. Indeed these two sections may provide the weakest link in the present analysis. For this reason, among others, it is impossible to ignore the conclusions of source criticism concerning these verses. There is a consensus that 11:9-10 is from the P source.[16] The section which follows, 12:1-20, is assigned to P with somewhat less certainty. This links 11:9-10 with the material after it from the perspective of source criticism,[17] while it fits more closely, in a narrative sense, with

---

[12]E. g. Gen 12:16, 20:14, 24:35, and 30:43.

[13]Cassuto attempted to minimize the difference between the two descriptions by stating, without providing supporting evidence, that the characteristic activity of prisoners in the dungeon was grinding corn, like the slave woman of 11:5. Ibid., 144-145.

[14]Durham, *Exodus*, 166.

[15]Pharaoh does refer to "Israel" in Exodus 5:2.

[16]See Durham, 146.

[17]Martin Noth, *Exodus*, OTL (Philadelphia: Westminster, 1962) 94-97.

the preceding verses in chapter 11.[18] In fact, 11:9-10 provides a fitting end to the entire plague narrative of 7:8–11:10.[19] Here is a good example of a place where source criticism may be used to highlight narrative artistry rather than to fragment the text.[20] If the above assignment of sources is correct, then the account in 11:4-8 and all that precedes it has not just been clumsily juxtaposed with 12:1-20, but has been skillfully connected by a narrative link.

Another important narrative connection, similar to the one just described, appears in 12:27b-28. This link lies at the junction between the Passover traditions (12:1-27a) and the report of the final plague (12:29-32). The source-critical debate concerning 12:1-28 is immensely complicated.[21] The assignment of v. 28 to P seems to be a majority opinion. Though v. 27b is not assigned to P, the majority of commentators do assign it to a different source (J) from vv. 24-27a (D).[22] Once again, the final writer has provided a brief, artful connection between two larger units.

Additionally, 11:9-10 and 12:27b-28 share a thematic connection. They contrast the disobedience of Pharaoh with the obedience of the Israelites. In 12:28, the Israelites respond to Yahweh's command to Moses and Aaron by doing (עשׂה) exactly as they are instructed. In 11:9-10, Pharaoh responds to the wonders done (עשׂה) by Moses and Aaron by refusing to let the Israelites go.

This brings us to the heart of the Passover complex, the paired descriptions of the ritual that this final plague will inaugurate. The narrative, which moves along briskly at the beginning and end of Exodus 11-12, comes to a grinding halt in the middle. 12:1-20 presents Yahweh's instructions to Moses and Aaron, and 12:21-27a Moses' subsequent instructions to the elders. Once again, an examination of similarities and differences between the two units will illuminate

---

[18]Durham, *Exodus*, 149.

[19]That some interpreters (See Childs, *Exodus*, 160-162) see 7:8–11:10 as a self-contained unit is perhaps the most serious challenge to the choice of a text for this chapter. Hopefully the present argument concerning 11:10 will justify the choice.

[20]Note Trible's encouragement to make use, when possible, of the results of source criticism to complement rhetorical analysis. See *Rhetorical Criticism*, 101. These two disciplines would seem to move in completely opposite directions. Hopefully, the present attempt to hold them together in a dynamic fashion is not too tortured.

[21]For a summary, see Durham, *Exodus*, 161-162.

[22]See Hyatt, *Exodus*, 136-137.

important themes.[23] Both 12:1-20 and 12:21-27a give instructions for choosing and preparing the lamb (vv. 3-6 and 21) and the putting of blood on the lintel and doorposts as protection against being struck down (vv. 7,13 and 22-23). Each unit specifically mentions the blood (דם) three times (vv. 7,13[2], and 22[2],23). In both cases Yahweh will pass through (עבר) Egypt (vv. 12 and 23) and pass over (פסח) the Israelites (vv. 12 and 23). Finally, both sets of instructions command that this celebration be observed faithfully in the future (vv. 14-20 and 24-27a).

The most striking difference between 12:1-20 and 12:21-27a is that the former passage is considerably longer and gives much more attention to details. These characteristics create a distinct change in tone between the two descriptions. Chapter 12:1-20 is slow-paced and deliberate. It seems more interested in the ritual itself than in the event it will commemorate. There are detailed instructions for eating in vv. 8-11 that are not paralleled in the second unit. On the other hand, 12:21-27a is hurried, almost frantic in tone. While the verbs in 12:1-20 are mostly in the third person, with a few second person forms, 12:21-27a begins with three stunning imperatives—separate (משך), seize (לקח), and slaughter (שחט). The second passage seems much more concerned with the coming event of deliverance than its future ritual commemoration. The narrative pace of the Passover complex slows down for the instructions in 12:1-20, but as the impending violence approaches, the pace accelerates in 12:21-27a, and the text takes on a sudden sense of urgency. The brief instructions from the mouth of Moses also match the nature of the story quite well. While the formal, intricate instructions in 12:1-20 sound like speech coming from a deity, the words in 12:21-27a seem to come from a man in a hurry.[24]

There are a number of curious changes in terminology within and between these two units. The lamb is specifically mentioned five times in 12:1-20.[25] The first four times (vv. 3,4[2],5) it is called שה, and the final time a פסח, literally a "passover." The lamb is specifically

---

[23]Of course, these two units have almost always been assigned to different sources, and this is one way to explain their differences. For a summary, see Durham, *Exodus*, 152, 157, 161.

[24]This feature is an example of Licht's assertion that "repetitive situations can be used to produce various mimetic effects in the narrative convention of the Hebrew Bible." See *Storytelling in the Bible*, 79.

[25]This excludes references to the lamb using a third person pronoun, which are numerous. Some of these pronominal references are rendered "lamb" in certain English translations, obscuring the count given here.

mentioned three times in 12:21-27a. The first time (v. 21) it is called a צאן, and the final two times (vv. 21,27) it is called a פסח.[26] In both cases the reference to the lamb uses a general term until it is slaughtered (שחט in vv. 6 and 21), at which time the ritual designation appears. This transformation takes place more quickly in 12:21-27a. Chapter 12:1-20 states one time that Yahweh will strike down (נכה) the Egyptian first born (v. 12) and again that Yahweh will strike down (נכה) the land of Egypt (v. 13). There will be no smiting (נגף) of Israel, however (v. 13). 12:21-27a twice mentions that Yahweh will smite (נגף) the Egyptians (vv. 23,27) and once that Yahweh will not smite (נגף) Israel (v. 23). While what will not happen to the Israelites is the same in both units, the description of the punishment of the Egyptians changes dramatically. Not only is a different verb used, but 12:2-27a makes no mention of the firstborn. The limits of the pending violence, present in 12:1-20, disappear as the event draws near. Though only the firstborn will actually die, the second unit more accurately portrays the plague as a strike at every Egyptian.

Finally, the most dramatic difference between 12:1-20 and 12:21-27a is the attempt to distance Yahweh from the act of violence in the latter passage. Until the end of v. 23, Yahweh has been the subject doing the striking and smiting. At this point, however, a new figure, the destroyer (המשחית) appears.[27] Yahweh is not removed as the ultimate cause of the action, but is protected from direct involvement in the act of killing.

Theological Conclusions

The above analysis has moved from the outside to the center because that is what the text forces the reader to do. The movement of the narrative is from the aftermath of the plague (11:1-3) to the plague itself (11:4-8) to the plan to protect the Israelites from the plague (12:1-27a) to the plague itself (12:29-32) to the aftermath of the plague (12:33-39). The act of violence itself is wrapped in acts of deliverance.

---

[26]The first occurrence contains a definite article, הפסח. Some English translations may obscure the second occurrence. The Hebrew phrase in v. 27 literally reads, "This is a sacrifice of a passover to the LORD."

[27]Another form of this word, the infinitive המשחית, does appear in v.13, perhaps providing an early hint of the destroyer's presence. The last phrase literally reads, "But there will not be on you a smiting for destruction when I strike down the land of Egypt."

The previous chapter dealt with a text, Exodus 1:8-22, in which God was on the side of the victims of violence. In Exodus 11-12, the structures of oppression which characterize Egyptian society are turned upside down. Williams has argued that during the plague narratives in Exodus 7-12 "the total fabric of social order is rent."[28] Those who once perpetrated violence now become victims. The difference is that the Egyptians may not be considered innocent victims. The position of the text is quite clear. Pharaoh is obstinate (11:9-10) while the Israelites are obedient (12:27b-28). Therefore, the inflicting of death upon the Egyptian firstborn is justified. But those who die are children. Viewed in terms of Egyptian society as a whole, the punishment may be justified because they killed Hebrew babies (1:22). Williams has noted this "symmetry of the cycle of violence and revenge," which first appears in 4:22-23.[29] Nevertheless, those most directly affected by the plague appear to be innocent. The text may indicate at least some awareness of the problem of innocent suffering. The female slave who determines the lower boundary of the victim group in 11:5 is replaced by a prisoner in 12:29. The text struggles to keep Yahweh on the side of the innocent victim, while at the same time affirming Yahweh as a powerful deliverer who works terrible wonders to free the oppressed.

Paul D. Hanson has aptly chastened those of us from the "First World" who are offended by the Divine Warrior image for our attempts to deprive the oppressed of today's world of this powerful and sustaining aspect of God's presence.[30] It is essential that modern readers engage in this struggle along with the text, rather than deny its existence.[31]

The mechanism of substitution emerges in Exodus 11:1–12:39 as a means of minimizing violence and holding it within boundaries. First, the firstborn of Egypt are killed as a replacement for the entire nation. Second, the death of the Passover lamb serves as a substitute for the

---

[28]Williams, *The Bible, Violence, and the Sacred*, 73. Williams further argued that the violent conflict taking place within Egyptian society is a reflection of a cosmic conflict between the God of Israel and the gods of the Egyptians, who are represented by Moses and Pharaoh respectively (p. 76).

[29]Ibid., 77.

[30]Paul D. Hanson, *The Diversity of Scripture: A Theological Approach* (Philadelphia: Fortress, 1984).

[31]For a concrete illustration of this very struggle, see Frank Chikane's defense of the South African "Kairos Theologians" in "Where the Debate Ends," in *Theology and Violence: The South African Debate*, ed. Charles Villa-Vicencio (Grand Rapids: Eerdmans, 1988) 304-306.

firstborn of Israel.[32] The blood on the doorposts, which appears prominently in the text, satisfies the destroyer, in place of the Israelite firstborn. Again, the text struggles to contain and control the impact of violence. The pending storm of the final plague is slowed by the detailed ritual material in 12:1-20, but the frantic retelling of this material in 12:21-27a accelerates the storm's arrival. The death of the firstborn, first mentioned in Yahweh's Passover instructions to Moses and Aaron (12:12), breaks out of control and threatens all Egyptians in Moses' instructions to the elders (12:23,27). The plague is contained in the actual report of the deaths (12:29), but threatens to break out of its boundaries again in the terrified statement of the Egyptians, "We shall all be dead" (12:33). The control of violence is a precarious process.

Changes of identity once again accompany violent activity, just as in the texts studied in chapters two and three. The most important is the change in the Israelites' identity in the view of Pharaoh. Throughout the plague narratives, Pharaoh had not called the Israelites by name except for the one partial exception noted in 5:2, but after the death of his firstborn son they become "the children of Israel" to him. It would be a mistake not to notice that the change of identity inflicted by violence affects the sheep in this text as well. In both sets of Passover instructions, the act of slaughtering alters the sheep from שׂה (11:3-5) or צאן (12:21) to ritual objects (פסח – 11:11, 12:21).

The final, and most crucial, issue is the question of Yahweh's involvement in the events of Exodus 11:1 – 12:39 and the subsequent effect on the biblical portrait of Yahweh's character. There are both intra-biblical and extra-biblical attempts to distance God from the troubling activity of infanticide. The plague is foretold five times (11:4-5, 12:12,13,23,27) before it happens. Each time Yahweh is the direct agent. Three times (11:13, 12:23,27) Yahweh's sparing of the Israelites is foretold, and in the middle reference only (12:23) the "destroyer" is described as the agent of violence. The text does not overtly remove Yahweh from direct responsibility, but subtly hints at another possibility. Many interpreters have offered naturalistic explanations of many of the plagues, and this final plague is no exception. There are no clues in the text for understanding this as anything like a disease which

---

[32]Williams, *The Bible, Violence, and the Sacred*, 78. Williams has developed this theme significantly in terms of sacrifice, as it is a key theme in the Girardian paradigm. See *Violence and the Sacred*, 4-6. Just as sacrifice operates generally as a limitation of violence, so the death of the firstborn of Egypt is "a limitation of the disease and disorder that a massive plague could produce." See Williams, *The Bible, Violence and the Sacred*, 120.

struck only children. While it is possible that this is what happened, such an explanation falls within the realm of historical analysis that has nothing to do with the text or the theology it presents.[33] While the blow is somewhat softened by the text (12:23), the realization that Yahweh has acted violently to deliver the Israelites nonetheless hits home. The striking final phrase in 12:36, that the Israelites "plundered the Egyptians," marks the end of a war which the underdogs have won with the help of their God. Girard's observations about reprisal and the rapidity with which victor and vanquished exchange roles are poignant and powerful.[34] This exchange has already begun to characterize Israel's story even as the new nation is in the process of being birthed.

To summarize, Exodus 11:1 – 12:39 reveals four important facets of violence. First, Yahweh emerges as the perpetrator of violence – the Divine Warrior – and this role cannot be denied. Second, substitutions act to contain violence, but violence always threatens to explode out of the boundaries arranged for it. Third, as noted in previous chapters, violent activity changes the identity of characters in the story. Finally, the act of deliverance has changed the oppressed into conquerors and they act like conquerors. The question left hanging is "How is the identity of Yahweh as a God of victims threatened when Yahweh's people begin to act more like conquerors than victims?"

---

[33]I find the explanation of George A. F. Knight particularly bizarre and perverse. Through a process of demythologizing and remythologizing, Knight arrived at the conclusion that "Evil produces situations in history from which there is no way out – except suffering love. So even the deaths of babies are caught up into the great plan that God is working out in human history." This statement suffers the dual distinction of both not taking the text of Exodus seriously and, while trying to defend God, making God into an even greater monster. See *Theology as Narration: A Commentary on the Book of Exodus* (Grand Rapids: Eerdmans, 1976) 92-93.

[34]Girard, *Violence and the Sacred*, 158.

INTERLUDE THREE:
GOD'S PEOPLE IN THE
WILDERNESS

The textual distance between the first Passover and the conquering of Jericho is great, but the chronological and geographical distances are relatively small. The children of Israel are liberated from slavery in Exodus 12, but not until the conquest in the book of Joshua do they have a place in which to begin to exercise their freedom. The in-between-time depicted by the biblical story from Exodus 13 to Joshua 5 begins with the movement of the Israelites into the wilderness and ends with their movement out of the wilderness. The move into the wilderness begins with the crossing of a sea (Exodus 14-15) and the move out of the wilderness begins with the crossing of a river (Joshua 3-4). The texts within this large portion of the Bible can be roughly divided into three types: (1) the Sinai legal material comprising almost all of Exodus 20 to Numbers 10, (2) the speeches of Moses which make up much of the book of Deuteronomy, and (3) wilderness narratives interspersed throughout the unit. The Passover complex sets the precedent for this combination of elements. It contains the first ritual legislation (Exodus 12:1-20) and the first speech of Moses to the Israelites (12:21-27), set within the narrative framework of God's liberating activity.

The preceding chapter of this study concluded with four obser-vations about violence in the Passover narrative. Each of these carries forward into the wilderness tradition. First, Yahweh, the God of the Israelites, commits acts of violence and the Divine Warrior image emerges. The violent retribution of Yahweh appears numerous times in the wilderness. Yahweh routs the Egyptians at the sea in Exodus 14-15, commands the slaughter of the Israelites worshipping the golden calf in 32:25-29, strikes Miriam with leprosy in Numbers 12:1-16, threatens to kill all of the Israelites in 14:10-12, destroys the Korahites in 16:23-35, kills 14,700 Israelites with a plague in Numbers 16:41-50, commands the impaling of the Baal worshippers in 25:1-5, commands the Israelite army into battle against the Midianites in 31:1-12, and commands

Joshua to conquer the land of Canaan in Joshua 1:1-9. This list contains some of the narrative acts of violence. The potential acts of violence commanded as enforcement of the laws of the Sinai covenant are much greater in number.

Second, violence threatens to break out of the boundaries set for it. Control over violence is always tenuous. The primary purpose of the legal material which dominates this section seems to be to establish a well ordered society, but the wilderness experience is anything but well ordered. Plague, calamity of nature, and war are the means of liberation and land acquisition for the people of Israel. But these violent forces claim Israelites as their victims as well. The plagues by which God destroys thousands of Israelites (Numbers 14:10-12, 25:6-9,) mirrors the plagues which subdued the Egyptians. The covering (כסה) of the Egyptian army by the sea (Exodus 15:5) is matched by the covering (כסה) of the followers of Korah by the earth (Numbers 16:33). Yahweh leads the Israelite army to rousing victory in battle over the Midianites (Numbers 31:1-12), but allows them to suffer devastating defeat in battle against the Amalekites and Canaanites (Numbers 14:39-45)

Third, the identity of Israel as Yahweh's chosen people is under constant threat, as Yahweh threatens to annihilate them at least three times. The harshness of life in the wilderness causes the Israelites themselves to consider giving up their freedom and returning to the slavery of Egypt (Exodus 16:1-3, Numbers 11:1-6). Their murmuring and disobedience constantly brings them under the threat of destruction by the same God who had delivered them. A gain in status achieved by violence is difficult to maintain peacefully. The threat and fear of punishment are necessary to maintain order. The ultimate punishment is that those who were freed from slavery in Egypt are not permitted to experience the next change in identity, from wanderers to land-holders. Instead, they are condemned to die in the wilderness (Deuteronomy 1:34-40).

Finally, those who had lived as victims and were delivered by Yahweh quickly and easily assume the role of overseers, just as the Israelites so easily became plunderers on the way out of Egypt. The clearest illustration of this mechanism is the action of the Levites in Exodus 32:25-29 and Numbers 25:6-15. In the former text, the sons of Levi killed three thousand Israelites who had worshipped the golden calf. In the latter, Phinehas, a Levite and the grandson of Aaron killed an Israelite man and a Midianite woman who had married. Some of those who had been freed from foreign control are then put in charge of controlling the others.

The crises and conflicts of the wilderness maintain a high level of violent activity in Israel's story, even when there are no other people around. This leads up to the period of the conquest when the Canaanites become the outlet for Israel's violence.

4

GOD'S PEOPLE ACQUIRE
LAND BY VIOLENCE

JOSHUA 6:1-27

Thus far in the story of Israel, the people have been transformed twice, from free people to slaves (Exod. 1:8-22) and from slaves to wanderers (Exod. 11-12). The next transformation will change them from wanderers to landowners. Difficulties which began to surface in Exodus 11-12, and erupted from time to time in the wilderness, appear in full form here. Though it is best to reserve theological discussion until after the examination of the text, one issue must at least be mentioned at the start, for the חרם ("ban", i.e., holy war) tradition so overshadows this text that it cannot be put completely out of mind. Joshua's command to devote the city to destruction (חרם) for Yahweh creates a theological problem with which people have wrestled ever since Joshua "fit de battle."

The Text

Two rhetorical features dominate Joshua 6.[1] These are the alternation of speech and action and the repetition of material.[2] In fact, these two

---

[1]This chapter, along with the rest of the Book of Joshua, is beset by textual difficulties. The most prominent of these is that the Hebrew text is significantly longer than the Greek. Verse 4 in MT, for example, is entirely missing from LXX. For an extensive listing of the tendencies present in each of these textual traditions, see Trent C. Butler, *Joshua*, WBC (Waco: Word, 1983) xix-xx. The consensus seems to be that the Hebrew text is expansionist and the shorter Greek text is usually preferable. For explanation and examples, see Kyle P. McCarter, *Textual Criticism: Recovering the Text of the Hebrew Bible*, (Philadelphia: Fortress, 1986) 26-29. On the other hand, some differences are the result of the shortening of the Greek text. For example, see the explanation by Boling and

characteristics function together. After Yahweh speaks to Joshua at the beginning of the chapter, the story alternates between Joshua's spoken instructions and the enactment of those instructions. Joshua clearly becomes the central character of the conquest in this passage. This is even more apparent in the Hebrew text which can distinguish between singular and plural forms of the second person pronoun. Joshua 6:2-3 reads, "And the LORD said to Joshua, 'See, I have given Jericho into your (sg.) hand, its king and the men of the army. You (pl.) shall go around, all the men of war going around the city one time. Thus you (sg.) shall do for six days.'" The singular form of the initial second person pronoun in this sequence focuses clearly upon Joshua in a way that matches in force the final statement in 6:27. While the third occurrence is plural in LXX, its singularity in the Hebrew text brings the emphasis back to Joshua.[3] The text begins with Yahweh directly telling Joshua that Jericho has been given to him and ends with Joshua's fame as a result of Yahweh's presence with him. The chapter may be organized as follows:

6:1-5   Speech: Yahweh to Joshua
6:6-7   Speech: Joshua to the priests and the people
6:8-9   Narrative: The priests and people move forward
6:10   Speech: Joshua to the people

Wright of how haplography produced the shorter reading of 6:17 in LXX (*Joshua*, AB [Garden City, N.J.: Doubleday, 1983] 203). While this present study is a rhetorical analysis of the Hebrew text, the reader should be aware that such differences exist, and that such an analysis of another version (e. g. LXX) might yield different results.

[2]Such repetitions and the variations therein have given rise to extensive source analysis of the Book of Joshua, including this chapter. The possibility of successive editions of this story has also been raised. An extreme of this position has been offered by John Gray who pointed to a "dramatic" pre-Deuteronomistic narrative which was subsequently "ruined by continual accretions." *Joshua, Judges, Ruth*, NCBC (Grand Rapids: Eerdmans, 1986) 80-81. Gray, along with Boling and Wright (*Joshua*, 206), also made the more interesting proposal that the final form is a combination of a sacred tradition and a more military one. Boling and Wright further suggested that the "less liturgical source" underlies the text of LXX. As further evidence of this, they cited the LXX use of the divine warrior title, "Κυριω σαβαωθ," in v. 17.

[3]Boling and Wright did note that this illustrates "variation characteristic of orally transmitted material." See *Joshua*, 205. In this literary context, however, such a feature artfully removes attention from the central character and then forcefully returns it.

6:11-15 Narrative: The people circle the city
6:16-19 Speech: Joshua to the people
6:20-21 Narrative: The people attack Jericho
6:22   Speech: Joshua to the two men
6:23-25 Narrative: The two men safeguard Rahab's family
6:26   Speech: Joshua pronounces a curse
6:27   Narrative: Yahweh is with Joshua and his fame spreads

Joshua 4 reports the crossing of the Jordan River by the Israelites. Chapter 4:13 states specifically that the Israelite army is ready to go to war against Jericho. The movement of the plot is slowed by the circumcision ceremony and the celebration of the Passover described in 5:2-12. Joshua 5 ends with the report of Joshua's mysterious encounter with "the commander of the army of the LORD" (5:13-15). This sets the stage for the coming battle, the story of which begins with a brief statement about the condition of Jericho (6:1). This statement introduces Yahweh's instructions to Joshua in 6:2-5.

These instructions contain six basic elements: (1) The men of the army (אנשי המלחמה) are to go around (סבב) the city once a day for six days (v.3); (2) Seven priests with seven trumpets are to go before the ark (v. 4); (3)The group is to go around (סבב) the city seven times on the seventh day (v. 4);[4] (4) The priests are to make a long blast on the trumpets (v. 5);[5] (5) the people shall shout a great shout (תרועה גדולה, v. 5); and (6) when the walls fall the people are to go up (עלה) into the city. An examination of the rest of this chapter reveals a certain unevenness in the seemingly repetitive nature of this text. Of the six elements in Yahweh's instructions to Joshua, only three of them (numbers 1,2, and 5) are repeated in Joshua's addresses to the people. On the other hand, all six are performed in the narrative portions of the story.

---

[4]There are possible connections to creation and Sabbath here. The seventh day does stand out from the other six. See M. H. Woudstra, *The Book of Joshua*, NICOT (Grand Rapids: Eerdmans, 1981), 110. Determining whether the final author of the book of Joshua or the authors of any of the sources used in chapter 6 were aware of the creation account in Genesis 1 would be an immensely complex source-critical task, which could hardly lead to certain results. Such connections, therefore, should not be pressed. In addition, that the seventh day in Joshua 6 is not a day of rest, but actually the day of most intense activity, would seem to make any attempt to connect this narrative to Genesis 1 somewhat odd.

[5]Connections between this narrative and the Jubilee year have been noted frequently because of the similarity between this element and Leviticus 11:9. See Gray, *Joshua, Judges, Ruth*, 81.

The command to go around the city once per day for six days is repeated by Joshua in v. 7 and is performed in vv. 8-14. The most significant variation within these repeated descriptions is the identification of those who go around the city. V. 3 says the "men of the army" (אנשי המלחמה) are to accompany the priests and the ark. In v. 7, Joshua tells "the people" (העם) to go around the city, but says the "armed ones" (החלוץ) shall go before the ark. V. 9 and v. 13 identify the "armed ones" (החלוץ) in front of the priests and "the rear guard" (המאסף) behind them. Assuming that "the people" (העם) refers to the Israelites in general, the precise manner of involvement of those not included in the army is ambiguous.

The instructions concerning the priests accompanying the ark are repeated by Joshua in v. 6 and their enactment appears twice (v. 8 and v. 13). The wording of these various repetitions is essentially the same.

Yahweh's command to go around the city seven times is not repeated by Joshua, but the act is performed in v. 15. Likewise, the instructions concerning the sounding of the trumpets at the end of the second circuit are not included in Joshua's address, but are followed by the priests in v. 16. The only significant difference between the two descriptions is the more detailed description of the prolonging (משך) of the trumpet blast in v. 5, which is absent from v. 16. The "great shout" (תרועה גדולה) of the people following the trumpet blast is repeated in Joshua's commands in v. 10 and v. 16. This command is obeyed by the people in v. 20. The order to "go up" (עלה) into the city after the walls fall, while absent from Joshua's words, is carried out precisely by the people in v. 20. Bar-Efrat notes that these actions fulfill Yahweh's instructions in v. 5 identically. He further argues that the precise repetition functions to show that everything happens as God commands. Bar-Efrat also notes that sometimes there are important differences, such as "expansion," in repeated material, but he does not note the significant expansion which comprises v. 21.[6]

There are three basic elements to Joshua's instructions which are not part of Yahweh's speech to him: (1) The devoting to destruction (חרם) of the city and the warning to avoid the devoted things (חרם) in vv. 18-19; (2) the sparing of Rahab (v. 17 and v. 22); and (3) the gathering of all the gold, silver, and other metal objects (כלי) into the treasury (v. 19).

The order to devote the city and its contents to destruction is enacted in v. 21, which offers additional detail. The totality of the slaughter of the human inhabitants is illustrated by two merisms, which literally read, "from man to (ועד) woman" and "from young to (ועד) old." This

---

[6]*Narrative Art in the Bible*, 161-162.

structure suggests the two opposites and everything between them.[7] The same grammatical construction which relates the elements within these two pairs relates this list of types of human beings to the list of types of animals which follows. The entire phrase reads, "from man to (ועד) woman, from young to (ועד) old to (ועד) ox and sheep and donkey." The two smaller merisms denoting the thoroughness of the human slaughter lie within a larger merism emphasizing the complete destruction of life from human to animal. The extension of the *herem* (חרם) to include animals explicitly goes beyond the records of the practice in Deuteronomy 2:34 and 3:6.[8] Joshua's command to stay away from the devoted things, not surprisingly, is without a corresponding element in the action sequence since it is a negative command. Verse 18 is obviously a foreshadowing of the Achan story in chapter 7. Israelites are in danger of death as a result of the ban (חרם) just as Canaanites are.

Joshua's final instruction concerning the gold, silver, and other metal objects (כלי) is performed in v. 24. These materials, of course, would not be destroyed by the fire used to destroy the city and its other contents and must be accounted for in some other way. Taking these things into the treasury is another safeguard against personal looting. The repetition adds one word of explanation. "The treasury of the LORD" (v. 19) becomes "the treasury of the house of the LORD" (v. 24). These materials are to become involved in Israelite worship. The difference between the gold and silver, unmodified, and the bronze and iron "objects" (כלי) is somewhat puzzling.[9] One possible explanation is that most, if not all, of the gold and silver would be jewelry or money, items worn or carried by human beings. The subsequent stripping of dead

---

[7]Bar-Efrat, *Narrative Art in the Bible*, 217.

[8]Passages such as Deuteronomy 7:2 and 20:17 are vague, however, they seem to include only humans.

[9]The problematic כלי arose in the discussion of Exodus 11-12 in the preceding chapter. In the "despoiling" tradition (Ex. 3:22, 11:2, and 12:35) the Israelites took "objects (כלי) of silver and gold" from the Egyptians. כלי is a general term derived from the verb כלה, meaning "to be complete" or "finished." Therefore, כלי may be understood literally to mean a "finished" or "completed thing." James Barr's "root fallacy" may warn against pressing this understanding too far. See *Semantics of Biblical Language* (Oxford: Oxford University Press, 1961) 100. This word certainly has a complex history of development which may have taken it far from its root meaning. It is widely used in the Hebrew Bible, the vast majority of times in the construct state, paired with a word specifying the material of composition (as in Joshua 6:19, 24) or the purpose (Amos 6:5, כלי שיר = instruments of music).

bodies in order to collect these items would be a particularly delicate subject for the author, thus requiring this vague reference.

The account of the saving of Rahab is very brief here. Some important details which first appeared in the instructions of the spies in 2:17-21 are missing. The story in Joshua 6 has no time for such details. In the earlier account, Rahab was instructed to place a scarlet cord in the window and not to let anyone of her household leave the house during the invasion. Yair Zakovitch has noted the connections between these instructions and the Passover story in Exodus 11-12. The scarlet cord is reminiscent of the blood placed on the doorposts of the Israelites to protect their firstborn. The instructions not to go outside (2:19) match the instructions given to the Israelites by Moses in Exodus 12:22.[10] That Rahab and her family have survived in Joshua 6:22-23 would indicate that they have followed these instructions. In v. 22 the two men are told specifically to go into her house and bring out her family. They have stayed inside as they were told.

The entire narrative of Joshua 6 is a drama which unfolds through a series of repetitions, additions, and deletions. M. Woudstra has noted the narrative technique of adding new elements to repeated ones in order to build toward a climactic ending.[11] Thus, the details of the destruction do not appear at all in Yahweh's instructions to Joshua at the beginning of the story, but await Joshua's instructions to the people in the middle of the story. When the final destruction is performed at the end of the story, even greater detail appears. Further, Woudstra observed the acceleration of narrative in v. 15. This acceleration is followed by a suspenseful delay caused by Joshua's instructions in vv. 16-19, which in turn is followed by a second acceleration in v. 20.[12] The outline at the beginning of this chapter illustrates that the whole of Joshua 6 is a series of such accelerations and pauses leading up to the dramatic conclusion, the destruction of the city.

One additional set of alternations, again noted by Woudstra, heightens the emphasis on destruction. Verses 21-26 report in succession the slaughter of all living things in Jericho, the safeguarding of Rahab, the burning of the city, the continuation of care for Rahab, and the cursing of the city. Destruction and salvation are juxtaposed continually

---

[10]Yair Zakovitch, "Humor and Theology or the Successful Failure of Israelite Intelligence: A Literary-Folkloric Approach to Joshua 2," in *Text and Tradition: the Hebrew Bible and Folklore*, ed. Susan Niditch (Atlanta: Scholars Press, 1990) 92-93.

[11]Woudstra, *The Book of Joshua*, 111-112.

[12]Ibid., 112-114.

in this series, intensifying the contrast between the fate of Rahab's family and the fate of the rest of Jericho.[13] This juxtaposition is all the more striking because of the lack of any narrative link between v. 21 and v. 22. The saving of Rahab had to have happened at least during, if not before, the events described in v. 21. Yet, there is no attempt to synchronize the Rahab account here with any earlier events.[14] It is simply tacked on sequentially, adding to a scene which is already confused and chaotic.

If the overall presentation of Joshua 6 seems chaotic, that may be precisely what the author intended. Numerous commentators have observed the frequent departure from typical Hebrew syntax within this text.[15] All four verb forms in v. 1 are participles. Verse 9 contains three participles and two infinitives. Both v. 2 and v. 8 begin with imperfect verbs and shift to perfect forms. This is not the usual syntax for sequential narrative. The result of this unusual syntax is the presentation of a variety of activities, often taking place at the same time. The events recorded in this passage do not take place one after the other as in conventional narrative. If the reader feels that he or she is having difficulty keeping up with all of the action, that appears to be exactly the intended effect of the story both grammatically and structurally.[16]

Theological Conclusions

The primary theological issue for Joshua 6 is the nature of God's presence within all of the activity which occurs in and around Jericho. Not surprisingly, throughout the history of interpretation of this passage, there seems to be a tendency to avoid theological interpretation. Other concerns, such as history, archaeology, and source analysis dominate the discussion.

When theology is considered, the most common conclusion to which interpreters struggle to arrive is that what took place in Jericho was worship not warfare. E. John Hamlin labeled Joshua 6 "history

---

[13]Ibid., 115.

[14]Bar-Efrat has described various ways in which such synchronization can be accomplished in a narrative. See *Narrative Art in the Bible*, 172-173.

[15]See Butler, *Joshua*, 65 and Boling and Wright, *Joshua*, 206.

[16]Bar-Efrat has described how the "consecutive nature of language" places certain limits on all authors in their portrayal of events. See *Narrative Art in the Bible*, 141,166-167. The unusual syntax in this story may be an indication of the author's attempt to overcome those limits.

remembered through liturgy."[17] Butler described the role of priests in the passage: "Their role has been to transform the narrative from battle story to cultic drama."[18] According to J. Alberto Soggin, "This literary form is perfectly adapted to a liturgical celebration where Yahweh is the principal actor. The people are limited to carrying out the liturgical acts which God orders..."[19] To such attempts to ignore the violence of war here, I must respond, as in the discussion of Exodus 11-12,[20] that this story ends with a city full of dead bodies.

Even one so sensitively attuned to issues of violence as Walter Wink seems to hedge here. Wink wants to understand Israelite holy war as a precursor to what he identifies as "Jesus' third way of non-violence." To this end he states:

> Jericho's walls collapsed after ritual, not military, action (though the mopping-up operation was carried out by Hebrew warriors).... Even the "ban," the practice of "devoting" booty to God by destroying it, can be seen as the imposition of extremely ascetical limits on the enjoyment of the fruits of war. (It also illustrates the depth to which the myth of redemptive violence had penetrated Israel's theology and politics)."[21]

Wink does not ignore the violence in this text, but he does attempt to contain it within parentheses.

The preceding rhetorical analysis does not support the theological conclusion that the focus of this text is on worship. To be sure, the text does contain liturgical elements, such as processions, horns, priests, and shouting. These elements, however, fade away as the story progresses. The violent warfare, concentrated in vv. 21-24, is not fully contained by liturgy. It escapes in a rampage of destruction. The story does not conclude with worship, but with death, curse, and the glory of conquest. Indeed, the only possible tempering of the violence at the end of the story is the Rahab tradition which may, as Woudstra suggested, even intensify the destruction by contrast.[22] The Rahab tradition may

---

[17]Hamlin, *Joshua: Inheriting the Land*, ITC (Grand Rapids: Eerdmans, 1983) 46.

[18]Butler, *Joshua*, 86.

[19]Soggin, *Joshua*, OTL (London: SCM, 1972) 86.

[20]See chapter 4, note 9.

[21]Wink, *Engaging the Powers*, 188.

[22]Woudstra, *The Book of Joshua*, 115.

exacerbate the problem of violence in other ways, as Danna Nolan Fewell points out:

> Rahab's faith and kindness raise serious questions about the obsession with holy war in the book of Joshua. How many Rahabs are killed in the attempt to conquer the land? How many people with vision and loyalty surpassing that of the Israelites are destroyed in the attempt to establish a pure and unadulterated nation?[23]

Not only can violence not be overshadowed by worship in this story, violence overtakes the story.

In light of this understanding of violence in the story, the problem of God's presence becomes critical. God's presence with Joshua is explicit both at the beginning of the story (vv. 2-5) and at the end (v. 27). God's presence with the people is never direct. Instead, God's presence is mediated through the presence of the ark. Its identification varies from "the ark" to "the ark of the covenant" to the ark of the LORD" to "the ark of the covenant of the LORD," with no recognizable pattern. Most importantly it is mentioned nine times in the chapter, all nine occurring in vv. 4-13. The first designation, "the ark," appears twice. "The ark of the covenant occurs only once, emphasizing the ark's function as a the container holding the tablets of the law.[24] "The ark of the LORD" occurs five times and, as the title which most emphasizes this object as a symbol of Yahweh's presence,[25] is the dominant designation in this text. Just as striking as the intensity of the ark's presence in vv. 4-13 is its complete absence in vv. 15-27. Yahweh's presence in this story changes progressively. Yahweh is fully present in vv. 2-5, speaking to Joshua. In vv. 6-14, Yahweh is present in a mediated way, through the ark. Verses 15-26 contain only the mention of Yahweh's name. Yahweh reappears directly, as the subject of a verb, only in the epilogue in v. 27. The author effectively places Yahweh at some distance from the acts of violence in this story, in a way even more thorough than the author of Exodus 11-12 did using "the destroyer." The most violent of the instructions given to the people, in vv. 17-19, are given by Joshua alone. They are not contained in Yahweh's spoken instructions. Nevertheless, God is not completely absent from Jericho. The divine warrior

---

[23]Fewell, "Joshua" in *The Women's Bible Commentary*, ed. Newsom and Ringe, 66.

[24]Terrien, *The Elusive Presence*, 162-163.

[25]Ibid., 163-166.

lurks in the shadows. Once again, "First World" readers must heed Hanson's warning not to deny the power of this image for the oppressed.[26] In this story, however, as Fewell notes, the line between oppressor and oppressed is blurred.

A related problem to God's involvement in warfare is the enactment of the "ban" (חרם). In her illuminating study of war ideologies in ancient Israel, Susan Niditch isolates two different basic understandings of the ban. In one set of biblical texts, the ban is understood as a sacrifice to God of God's share of the spoils of war. Human warriors sacrifice their opponents to God in return for God's assistance in the victory.[27] In the other set of texts, the ban is divine punishment of Israel's enemies which tend to lead it into sin. The victims are idolaters who justly deserve such punishment.[28] Niditch places Joshua 6 into the former set of texts. Further, she places Joshua 6:17-21 into a group of texts in which "no matters of justice are discussed."[29] Niditch argues that these understandings of the ban function to remove the human guilt which results from killing. Viewing the victims as either an offering to God or as ones deserving punishment helps to remove the guilt from the killer. This is an attractive psychological explanation that Niditch bases on sound anthropological understanding. From a literary perspective, however, it does not answer fully the problem the reader of Joshua 6 encounters when confronted with a story in which God is a speaking character who orders the destruction of a city. More helpful is Niditch's assertion that the various war ideologies in the Hebrew Bible struggle, uncomfortably, with the idea of the ban.[30] I will return to the view of violence taken by the Hebrew Bible as a whole in the final chapter of Part I.

The Israelites are not fully transformed into landed people in Joshua 6. As the curse in v. 26 makes clear, the purpose of the destruction of Jericho is not to occupy the city. This story is, however, paradigmatic of the conquest.[31] The people of Israel, led by Joshua, begin the process of taking the land by murder and plunder.

[26]Hanson, *The Diversity of Scripture*, 101-102.
[27]Susan Niditch, *War in the Hebrew Bible: A Study in the Ethics of Violence* (Oxford: Oxford University Press, 1993) 42.
[28]Ibid., 45.
[29]Ibid., 34. The other texts in this small group are Deuteronomy 2:34-35 and 3:6-7, and Joshua 8:24-40 and 11:11-14.
[30]Ibid., 150-155.
[31]Butler, *Joshua*, 75.

In summary, three things can be said about violence in Joshua 6. First, violence breaks out of boundaries, in this case liturgical boundaries, and becomes uncontrolled. Second, God is present at the scene of violence, but is so at a distance. Third, the people of Israel, who begin to act as conquerors in Exodus 12, perfect the practice here. Their status as victims has all but disappeared.

INTERLUDE FOUR:
TRIBES IN CONFLICT

The period in Israel's story known as the tribal confederacy is often portrayed as an almost idyllic time. The values which supposedly dominated Israelite society were social egalitarianism and allegiance to the kingship of Yahweh.[32]

An evaluation of this part of Israel's story which focuses on violence in biblical texts leads to quite different conclusions. The first conclusion in the previous chapter of this study concerning violence is that it has a tendency to break out of established boundaries and become uncontrolled. The book of Joshua is very much about the establishment of boundaries. These boundaries are geographical, social, and religious. In Joshua 8-10, Israel carves out a space for itself. Joshua 10:41 states the geographic boundaries of Israel's Promised Land quite specifically. At the same time, the children of Israel are busy driving out the Canaanites in order to establish a separate society. Joshua 12:7-24 relentlessly lists the defeated kings and their peoples. The external boundaries having been established, Joshua 12-22 establishes Israel's internal, tribal boundaries. Land is apportioned to the tribes in great geographic detail by means of an orderly process. Joshua 23-24 form the appropriate capstone to all of this boundary formation. The covenant language of 24:14-28 establishes the religious boundaries for Israel.

The meticulous control of the book of Joshua is only occasionally disrupted. Evaluations of the conquest in 11:23 and 13:1 are in tension with each other. The complaint of the tribe of Joseph in 17:14-18 indicates that both the internal and external boundaries may be in question. Nevertheless, the dominant impression of the book of Joshua is that all is well and in good order.

The book of Judges offers a stark sense of contrast to the book of Joshua. The clearly established boundaries of the book of Joshua seem non-existent. The lack of geographic and social boundaries is exposed in

---

[32]For influential examples of this view, see Hanson, *The People Called*, 30-86 and Norman Gottwald, *The Tribes of Yahweh: A Sociology of the Religion of Liberated Israel, 1250-1050 B.C.E.* (Maryknoll, N.Y.: Orbis, 1979) 608-621.

Judges 1 and 3:1-6. The well established cycle of the book of Judges (2:11-19) contends that because Israel fails to maintain the religious boundary between themselves and the Canaanites, the geographic and social boundaries are violently disrupted. Even the internal peace and unity among the Israelite tribes is exposed as a false hope in 5:15c-17, 9:7-56, and chapters 17-21. The ambiguous statement in 17:6 and 21:25 sums up the tenuous nature of boundaries established by violent means. Does "every man did what was right in his own eyes" mean that people lived in an orderly fashion, guided by their own internal moral compasses, or does it mean that a period of lawlessness ensued? The book of Judges is dominated by stories of bloodshed, both between Israel and its neighbors and among the tribes of Israel itself. Boundaries established against violent disorder do not hold.

The second conclusion form the previous chapter is that God is present at violent events, but is kept at a distance. The ambiguous, mediated nature of God's presence at Jericho is paradigmatic. Yahweh quite plainly lies behind the cycle of servitude and deliverance in the book of Judges. In numerous general statements, victory in battle is attributed to the presence of God (3:28, 4:23, 11:32, etc.). At the scene of detailed acts of violence (3:15-23, 4:17-22, 9:42-45, etc.) God is typically absent.[33] The term "spirit of Yahweh" (רוּח יהוה) makes its first appearance in the book of Judges (3:10, 11:29, 13:25, 14:6,19, 15:14) as a way of speaking about God's presence with the deliverers. The ark, mentioned some twenty-nine times in the book of Joshua, is noticeably absent from the book of Judges. The single reference, in 20:27, reveals that this is because the ark is now stationary at the shrine of Shiloh. The presence of God with the Israelite army is now mediated through the "spirit of Yahweh" which accompanies the leaders.

The third conclusion in the previous chapter concerned the disappearance of clear lines of distinction between victim and oppressor. In the book of Joshua, Israel is portrayed as conqueror. The battle of Jericho sets the tone. In the book of Judges, Israel's identity fluctuates. The people of Israel essentially become one more group in the ancient Near East vying for autonomy, subject to a continuous cycle of victory and defeat. The order established so carefully in the book of Joshua is exposed as a facade in the book of Judges. The chaos of external threat and internal strife will come to a head in the early chapters of 1 Samuel as the very existence of the people of Israel is threatened. This crisis will lead to another major shift in the identity of Israel.

---

[33]Yahweh's confusion of the Midianite camp in 7:19-23 is a possible exception to this rule.

5

GOD'S PEOPLE BECOMES A NATION BECAUSE OF VIOLENCE

1 SAMUEL 4:1-22

At first glance, this may seem to be an odd choice of text for the next turning point in Israel's story. The next significant change in Israel's status is from a people to a nation. It is somewhat difficult to choose a single text in which this transformation takes place. One might argue that it happens in 1 Samuel 8 when Israel voices its need for a king, or in 1 Samuel 9 when Saul is chosen king, or in 1 Samuel 10 when Saul is anointed. Clearly, the book of Samuel presents the change from a loosely affiliated group of tribes to the united monarchy as a gradual process. No single text encapsulates it. Nevertheless, there is one single event which seals the fate of the tribal confederacy and instills within Israel its desire to be "like other nations" (1 Samuel 8:5). This transforming event is the devastating defeat of Israel's army by the Philistines at Aphek in 1 Samuel 4.[1] This passage is often grouped with the next two chapters as part of "The Ark Narrative." While this may be an

---

[1]Brueggemann stated that this passage prepares the way for the "narrative of kingship." See *First and Second Samuel*, (Louisville: John Knox, 1990) 29. Robert Polzin proposes reading 1 Samuel 4-7 as a parable in which the decrepit Eli represents the ultimate failure of the monarchy and the ark of the covenant represents Israel under the leadership of Yahweh alone. See *Samuel and the Deuteronomist: A Literary Study of the Deuteronomic History, Part 2, 1 Samuel* (San Francisco: Harper & Row, 1989) 55-79. Peter D. Miscall, following Polzin, proposes that the delay in the development of the monarchy within the book of Samuel is an indication of this narrative's uneasiness about kingship in Israel. See "Moses and David: Myth and Monarchy," in *The New Literary Criticism and the Hebrew Bible*, ed. J. Cheryl Exum and David J. A. Clines (Valley Forge: TPI, 1993) 190-191.

accurate literary assessment, there is much more at stake in 1 Samuel 4 than the possession of the ark. The Philistine threat endangers Israel's autonomy and possibly even their future existence.

The Text

The strangeness of 1 Samuel 4 is not immediately apparent to the English reader. The Hebrew text, however, contains several features which keep the reader off balance. First, there is a striking abundance of unusual vocabulary. One measure of this feature is the existence of many words and word combinations which appear only here within the entire Hebrew Bible. The Masoretic Text notes these in the margin of each page of text. 1 Samuel 4 contains 24 such notations, while 1 Samuel 3 has none and 1 Samuel 5 has only three.[2] Second, like the previously examined text in Joshua 6, 1 Samuel 4 is beset by textual problems. Consequently, there is more than one potential text which could be analyzed. Third, 1 Samuel 4 is characterized by awkward syntax which distracts from the flow of the Hebrew narrative.

1 Samuel 4 is typically understood to be part of an "Ark Narrative." According to various analyses, this narrative may have included all or parts of 1 Samuel 4-6, some of 1 Samuel 2 and perhaps even 2 Samuel 6.[3] The striking feature which has initiated much of the discussion is the absence of Samuel from 1 Samuel 4-6.[4] This issue is relevant for the present study only in determining the extent of the passage to be examined. While 4:22 clearly ends one episode and 5:1 begins another, the situation at the beginning of chapter four is not nearly so simple. Virtually every commentator on 1 Samuel rejects the current verse division in MT and either puts the first sentence in 4:1 with the end of chapter three or omits it altogether, thus defining the extent of the story of the capture of the ark as 4:1b-22.[5] The choice for rhetorical analysis

---

[2]This does not make chapter four unique in the entire book of Samuel. 1 Samuel 6, which is considerably shorter, has twenty of these notations.

[3]This has become an immensely complex source-critical debate. For a brief, but thorough, summary, see Ralph W. Klein, *1 Samuel*, WBC (Waco: Word, 1983) 38-40. For a lengthier discussion, see Anthony F. Campbell, *The Ark Narrative* (Missoula, Montana: Scholars Press, 1975) 6-54. No consensus has been reached concerning the existence or extent of a pre-canonical narrative.

[4]The mention of Samuel in 4:1 will be discussed below.

[5]The text-critical situation at the end of 1 Samuel 3 and the beginning of 1 Samuel 4 is a tangled one. In LXX, 3:21 reads, "The Lord continued appearing in Shiloh, for the Lord revealed himself to Samuel. And Samuel was accredited as a prophet of the Lord from one end of the land to the other end. And Eli was very

does not involve simply deciding whether 4:1a belongs in the Hebrew Bible, but also whether it is part of the story told in chapter four. Text-critical considerations aside, does the present Hebrew text make sense with "And the word of Samuel was unto all Israel" as the introduction to the story? The analysis offered here will attempt to maintain an affirmative answer to this question. The impact of the decision is no small one. If 4:1a is included then Samuel is a character in the story. If not, then he is absent.

With the extent of the passage tentatively determined, the story can now be divided as follows:

4:1-2   The Philistines win the first battle
4:3-5   The Israelites bring the ark to their camp
4:6-9   The Philistines react to the arrival of the ark
4:10-11 The Philistines win the second battle
4:12-18 Eli hears news of the defeat and dies
4:19-22 The wife of Phinehas declares the departure of the glory

The story can and has been divided in numerous ways. This scheme is based on shifts is setting from the battlefield to the Israelite camp to the Philistine camp to the battlefield to the streets of Shiloh to a birth chamber.[6] The story begins with the appearance of Samuel before Israel and ends with the disappearance of the ark from Israel. While the ark permeates the entire account, being mentioned twelve times, Samuel presides silently over this event in Israel's story.

---

old and his sons kept on going their way, and their way was evil before the Lord." In MT, 3:21 says, "The LORD continued to appear at Shiloh, for the LORD revealed himself unto Samuel at Shiloh by the word of the LORD." Likewise, at the beginning of 4:1, LXX adds "And it happened in those days that the Philistines gathered for war against Israel." MT does not contain this phrase but begins 4:1 with "And the word of Samuel was unto all Israel." P. Kyle McCarter argued that the extra material in LXX dropped out of the Hebrew text by haplography. His explanation requires maintaining the present 4:1a of MT as the end of 3:21 in the original text, while inserting the end of 3:21 from LXX at the beginning of chapter 4. See McCarter, *1 Samuel: A New Translation with Introduction and Commentary*, AB (Garden City, N. Y.: Doubleday, 1980) 97-104. Klein offers a simpler explanation omitting 4:1a of MT and retaining all of the additional material from LXX. See Klein, *1 Samuel*, 30, 37.

[6]These changes in setting and the storyteller's style of taking the reader into each of them creates in 1 Samuel 4 a perfect example of what J. Licht has called "scenic narrative." See his discussion in *Storytelling in the Bible* (Jerusalem: Magnes, 1978) 29.

The opening scene is the first battle. The defeat is devastating. In v. 2 Israel is "struck down (נִגַף) before the Philistines." In light of the question the elders of Israel will ask in v. 3, the passive form (*niphal*) of the verb is significant. The text already provides the reader a hint that the military power of the Philistines is not Israel's problem. The Philistines do not strike them down, but some unnamed subject does. The linguistic connection between this text and the Passover narrative in Exodus 12 is quite suggestive. Yahweh's promise to strike down (נָגַף) the Egyptians (12:23,27) and not to strike down (נָגַף) the Israelites (12:23) is nullified in 1 Samuel 4:2.[7]

In vv. 3-5, the setting shifts to the Israelite camp at Ebenezer. The name of this place, which means "stone of help," produces a particularly ironic setting in which to contemplate the crushing defeat. The conclusion which was hinted at in v. 2 now appears plainly on the lips of the elders of Israel. The elders immediately answer their own question in v. 3 by suggesting that the ark be taken (לְקַח) from Shiloh. The ark's absence from the battlefield is something of a mystery. During Israel's first battle in the land of Canaan, described in Joshua 6, the presence of the ark is presented as the decisive element. After the battle of Jericho, however, the ark is only mentioned three times in the remainder of the book of Joshua (7:6, 8:33[2]), and only then as an implement of worship. The entire book of Judges contains only a single reference to the ark (20:27). This occasion does not directly involve the battle against the Benjaminites. The army comes to Bethel to inquire of the ark as of an oracle, but the ark does not accompany the troops into battle. Prior to 1 Samuel 4, the book of 1 Samuel mentions the ark only one time (3:3). Again, it is inactive, sitting in the temple at Shiloh being attended to by Samuel. The statement of the elders in 4:3, concerning the function of the ark, is quite clear. Along with the ark shall come the presence of Yahweh into their midst. The ark's military function is stated clearly as well. This is "the ark of the covenant of the LORD of Armies (יהוה צבאות), the one sitting on the cherubim."[8] The ark is the throne of the divine warrior.[9]

---

[7]The numerous connections between 1 Samuel 4 and the Exodus traditions have been notice by many commentators. See Brueggemann, *First and Second Samuel*, 34, and McCarter, *1 Samuel*, 106.

[8]The various names given to the ark were discussed in the previous chapter of this study. The use of the word "covenant" in the title emphasizes its contents (the tablets of the law). The enlarged title here provides the ark its most military designation. See Terrien, *The Elusive Presence*, 162-163. The title יהוה צבאות presents difficult problems. "LORD of Hosts" or "LORD of Armies" cannot be

The reader is left wondering why they did not bring it along in the first place. An ominous hint is dropped at the end of v. 4, however. This powerful object, "the ark of the covenant of the LORD of armies," becomes merely "the ark of the covenant of God" (אלהים). It has become a passive, sessile object, its potential power nearly forgotten. In addition, the text now acknowledges that the ark has been brought by Hophni and Phinehas, whose eventual fate was already announced in 1 Samuel 2:34.[10] But in v. 5 the arrival of the ark in the Israelite camp creates an eruption of celebration. The victorious days of Jericho are recalled in the "great shout" (תרועה גדולה) of Israel,[11] a shout so great it stirs (הום) the earth itself. This word appears in its verb form only six times in the Hebrew Bible. The only use which precedes this one is the promise in Deuteronomy 7:23 that God will "discomfit" (הום) Israel's enemies in Canaan.[12] The designation of the ark changes back, upon its arrival in v. 5, to "the ark of the covenant of the LORD."

In vv. 6-9, the scene shifts to the Philistine camp. Brueggemann aptly noted the imagination of the author here, who brings the reader into the Philistine camp to witness the response to the arrival of the ark.[13] This is an ideal example of movement from one scene to another by means of a physical phenomenon, the traveling of a sound wave.[14] The Philistines have heard the "great shout" (תרועה גדולה) and they are afraid. Somehow the Philistines know that the arrival of the ark has

---

grammatically literal translations since proper names cannot be placed as the first element in Hebrew construct chains. Frank Moore Cross proposed that originally יהוה had a verbal function in this title. He thus offered "he creates the hosts" as a possible translation. As יהוה developed into a proper noun, the title became a grammatical anomaly which some texts, such as 1 Kings 19:15, tried to repair. See Cross, *Canaanite Myth and Hebrew Epic: Essays in the History of the Religion of Israel* (Cambridge: Harvard University Press, 1973) 65-70.

[9]McCarter, *1 Samuel*, 105-106.

[10]Yehoshua Gitay cites this feature of the story as an example of the elliptic nature of narrative in the Bible saying, "A reference mentioned at a specific place may remain undeveloped, only to reappear later in its full sense. The narrator trusts the audience's familiarity with this literary technique." See "Reflections of the Poetics of the Samuel Narrative: The Question of the Ark Narrative," *CBQ* 54 (1992): 222.

[11]See Joshua 6:5, 20.

[12]While a reference back to Deuteronomy here seems less likely than the reference to Joshua 6, it would be entirely appropriate.

[13]Brueggemann, *First and Second Samuel*, 31.

[14]Bar-Efrat describes this technique using the movement of the trumpet blast in 1 Kings 1:39-41 as an example. See *Narrative Art in the Bible*, 168-169.

caused this response. Verses 7-9 report a conversation taking place in the Philistine camp and the reader is in a position to overhear it. Separate speakers are not identified, but the group which speaks in vv. 7-8 can hardly speak the words of v. 9. It is with this overheard conversation that another decisive turn takes place in the story. The arrival of the ark has turned devastation to triumph in the Israelite camp and it initially turns triumph into fear in the Philistine camp. This fear is reversed, however, by the unnamed speaker(s) in v.9. This speaker also knows precisely what is at stake in the battle. The winner will be the master whom the loser will serve (עבד). Throughout vv. 6-9, the conversation reminds the reader and the Philistines themselves who their opponents really are. They are not Israel, a great people or nation, but they are Hebrews (עברים), a band of escaped slaves.[15] The speakers in vv. 6-8 remember the story of this group defeating the mighty Egyptians with divine assistance. The Philistines may not understand monotheism, but they know that a divine power "struck (נכה) the Egyptians with every blow" (מכה from נכה).[16] They are close to being thrown into the panic (מהומה) caused by Yahweh's discomfiting (הום) of the enemy, as promised in Deuteronomy 7:23. But while הום appears in v. 6, it is the earth which is "stirred" or "discomfited." The noun form, מהומה, never appears, and the panic never afflicts the Philistines because the encouragement of the speaker in v. 9 reverses the mood.[17]

---

[15]See the discussion of the use of the term, עברים, in Kautzsch and Cowley, *Gesenius' Hebrew Grammar*, 8-9 and N. Na'aman, "Habiru and the Hebrews: The Transfer of a Social Term to the Literary Sphere," *JNES* 45 (1986): 271-88.

[16]Various attempts have been made to solve the perceived problem created by the reference to the wilderness here in v. 8. The problem is apparent in the rendering found in the NRSV: "struck the Egyptians with every sort of plague in the wilderness." LXX inserts a conjunction in order to produce "struck Egypt with every plague and in the wilderness." McCarter emends the Hebrew text in order to read "struck Egypt with every kind of scourge and pestilence" (McCarter, *1 Samuel*, 102-104). No emendation is necessary to produce a sensible text unless one insists on translating מכה as "plague" and if one believes the Hebrew scribe to have been too dense to realize that the plagues did not happen in the wilderness. The simple translation "struck the Egyptians with every blow in the wilderness" avoids reference to the plagues which happened in Egypt and would seem more likely to refer only to the Reed Sea event. This understanding is, in fact, more consistent with the biblical tradition that the defeat of the Egyptians at the sea is the event which becomes known and creates fear in Canaan (Exodus 15:14-16). In fact, מכה does not appear in the plague narratives, nor at any place in the book of Exodus.

[17]Contra McCarter, *1 Samuel*, 109.

Striking in this narrative is the absence of the traditional elements of holy war, as outlined by von Rad,[18] including the divine panic. This war is not presented by the writer as a holy war.

In vv. 10-11 the story returns to the battlefield. The results of the second battle are even more devastating for Israel. 30,000 die compared to 4,000 in the first battle. Those fleeing the second battle do not retreat to the camp, but return "each to his tent."[19] As at Jericho, the lines between the people and the army are blurred. In v. 1 "Israel" goes out to battle the Philistines. In v. 2, the 4,00 killed are simply "men" (אִישׁ). Those who return to the camp in v. 3 and send for the ark in v. 4 are "the people" (הָעָם). In v. 5, "all Israel" shouts when the ark comes to the camp. In v. 10, "Israel" suffers defeat and flees. The 30,000 who die in the second battle are called "ones on foot" (רַגְלִי).[20] They are "struck down" (נגף)[21] again, and are victims of a great blow (מַכָּה), just as the Egyptians were in v. 8. In v. 11 the ark becomes "the ark of God" (אֱלֹהִים), its simplest and least theological designation thus far, and it will maintain this designation for the remainder of the story. The ark is taken (לקח) by the Philistines, just as it was taken (לקח) from Shiloh by the Israelites in v. 4. The three consequences of the battle are listed in vv. 10-11 as the defeat of the army, the capture of the ark, and the death of Hophni and Phinehas.

Verses 12-18 present the reaction to the battle report in Shiloh, the longest of the six scenes in the story. Eli dominates the scene.[22] He is mentioned by name seven times in the chapter, six of which are in vv. 12-18. The Benjaminite messenger arrives in a visible state of mourning. Just as the shout transports the reader to the Philistine camp in v. 6, the messenger carries the reader to Shiloh.[23] His clothes are torn and there is dirt upon his head. Commentators generally go to some length to explain why the message reaches the other inhabitants of Shiloh before it reaches Eli. There are textual difficulties at v. 13 and v. 18 in

---

[18]von Rad, *Holy War in Ancient Israel*, trans. Marva J. Dawn and John Howard Yoder (Grand Rapids: Eerdmans, 1991) 41-51.

[19]McCarter, *1 Samuel*, 107.

[20]NRSV suggests "foot soldiers."

[21]See comparisons with Exodus 12 above.

[22]Berlin argues that the text does not shift merely from the battlefield to Shiloh, but intentionally presents the Shiloh scene from Eli's point-of view. See *Poetics and Interpretation of Biblical Narrative*, 68-69.

[23]Both of these devices fit what Licht describes as "a suitable link to keep the story in one piece" when more than one setting is involved in a single narrative. See *Storytelling in the Bible*, 41.

the descriptions of where Eli was sitting.[24] The rhetorical strategy of the author is quite apparent, however. Upon hearing the bad news in v. 13, the residents of Shiloh cry out (זעק). In v. 14, Eli hears the cry (צעקה), which is reminiscent of the cry (צעקה) in Egypt after the death of the firstborn (Exodus 12:30). When Eli hears the cry, he responds with a question, "What is the sound of this uproar?" This question parallels remarkably the question asked by the Philistines in v.6, "What is the sound of this great shout?" The messenger then comes to Eli and Eli asks a direct question about the battle in v. 16. Eli's questions are not met with words of encouragement, as were those of the Philistines. Instead, the report destroys him.[25] The drama builds throughout the messenger's report.[26] At first glance, the messenger's statements in v. 16 seem repetitive. Bar-Efrat has described this as "a rare instance in which agitation is reflected in speech."[27] Even if two different readings of the man's statement have been combined,[28] the two statements work together as part of the overall dramatic affect of the report.[29] The first statement is neutral, "I have come from the battle." The second suggests disaster, "I have fled from the battle today." In v. 17, the magnitude of the disaster continues to build as he reports the specific details. The order of the disasters has changed from vv. 10-11.[30] The army has been defeated, Hophni and Phinehas are dead, and the ark has been taken (לקח). From Eli's reaction, it is the final element

---

[24]See the explanations in McCarter, *1 Samuel*, 111-112.

[25]McCarter's comparison of this report and the report to David in 2 Samuel 1:3-4, which brings the news of the deaths of Saul and Jonathan, is quite striking. The subsequent argument that a common literary motif lay behind such reports is convincing. See *1 Samuel*, 113.

[26]John Mauchline, *1 and 2 Samuel*, NCBC (Oliphants: London, 1971) 74.

[27]Bar-Efrat, *Narrative Art in the Bible*, 65-66.

[28]There are numerous textual problems in vv. 14-16. The LXX reading is much longer. McCarter suggested that the present reading of v. 16 in MT is a conflation of variants. See *1 Samuel*, 111-112.

[29]Bar-Efrat has proposed that the apparent confusion in the messenger's statement reflects his sense of discomfort with the message he has to deliver. See *Narrative Art in the Bible*, 65-66.

[30]Berlin demonstrates that this kind of alteration in the order of elements may represent the varying viewpoints of characters within the story (*Poetics and Interpretation of Biblical Narrative*, 72-73). Sternberg argues that this ordering of the list from Eli's perspective produces a favorable view of the elderly judge. See *Poetics of Biblical Narrative*, 421.

which is most devastating and which causes him to fall to his death.[31] The final note on Eli's death in v. 18 has an odd sound to it. The reference to his weight might appear to be disrespectful. The only other person in the Hebrew Bible described in a manner similar to this is Eglon, the King of Moab in Judges 3:17. Like Eli, Eglon's weight is related to the circumstances of his death. The story of Eglon's murder by Ehud in Judges 3 is clearly comical. Is the reader of 1 Samuel 4 supposed to laugh at fat, old Eli? Probably not. The word used to describe Eglon in Judges 3:17 is בריא, a word most commonly used to refer to the "fat portions" of animals. Eli, on the other hand is described in 1 Samuel 4:18 as כבד (heavy). The authors' choice of this word is quite significant because it is a form of the same word used for "glory" (כבוד) in 1 Samuel 4:21-22.[32] This reference to Eli as "heavy" (כבד) may be an attempt to identify him with the ark which represents God's glory (כבוד). In addition, v. 22 ends with a final note of respect for Eli. The forty years of his leadership as judge match the forty year reigns of David and Solomon.

The final scene of the story in 1 Samuel 4 stands in sharp contrast to the others. The first five scenes take place in public arenas—a battle-field, military camps, and a city gate. In vv. 19-22, the author takes the reader into the privacy of a birth chamber. Like Eli, his daughter-in-law dies of grief at the report of the disaster. The news of the taking (לקח) of the ark and the deaths of Eli and Phinehas first hasten the birth of her son. But even the blessing of the birth of a male child cannot ease her despair. She names the child for the catastrophe which has just befallen Israel. The construction of vv. 21-22 is quite difficult. The problematic name, "Ichabod,"[33] and the double saying from the mouth of the

---

[31]S. Hertzberg noted the similarity between this report and the report of increasingly devastating disasters to Job in Job 1:14-19. See *I & 2 Samuel: A Commentary*, OTL (Philadelphia: Westminster, 1964) 49.

[32]The glory (כבוד) of God in the Hebrew Bible was typically understood as the density or heaviness of God's presence in the temple. See G. Henton Davies, "Glory," in *The Interpreter's Dictionary of the Bible*, vol. 2, eds. G. A. Buttrick et al. (Nashville: Abingdon, 1962) 401ff. According to Sternberg, this physical description of Eli does not follow the normal biblical pattern in which descriptions are given early in a narrative to provide a cause for a future event. The description of Eglon's obesity and Ehud's left-handedness in Judges are examples of the typical pattern which Sternberg calls "proleptic portraits" (*Poetics of Biblical Narrative*, 338).

[33]Attempts to interpret the name go back at least as far as Josephus (*Antiquities* 5.360). For a thorough discussion of the alternatives, see McCarter, *1 Samuel*, 115-116.

woman[34] have both elicited much discussion. The speech of this unnamed woman is quite dramatic, and the effect is emphasized by the repetition and further explanation in v. 22. Her first statement, explaining the name Ichabod in v. 21, "Glory has departed from Israel," is explained by the author as a reaction to the loss of the ark, Eli, and Phinehas. Despite her personal loss, this woman sees clearly the larger implications for Israel and she clarifies her first statement with her dying breath, "Glory has departed from Israel, for the ark of God has been captured." The birth of the child cannot ease the pain of this event. Further, this boy will not inherit the authority of his grandfather or his father. The figure of Samuel, from v. 1, looms large over the end of the narrative. With the deaths of Eli, Hophni, and Phinehas, Samuel has ascended. With the loss of the ark, the representation of Yahweh's presence, Samuel steps forth as Yahweh's representative. The ark will be recovered in 1 Samuel 5:1–7:1, but with the continuing rise of Samuel in chapter seven and the monarchy in chapter eight, the ark will again slip into relative obscurity.

Theological Conclusions

The story in 1 Samuel 4 must be read with the Exodus and Conquest narratives in mind. The world which Israel inhabits is a violent and dangerous one. The most important question for Israel is, "On whose side does God fight?" While God's action on behalf of the oppressed Israelites comes as a surprising revelation in Exodus, by the time the Israelites attack Jericho God's position is clearly understood and accepted. The defeat at the hands of the Philistines in 1 Samuel 4:1-2 brings about a profound theological crisis. The speakers in v. 3 state that Yahweh has fought against Israel. The assumptions on which the Israelites have come to rely are no longer valid.[35] The immediate theological crisis is forestalled in vv. 3-5 by the decision to bring the ark to the scene of the battle.

The Israelites seem to recognize that they have taken Yahweh's presence for granted. Yahweh's help must be insured more carefully. The story goes well for a few verses, as the arrival of the ark encourages the Israelite camp (v. 5) and fills the Philistine camp with fear (vv. 6-8). Only the dubious presence of Hophni and Phinehas and the subtle

---

[34]The quotation in v. 21 is missing in LXX and is thus omitted by McCarter. Ibid., 113. Hertzberg argues for the intentionality of the double saying, based on its literary force. See Hertzberg, *I & II Samuel*, 50.

[35]Brueggemann, *First and Second Samuel*, 29.

change in the name of the ark in v. 4 hint that all is not well. The second battle devastates Israel.[36] The presence of the ark does not bring victory. On the contrary, the second defeat is much worse. The earth is "discomfited" (הוּם) by the arrival of the ark (v. 5) but, in the end, the Philistines are not. As Brueggemann states, "Israel's presumed world has failed."[37] According to the words of the dying woman in v. 22, the ark, and the glory of Yahweh it represents, is literally taken into exile (גלה).[38] Terrien characterizes this event as a "divine humiliation."[39] In the process Israel learns a costly lesson. In the words of Hertzberg, "Yahweh is not bound by the ark; he shapes history independently of the symbol of his constant presence."[40] Indeed, Psalm 87:59-61 suggests that God is willing to suffer humiliation, to "give his strength to captivity, his magnificence into the hand of the enemy."[41]

God's people have become victims of violence again in 1 Samuel 4. Psalm 87 may understand that God suffers in the defeat as well, but this is not the understanding of the elders in 1 Samuel 4:3. God does not simply withdraw from the situation and let nature take its course. Rather, God directly strikes down (נגף) Israel.[42] Once the Israelites discover that God's presence cannot be guaranteed by the presence of the ark, they determine that the only course for their future is to become like other nations (1 Samuel 8:4), with a king who can employ a standing army which can compete in the violent world of the ancient Near East.

Once again, in this passage, violence influences identity. The people who have struggled with the help of God to be Israel are threatened, in the absence of their God, with a return to being Hebrews (vv. 6-9). The

---

[36]The eventual effect of the ark narrative (1 Samuel 4-6) may have been partially humorous (See Terrien, *The Elusive Presence*, 167), but the story in 1 Samuel 4 in undoubtedly tragic.

[37]Brueggemann, *First and Second Samuel*, 33.

[38]It is not within the provence of this study to argue for or against a post-exilic date for the book of 1 Samuel, and the added significance it might give this term. I simply would acknowledge the tremendous theological weight it came to carry in Israel.

[39]Terrien also found a strong theological connection between 1 Samuel 4 and the captivity of God's power in Psalm 78:59-61. See *The Elusive Presence*, 265-266. See also Fretheim's description of "the capture of God" in *The Suffering of God*, 145.

[40]Hertzberg, *I & II Samuel*, 51.

[41]That Psalm 78:59-61 refers to the Israelite's defeat at Aphek in 1 Samuel 4 seems certain. See Terrien, *The Elusive Presence*, 265.

[42]Brueggemann, *First and Second Samuel*, 32.

defeat threatens to return Israel to slave status. Throughout the story, the identity of those who are involved in the events is ambiguous. They are Israel (v. 1), men (v. 2), the people (v. 3), all Israel (v. 5), Israel (v. 10), and ones on foot (v. 10). Violence, in this case warfare, blurs the lines of identity within the groups involved. There is no clear division between civilian and military.

The identity of Israel's deity seems also to be at stake. The one who would fight and defeat Israel's enemy in v. 4 is Yahweh, or even "Yahweh of Armies" (צבאות). The one who fails to do so is God (אלהים). Israel's deity is not transformed directly in this story. In fact, their deity is never present directly.[43] It is the name of the object which represents this deity which undergoes transformation. As in Joshua 6, Yahweh is kept at a discreet distance from the violent events in 1 Samuel 4 by the mediation of the ark.

Finally, the most painful effect of violent oppression is the destruction of hope, which is reflected in vv. 19-22. For the wife of Phinehas the birth of a son, one of the greatest blessings an Israelite woman can receive, becomes a sign of God's absence, the exile of God's glory from Israel. Her despair must represent the despair of all Israelites over what seems to be a giant step backwards in their quest to possess the Promised Land. Their God has abandoned them.

In summary, God's involvement in the violence of the world continues to be a troubling question for Israel. Certainly, 1 Samuel 4 asserts that God's involvement cannot be manipulated by human beings. What involvement God has is only indirect, mediated by the presence of the ark. The uncertainty created by this experience will eventually lead Israel towards nationhood and the enhanced military might which comes with it. Violence is a threat to identity. In order not to have its identity revert back to slavery, Israel will become something new, a nation with a king. Violence involves everyone in a society. Lines of distinction blur as the influence of violence grows. Those who suffer loss in violent conflict lose hope and the question of God's presence becomes critical.

---

[43]Brueggemann says that the ark is a "narrative vehicle" for Yahweh's action in 1 Samuel 4. See *I and II Samuel*, 29. If he means by this that the ark is a way of keeping Yahweh at a distance in the story, I agree, but would go further. The ark is a way of keeping Yahweh at a distance from the bloody violence which characterizes Israel's world. For the modern reader, it is a "narrative vehicle," but for Israel it serves a theological and moral purpose.

INTERLUDE FIVE:
CONFLICT OVER THE THRONE

The common designation of this period as the "united monarchy" leads to two potential misunderstandings. First, the extent to which the monarchy was united under each of the three great kings — Saul, David, and Solomon — is in serious doubt. Second, this period is often taken to be the norm for Israel. This may be because of the tremendous ideological role the Davidic monarchy plays in all the rest of the Bible and in Israel's history beyond the biblical period. Within the scope of Israel's story, this is a relatively brief period. The stories of Saul, David, and Solomon consumes a major portion of the biblical text, 1 Samuel 8 — 1 Kings 11 in the Deuteronomistic History and I Chronicles 10 — 2 Chronicles 9 in the Chronistic History.

There has been significant dispute concerning how to divide and classify this material. Critical study of this portion of the Hebrew Bible has been largely dominated by the view that its core is formed by a carefully constructed "Succession Narrative" in 2 Samuel 9-20 and 1 Kings 1-2. The idea that the primary issue of this portion of scripture is the question of who will succeed David on the throne is largely attributable to the substantial 1926 essay of L. Rost.[44]

The literary focus of this present study has much greater affinity with David Gunn's evaluation of the David story. Gunn has expanded the traditional boundaries to include some material from the early chapters of 2 Samuel, though his "Story of King David" still forms a somewhat separate core within the larger block of material with which this interlude is concerned. More importantly he has offered convincing alternative explanations of the genre and purpose of the story. Gunn calls it a traditional story, which is primarily concerned with the life of David.[45] Gunn's interpretation of the story, which I find convincing, leads me to the further conclusion that there is no significant

---

[44] See L. Rost, *The Succession to the Throne of David*, trans. M. D. Rutter and D. M. Gunn (Sheffield: Almond, 1982).

[45] See *The Story of King David: Genre and Interpretation* (Sheffield: JSOT, 1978) 35-111.

advancement of Israel's story in this section of the Hebrew Bible or the chapters around it, which contain narratives of Saul and Solomon. It represents the high point of Israel's story. From the perspective of this study, however, it is a period in which Israel's identity remains relatively constant. There are fluctuations in Israel's ability to control territory and resist the force of foreign empires. There are disputes and divisions, particularly at the times of the deaths of Saul and David. Indeed, the monarchic mantra of Saul-David-Solomon gives way under the burden of a close reading to reveal an Israelite king list that looks more like Saul-Ishbosheth-David-Absalom-David-Adonijah-Solomon. But such expansion and contraction and court intrigue are at least as much the result of being a monarchy as they are part of the process of becoming one. Therefore, the tone for the monarchy is set with the decision to become one in 1 Samuel 8, and this decision is forged by the devastation of Aphek, which was examined in the previous chapter.

The study of 1 Samuel 4 in the previous chapter arrived at a number of conclusions about the violent trends which led to the establishment of the Israelite monarchy. The question with which this interlude is concerned is the way in which these trends continue to shape the story of Israel throughout the period of the early monarchy. First, the battle of Aphek called into question the nature of God's involvement in the violent world in which Israel is attempting to carve out its existence. The lesson of Aphek for the people of Israel is that the support of God for Israel's war efforts can be neither simply expected or easily manipulated. The cycle of subjugation and deliverance which dominated Israel's story in the book of Judges is turned on its head. According to Judges, the way for Israel to prosper was to be different and separate from the other nations. The conclusion of the Israelites at Aphek is that to compete in Canaan they needed to be "like the other nations." The monarchy establishes an army and the idea of holy war comes to an end. Under David's direction the ark becomes permanently ensconced in the temple and eventually forgotten. Israel learns to rely, for better or worse, on conventional military might. Though the warfare stories from the reign of Saul are concerned to some extent with the sacral element of war (1 Samuel 13:2-15), this element fades away. God is removed from the battlefield and eventually closed off in the temple along with the ark. The desire for a monarchy runs its full course so that the presence of God is no longer an essential element of a battle. Israel fights wars "like the other nations" too. Likewise, though the first two kings, Saul and David, are chosen and anointed by a prophet representing God, succession becomes an entirely human endeavor, one accomplished by violence (2 Samuel 2:12-23, 4:9-12, and 1 Kings 2:19-25) and intrigue.

The costs of maintaining an effective monarchy are high. In 1 Samuel 4, Israel is threatened with the prospect of becoming enslaved again. In 1 Kings 5:13 (5:27 in the Hebrew Bible) this takes place, in part. Solomon places 30,000 of his own people into מַס (forced labor). מַס appears previously at 2 Samuel 20:24 and 1 Kings 4:6, but it is not clear in these texts whether these slaves are foreigners, Israelites, or both. More significantly, this word appears in plural form in the narrative of oppression in Exodus 1:11. The monarchy saves the entire people from being enslaved by foreigners, but 30,000 Israelites lose their identity as free persons in order to support the monarchy. In reality Israel is only partly free.

The next text to be examined closely, 1 Kings 12, reveals that it is this practice of enslaving part of the nation internally to keep the whole free creates two separate identities. This sense of separation will lead to the division of the nation.

6

GOD'S PEOPLE DIVIDED
BY VIOLENCE

1 KINGS 12:1-20

The united monarchy, which arose as a result of Philistine aggression, would not exist for long in Israel. The combined reigns of Saul, David, and Solomon last for eighty-two years, if the chronology of the Hebrew Text is accepted. The signs of tension between the north and the south are present throughout this period. In fact, the simultaneous reigns of David and Ishbaal (2 Samuel 2:8-10) form an early two year break in the united monarchy immediately following the death of Saul. The rebellions of Absalom and Sheba and the self-declared kingship of Adonijah also reveal the fault-lines within the kingdom during the reign of David. Solomon manages to hold the kingdom together during his reign through heavy-handed tactics, but at his death the rupture again comes to the surface. First Kings 12:1-20 describes the end of the united monarchy, an end brought about by the oppression of forced labor and punctuated by a reciprocal act of mob violence.

The Text

The precise boundaries of this text are not obvious.[1] A crisis arises as Rehoboam attempts to begin his reign. The crisis begins when "all

---

[1]Commentators divide the text differently. For example, Simon J. DeVries treated vv. 1-24 together as the Rejection of Rehoboam." See *1 Kings*, WBC (Waco: Word, 1985) 152. John Gray divided these same verses into three parts. According to his division, vv. 1-19 report "The Rejection of Rehoboam at the Assembly at Shechem," v. 20 "the Adoption of Jereboam as King," and vv. 21-24 "Rehoboam's Reprisals Checked by Prophetic Intervention." See *I & II Kings: A Commentary*, 2nd ed., OTL (London: SCM, 1970) 301-309. G. H. Jones placed all

Israel" comes to "make him king" in v. 1. The situation concludes in v. 20 when "all Israel" makes Jereboam king and "Judah alone" follows Rehoboam as successor to Solomon. V. 20 makes it clear that "all Israel" there refers to the northern tribes, apart from Judah. The position of Benjamin is ambiguous and will be discussed below. This narrative is characterized by verbs of movement. Individuals and groups come (בוא), go (הלך), return (שׁוב), flee (נוס/ברה), and are sent (שׁלח). Rhetorical analysis should give careful attention to these verbs and how the narrator uses them to communicate the message of the text.[2]

The story in 12:1-20 can be divided into a narrative introduction, three major scenes, and a narrative conclusion. Each of the major scenes contains a significant amount of dialogue.

     vv. 1-2   Introduction
     vv. 3-5   The Northern tribes meet with Rehoboam
     vv. 6-11   Rehoboam consults two groups of advisors
     vv. 12-16 The Northern tribes meet with Rehoboam again
     vv. 17-20 Conclusion

In v. 1, Rehoboam "goes" (הלך) to Shechem while all Israel "comes" (בוא) to this northern town. The significance of this distinction will become clear in the next few verses. Though this story opens with the possibility of keeping the nation unified still in view, this separate action of the Northern tribes is ominous. The reappearance of Jereboam in v. 2 heightens the tension, in light of the previous narrative in 11:26-40. V. 2 contains an important textual problem. The Hebrew text reads "and Jereboam dwelt (ישׁב) in Egypt." Because of the importance of verbs of movement mentioned above, one is tempted to read with the Latin text and the Greek text of Origen, "and Jereboam returned from

---

of vv. 1-32 under a single heading, "The Division of the Kingdom." See 1 and 2 Kings, vol. I, NCBC (Grand Rapids: Eerdmans, 1984) 247.

[2]The historical-critical consensus holds that 1 Kings, in its present form, is part of the Deuteronomistic History. This work was composed in late seventh century Judah, long after the destruction of the Northern Kingdom. As such, it is a history reported from a Southern point of view. It is not entirely unsympathetic, however, to Northern concerns. This is best understood in comparison to the book of Chronicles. 2 Chronicles 10:1-19 duplicates 1 Kings 12:1-19 almost word for word. Thereafter, however, the book of Chronicles ignores the Northern Kingdom, except when it acts against Judah. This creates a thoroughly Southern point of view. It remains to be seen whether the present analysis will produce the same conclusions about the perspective of the book of Kings.

Egypt."[3] The corresponding reading in Hebrew requires simply a repointing of the verb, but the necessary change of the accompanying preposition would be consonantal.[4] This choice might either be clarified or further complicated by the resolving of another textual problem in v. 3. There are two alternative Hebrew forms for the verb of movement, בוא, in this verse. The consonantal reading in the text of MT (the *kettib* reading) is plural, but the reading in the margin of MT (the *qerê* reading) and the vocalization in the text are both singular. Choosing the singular reading emphasizes the coming (בוא) of Jereboam to Shechem, which makes the possible verb of movement in v. 2, שׁוּב, redundant. The whole of v. 3, which comes through somewhat awkwardly in English, subsequently says, "And they sent and called to him, and Jereboam came and all the assembly of Israel, and they spoke unto Rehoboam."[5] Jereboam's coming (בוא) to Shechem associates him with the Northern tribes, which also come (בוא) to Shechem in v. 1. Rehoboam, on the other hand, is portrayed as an outsider who goes (הלך) to Shechem.

Verses 4-5 contain the first of a series of dialogues within this narrative. The problem which makes the meeting necessary comes into clear view here. The request of the people in v. 4 seems more than reasonable. They offer to continue to serve the Davidic dynasty if only Rehoboam will make their service a little easier. The people's request is laced with oppressive words. Solomon made their yoke (עֹל) difficult (קשׁה). They ask Rehoboam to lighten their difficult (קשׁה) service (עבד) and the heavy (כבד) yoke (עֹל) Solomon placed on them. The burdensome language of slavery is reminiscent of the suffering of the Hebrews in Egypt in Exodus 1:11-14. The reader feels the weight of their toil. In contrast, Rehoboam's reply in v. 5 is quick and easy. Verbs of movement dominate and, again, the narrator's Shechem-centered point of view is emphasized as Rehoboam tells them to go (הלך) away and to return (שׁוּב) to him there in three days.

In vv. 6-7, Rehoboam asks for and receives counsel from the elders who had been with Solomon. Literally, he asks them how he should "return (שׁוּב) a word" to the people. Even the words travel using the same verb of movement as the people. Ironically, Solomon's old

---

[3]It should also be noted that 12:2 in MT matches 11:43 in LXX, making 11:43 of MT equal 11:44 in LXX.

[4]See note 3c-c in BHS.

[5]This reading of v. 3 is further supported in MT by a disjunctive accent, albeit a weak one, separating the phrases "and Jereboam came" and "and all the assembly of Israel."

advisors suggest a gentle approach. Their reply is dominated by forms of the word עבד. They tell Rehoboam he should be a servant (עבד) and that he should serve (עבד) the people so that they will be his servants (עבדים). The hard service described in v. 4 stands in stark contrast to the sense of reciprocity suggested here.

Unfortunately, Rehoboam does not accept the advice of the elders. Verse 8 reports his rejection of their counsel and serves as a turning point in the story. The last hope of keeping the kingdom united, which lingers in the advice of the elders, disappears as Rehoboam turns to the other group. The contrast between the young men and the elders consists of more than age alone. Just as the elders in v. 6 are described as "standing before Solomon," the young men in v. 8 are ones who "stand before Rehoboam." The narrator subtly informs the reader with which group Rehoboam identifies and whose advice he will likely accept. Rehoboam's question to the elders in v. 6 is, "How do you advise to return a word to this people?" To the young men he asks, "How do you advise that *we* return a word to this people?"[6] Unlike the "good words" which the elders advise him to use, the words the young men propose in vv. 10-11 are harsh, crude, and inflammatory. This harsh manner is highlighted by the narrator who reports by direct quotation the precise words the young men wish to place in Rehoboam's mouth.

The counsel of the elders in v. 7 is reported in a general fashion. The narrator does not provide the precise words they wish him to repeat. The feelings of the narrator about the foolishness of Rehoboam's choices come through powerfully. Rehoboam rejects the counsel of experienced elders and accepts that of brash youngsters.[7] In fact, he literally "forsakes" (עזב) the advice of the elders in v. 8 before even hearing the advice of the young men.[8] The narrator clearly indicates that this decision will result in failure. The words of Rehoboam in v. 9 and those of the young men in v. 10 repeat only the request of the people in v. 4 to lighten their yoke. They fail to repeat the promise of service the people have offered in exchange. In addition, the young men not only refuse to make any concession, but want to make the service even harder. The folly of Rehoboam's eventual choice builds throughout vv. 6-12.

---

[6]Jones, *1 and 2 Kings*, vol. I, 251.

[7]ילדים might even be translated as "children," intensifying the sense of contrast between the groups. See Bar-Efrat, *Narrative Art in the Bible*, 33-34.

[8]Gene Rice, *1 Kings: Nations Under God* (Grand Rapids: Eerdmans, 1990) 100.

The third major scene of the story is linked to the previous two by important elements in vv. 12-13.[9] In a reversal of v. 5, in which the people went (הלך) from Rehoboam, they now come (בוא) to him just as he told them to. An ominous note is again sounded by the presence of Jereboam, who had rebelled against Rehoboam's father, and had been promised a kingdom in 11:31. The people's willingness to cooperate with the Davidic dynasty is underscored by the repetition of the command, "Return (שׁוּב) to me on the third day," which they have obeyed dutifully. Verse 13 repeats Rehoboam's forsaking (עזב) of the advice of the elders in v. 8. In v. 14, Rehoboam repeats the words of the younger advisors from v. 10, omitting the vulgarity in reference to his father. That the meaning of this statement involves the comparison of genital size seems plain enough, and Rehoboam's choice not to repeat it may be the only bit of wise discretion the narrator adds to his portrayal of Solomon's son.[10]

Verse 15 is perhaps the most difficult element to reconcile with the rest of the story. The narrator boldly steps forward here to offer a theological evaluation of events.[11] This kind of statement falls into the category Bar-Efrat has called "overt" narration.[12] The narrator runs a certain risk in using such overt narrative judgments. In Bar-Efrat's words, such interventions "mar the illusion of reality in the narrative, diverting attention from the events of the narrative to the craft of narration and from the incidents themselves to the attitude toward them."[13] This is exactly what happens in v. 15.[14] The narrator's sudden

---

[9]These elements are clear examples of what Bar-Efrat labeled "resumptive repetitions" (*Narrative Art in the bible*, 215-216).

[10]Numerous explanations have been offered for the Phrase, "My little finger is thicker than my father's loins," in v. 10. Some commentators have made an effort to avoid the apparent crassness of the statement. Though Martin Noth seems to be alone in arguing for a clear reference to genitals, this conclusion is difficult to escape. See *Konige*, BKAT (Neukirchen-Vluyn: Neukirchen Verlag, 1968) 267. Gray's description of a "homely hyperbole" is vague (*I & II Kings*, 306).

[11]There is, of course, a source-critical explanation for this verse, that it is a pious insertion into the story from the hand of a Deuteronomistic editor. For a characteristic discussion, See DeVries, *1 Kings*, 157. Regardless of the historical veracity of such analyses, they do not satisfactorily explain how the verse fits with the rest of the narrative in its final form.

[12]See his discussion in *Narrative Art in the Bible*, 23-32.

[13]Ibid., 31.

[14]In the author's defense, it may be noted that Yahweh is not a character in this story. Therefore, overt narration is one of the few remaining options for expressing Yahweh's will. Von Rad described a tendency in the writing of the

appearance brings the narrative to a halt and leaves the reader puzzled. How can this evaluation fit with the story that has been told so far? The narrative, thus far, has presented Rehoboam's actions as brash and foolish, yet now attributes them to God's design. This verse reveals a theological tension which matches the political tension in the story.[15] This narrative, through v. 14, describes events in a way that makes human decisions, in this case bad ones, determinative for Israel's history. This is precisely why the narration must become overt in v. 15. The "covert narration"[16] is taking the story in an unacceptable direction theologically. Through the first fourteen verses there is no acknowledgment of divine action or presence, and a reassertion of Yahweh's involvement is necessary. At the same time, v. 15 is artfully woven into the story. At the beginning of v. 16, the people observe what the narrator observes at the beginning of v. 15, that Rehoboam has not listened to them. Verse 16 continues to parallel the preceding verse as the people enact the prophecy of Adonijah, mentioned in v. 15, by separating themselves from the Davidic dynasty.

The poetic speech, delivered by the people collectively to Rehoboam in v. 16, puts an end to the dialogue in this story. The narrative hurries towards its conclusion in a rapid series of actions, again dominated by verbs of movement. The torrid pace of the action is enhanced by elements of confusion in the narrative. Israel goes (הלך) away from Shechem again, just as in v. 5. The note concerning Rehoboam's reign over Judah in v. 17 sounds as if he has returned to the south, but the description of him fleeing (נוס) to Jerusalem in v. 18 belies that assumption. When Rehoboam sends (שלח) Adoram in v. 18, the reader is told neither where he sends him nor why. "All Israel," which seems to have dispersed at the end of v. 16 is suddenly gathered again in v. 18 to execute Adoram collectively in the unnamed location.

A story which began with careful, ordered dialogue and movements of people deteriorates into total chaos. The rash words of Rehoboam

---

historical books to move toward a less direct portrayal of Yahweh's action in history (*Old Testament Theology*, vol. 1:51-52).

[15]Trible has described tension between the narrator and the characters as a basic rhetorical feature of biblical stories. See *Rhetorical Criticism*, 103. Here, the tension seems to go deeper, existing between the narrator's portrayal of characters and the narrator's theology. Sternberg acknowledged the possibility of conflict within the narrator, revealed by such theological statements as v. 15. The narrator's struggle is to "harmonize rhetoric and ideology" (*The Poetics of Biblical Narrative*, 483).

[16]Bar-Efrat, *Narrative Art in the Bible*, 32.

generate rash action on the part of the northern tribes. The narrator, who seems to have sided with the Northerners early in the story, accuses them of rebellion in v. 19. Rice has aptly summarized the narrator's ambivalence: "The passage strongly condemns repressive government, but it does not romanticize revolt."[17] Historical-critical readings would credit this sense of duality to the presence of various sources and layers of tradition within the text.[18] Regardless of the process which may have brought about the formation of this text, the effect of the present form is powerful. This is a story which has two sides. The two sides of the story are as irreconcilable as the political differences between the northern and southern kingdoms. The author makes no attempt to settle in the text what was never settled in reality. The form of the story reflects the content it presents. The cumulative effects of years of inequity and forced labor, as described in the lengthy dialogues of vv. 1-16, bring about an explosive division characterized in a hurried and murderous frenzy of action in vv. 17-19.

Verse 20 provides the final results. The kingdom is divided. Just when it seems that v. 19 has brought the story around to a southern point-of-view, the northern perspective reemerges. The reader catches a glimpse of the return (שׁוּב) of Jereboam and his coronation. Rehoboam is mentioned only indirectly, as "house of David," and from afar. The grandeur of the united monarchy is a distant memory.

Theological Conclusions

First Kings 12:1-20 is not, on the surface, a very theological text. Were it not for the troubling evaluation of the events in v. 15, Yahweh would be absent in name from the story. Nevertheless, this story is intimately tied to Israel's theological traditions.

The division of the united monarchy into two kingdoms is caused by the oppressive violence of slavery. The division is signaled by a collective murder. First Kings 12:1-20 reveals, perhaps better than any other biblical text, the dark underside of the seemingly idyllic reigns of Solomon and David. The formation of the Israelite monarchy is motivated by the military threat of the Philistines. The decisive display of this threat is the battle of Aphek in 1 Samuel 4. In 1 Samuel 8 the people demand a king. In the process of fulfilling the people's request,

---

[17]Rice, *1 Kings: Nations under God*, 98.

[18]See typical discussions in Jones, *1 and 2 Kings, vol. 1*, 247-249 and J. Robinson, *The First Book of Kings*, CBC (Cambridge: Cambridge University Press, 1972) 152.

reluctantly, Samuel recites the conditions which would eventually characterize Israel's monarchy in 1 Samuel 8:11-18. This recitation sounds suspiciously like a description of Solomon's kingdom. 1 Kings 11 foreshadows the eventual split by reporting Ahijah's promise of ten tribes to Jereboam. The monarchy, as a response to an external violent threat, gives rise to a destructive pattern of internal violence. Israel's history seems to follow something of a cycle. The threat of famine led the people into Egypt and eventual slavery. Deliverance from slavery then made way for the tribal confederacy described in the book of Judges. Philistine power, another threat, led to a new kind of slavery — subjection to a monarch. Like the period in Egypt the monarchy did not begin as a period of harsh enslavement, but evolved into such. First Kings 12 might be viewed as a kind of Exodus for the Northern tribes, a deliverance from slavery. Indeed, this text shares many points of contact with the Exodus tradition. Hanson has noted that Jereboam rises from among his own people to a position of privilege above them, and that he leaves that position to lead a rebellion.[19] Jereboam travels from Egypt to Israel at the beginning of 1 Kings 12. Rehoboam's refusal to lighten the service of the Northern tribes mirrors Pharaoh's intransigence in response to the demands of Moses. The killing of Adoram recalls the murder of the Egyptian taskmaster by Moses. Finally, Rehoboam is again portrayed in a manner reminiscent of Pharaoh as he mounts his chariot to flee from Shechem.

In the Exodus story, elements of good and evil are relatively easy to distinguish, but in this story of the division of the Israelite monarchy the lines are not so clear. This seems to be the deliberate intention of the author, who does not take sides. The episode of forced labor, which is discussed by the characters in the first part of the story, does have a definite perpetrator and definite victims. The murder that brings the story to a close, however, casts the former victims in the role of perpetrator and a representative of the former perpetrator in the role of victim. The parallels cited above, between this story and the Exodus are more than matched by differences between the two events. While the author of 1 Kings 12 clearly wishes to call the Exodus to the reader's mind by highlighting points of contact, this is by no means an attempt to equate the two events.

This story reveals much about how violence operates in an ordered society, and how it operates when that order collapses. In less than a century, the Israelite monarchy evolves from a system designed to liberate people from external threat to an oppressive force which creates

---

[19]Hanson, *The People Called*, 133-134.

a society stratified according to tribal affiliation. Those at the top of society, represented by Rehoboam, become accustomed to the privileges gained by a system of oppression. Rehoboam deals with the threat of an uprising in the same way as Pharaoh, by threatening even harsher conditions. Unfortunately, for Rehoboam, many of the Northerners apparently knew a way of life other than servitude. They treated it as an option. They were willing to bargain and accept a life of servitude if there was some benefit in it. The text emphasizes this by highlighting in v. 12 their precise obedience to Rehoboam's command in v. 5. Their oppressor, like all others, is unwilling to compromise, however. In oppressive societies, voices of moderation are ignored, and extremism becomes the dominant theme.

When the accepted order breaks down the action is brisk and sudden. Girard has compared the mechanism of kingship to that of scapegoating. He describes a king, like a sacrificial victim, as "a catalyst who converts sterile infectious violence into positive cultural values."[20] The problem for Rehoboam is that, like a sacrificial victim, a king must be chosen unanimously to be effective. As soon as the Northerners begin to see the prevailing conditions as something other than "positive cultural values," then the arrangement falls apart. Williams has argued further that The Israelite monarchy, like others, was formed at a time of crisis with the king chosen as a "victim of converging mimetic forces."[21] This certainly describes Saul, caught between the fear created by the Philistines and the anti-monarchical tendencies of the Israelite tribal confederacy, personified in Samuel. When the arrangement begins to break down, the king is in danger of becoming a true sacrificial victim. Fortunately, for Rehoboam, the rebellious Northerners follow a common pattern of unleashing there violent action upon a representative of the king rather than the king himself.[22] The stoning of Adoram is portrayed in a rapid, hurried fashion.[23] In this way it resembles the murder of Abel by Cain. The murder of Adoram becomes the act which founds the Northern kingdom. This is revealed in the text by the emphasis in v. 18 on "all Israel" acting together. The Northern tribes are named in this manner at the beginning of v. 16 as they consider Rehoboam's

---

[20]Girard, *Violence and the Sacred,* 107. I do not like the word "positive" here. It implies that such societies are somehow inherently moral. A more functional adjective such as "desirable" or "successful" might describe this phenomenon more accurately.

[21]Williams, *The Bible, Violence, and* the Sacred, 134.

[22]Ibid., 131.

[23]Hanson, *The People Called,* 133.

reply. At the end of v. 16, when they disperse, they are merely "Israel." They come back together in this act of violence, and their unanimity is highlighted in their designation. Verse 19 states plainly that the separate Northern kingdom began with the stoning of Adoram.

The ultimate theological question with which the reader of this text is left is "Where is God in this story?" Aside from the interpretive statement from the narrator in v. 15, God is not visible here. This is why v. 15 is so integral to the narrative. At so monumental a moment in the history of Israel, it is inconceivable that Yahweh could be uninvolved. The quandary that arises here with the division of the kingdom is determining on which side Yahweh stands. To this point, Yahweh has sided with Israel, the victim of oppression, the little brother among all the peoples of the ancient Near East.

Some early complications in this simple scheme have arisen in moments when Israel was not so clearly the innocent victim, such as at the end of the Passover narrative in Exodus 12 or during the destruction of Jericho in Joshua 6. The picture becomes considerably more complicated here in 1 Kings 12, as the favored victim becomes divided against itself. The author of the story has appropriately matched an ambiguous narrative with an ambiguous situation.[24] The discussion in the previous chapter on the capture of the ark in 1 Samuel 4 mentioned the humiliation[25] or capture[26] of God. In a similar way, 1 Kings 12 may be about the tearing apart of God. The heart of God is unable to follow either group alone. Thus, God accepts or even "brings about," in the language of the text, the tearing apart of God's people, initially symbolized in the tearing of Ahijah's garment in 1 Kings 11:30.

The reputation of Yahweh may be rescued, to some extent, in the larger context of this passage. In the text immediately following, 12:21-24, the word of Yahweh comes to Rehoboam via the prophet Shemaiah, commanding Rehoboam not to return to fight the Northern tribes. The word of Yahweh thus prevents a full scale civil war at this point. Indeed, Niditch has said of this text that "God is thus put on the side of

---

[24]The views of numerous commentators on the mixture of perspectives present in this text have been noted above. Brueggemann has perhaps stated his case a bit too clearly in saying that the writer of 1 Kings 12 "believes that the Word is allied with the powerless, against the regime." See 1 Kings (Atlanta: John Knox, 1982) 60. It is difficult to reconcile this distinctly one-sided view, no matter how appealing it is, with the evaluations in v. 15 and v. 19.

[25]Fretheim, *The Suffering of God*, 144-145.

[26] Terrien, *The Elusive Presence*, 265.

holding peace among Israelites."[27] This brings us back, however, to the murder of Adoram in 12:18. When Rehoboam fails to avenge Adoram's murder, thus tacitly accepting it, is Adoram made into a the scapegoat whose murder insures peace between the two peoples? Yahweh's role in the outcome of this episode remains in question.

In summary, the systems of violent oppression under which Israel suffered become internalized within the nation itself. The resentment caused by such inequity comes to a head in 1 Kings 12. As the society breaks down, violence erupts and an irreconcilable split takes place along class and ethnic lines. The relatively consistent theology which undergirded Israel's understanding of its own existence can no longer function. This text presents a powerfully ambiguous story which mixes themes of rebellion and liberation.

From this point, there will be no single story of Israel, but a divided story. The Northern half of the story will come to an end sooner, and the Bible will show declining interest in the North. The eventual fate of Israel is more poignantly captured in the Southern half of the story, and its conclusion will become the conclusion of the Hebrew Bible itself.

---

[27]Niditch, *War in the Hebrew Bible*, 97. In her classification of ancient Israelite war ideologies, Niditch places this text among several that put limits on war. In this case, the limitation is that one should not go to war against one's kin.

INTERLUDE SIX:

CONFLICT WITH OTHER NATIONS

The movement from one text to another in this case involves more than just passage of time in Israel's story. It is a movement from one parallel literary history to another. In this way the Hebrew canon reflects the story it tells. The Deuteronomistic/Chronistic schism is a division between two views of Israel's story. The Deuteronomistic History continues after the division of the kingdom, in 1 Kings 12, to report on political events in the northern kingdom of Israel until the fall of Samaria in 2 Kings 17-18. After the report of the division of the kingdoms, in 2 Chronicles 12, the Chronistic history ceases reporting on events in the northern kingdom, unless those events directly affect Judah. Thus, the Chronistic History completes the division from a literary perspective by regarding the continuing story in the north of no direct importance to the continuing story of God and God's people.

The patterns of violence observed in the story of the division of the kingdom in 1 Kings 12 and 2 Chronicles 12 continue as the story of the people of Israel progresses. The rift between North and South remains and violent conflict arises from time to time. After Rehoboam's death, Jereboam and Abijah go to war against each other (2 Chronicles 13:2ff). Asa of Judah and Baasha of Israel also fought each other (2 Chronicles 16). Even the brief alliance formed by Jehoshaphat of Judah and Ahab of Israel against Aram (2 Chronicles 18) ends in failure. Even in its final years, the northern kingdom made war against Judah (2 Chronicles 28). The division created by the oppressive reign of Solomon and Rehoboam's attempt to continue this pattern become a permanent situation. Not only are the two kingdoms permanently separated, but they are even incapable of peaceful coexistence. The relatively peaceful separation reported in 1 Kings 12, perhaps sealed by the blood of Adoram, gives way to perpetual conflict until the destruction of the northern kingdom by the Assyrians.

7

GOD'S PEOPLE DESTROYED BY VIOLENCE

2 CHRONICLES 36:15-21

Second Chronicles 36 is the final chapter of the Hebrew Bible. It contains brief reports of the last four kings of Judah. First, Jehoahaz, the son of Josiah, is kidnapped and taken to Egypt after reigning for only three months (v. 4). Second, Neco places Jehoiakim on the throne in place of Jehoahaz (v. 4). After eleven years, Nebuchadnezzar comes to Jerusalem and takes Jehoiakim away to Babylon (vv. 5-6). Third, Jehoiachin replaces Jehoiachim as king for just over three months before he, too, is carried off to Babylon (vv. 9-10). Finally, Zedekiah reigns for the final eleven years before the Exile (v. 11). In vv. 11-14, the writer of Chronicles characterizes the reign of Zedekiah as evil for four specific reasons. First, Zedekiah did not humble himself before Yahweh's representative, the prophet Jeremiah (v. 12). Second, Zedekiah rebelled against Nebuchadnezzar, to whom he had sworn allegiance (v. 13). Third, Zedekiah "hardened his heart against turning to Yahweh" (v. 13). Finally, the priests and people during the time of Zedekiah committed abominations in the temple (v. 14).

The report of the reign of Zedekiah leads up to the text to be examined in this chapter. Second Chronicles 36:15-21 is the account of the destruction of Jerusalem. The description of Israel's final plunge into disaster is brief and violent. The people whom God had created by delivering them from the hand of a foreign enemy in the book of Exodus are here delivered into the hands of another brutal empire.

Of course, the Exile is not the historical end of the life of Israel. The Hebrew Bible does record a history of the Restoration in the books of Ezra and Nehemiah. The Hebrew Bible, however, places the books of

Ezra and Nehemiah before Chronicles, making the destruction of Jerusalem the final event in the biblical story of Israel.[1] The historical
chronology of events and the literary story presented by the Hebrew
Bible are not equivalent. It is not quite accurate, though, to say that the
Hebrew Bible ends with the destruction of Jerusalem. The final two
verses, 2 Chronicles 36:21-22, report the Decree of Cyrus, a different
version of which appears at the beginning of the book of Ezra.[2] These
last two verse offer at least a hint that the story is not complete, and this
hint of the Restoration forms part of the literary context of 2 Chronicles
36:15-21.

The Text

At first glance, 2 Chronicles 36:15-21 is a surprisingly brief account of
what becomes a defining moment for Israel. This text is set off quite
clearly from the preceding verses, which form a fairly standard
evaluation of Zedekiah's reign.[3] Verses 15-21 need not be broken down
into any smaller sections. It is an unbroken, almost breathless report,
which matches in tone not only all of chapter thirty-six, but also all of

---

[1]The Greek tradition does place the four books of the Chronistic history in
their more natural historical order, and is subsequently followed by the Catholic
and Protestant Canons. This is not the place to analyze all of the arguments concerning explanations for the different sequences of the books. The problem of the
ordering of the books has become entangled with the even more complex issues
of authorship and unity of the Chronistic history. Thorough discussions of these
issues can be found in the introductions to the major commentaries on Chronicles, Ezra, and Nehemiah.

[2]The double appearance of the Decree of Cyrus has elicited a mountain of
scholarly debate. It has been used to argue both for and against the common
authorship of Chronicles and Ezra-Nehemiah. For the most representative
examples of the two opposing positions, see Menahem Haran, "Explaining the
Identical Lines at the End of Chronicles and the Beginning of Ezra," *BRev*, 2
(1986): 19 and H. G. M. Williamson, "Did the Author of Chronicles also Write
the Books of Ezra and Nehemiah?," *BRev*, 3 (1987): 56-59.

[3]Raymond Dillard has noticed a distinct pattern in the evaluations of the last
four kings. Two characteristic elements of previous evaluations, the identification of the king's maternal lineage and the death notice of the king, are missing from all four. Each of these passages, like the end of 2 Chronicles as a whole,
appears to be intentionally shortened. Each of the last four kings is taken into
exile and each pays tribute to a foreign ruler from the temple treasury. Thus, the
Davidic dynasty and the temple are plundered in parallel fashion. See Dillard, *2
Chronicles*, WBC (Waco: Word, 1987) 297.

the last eight chapters of 2 Chronicles.[4] This account begins and ends with notations which make reference to the long history of God's people, particularly to their long history of disobedience. God's people are never named in these verses. Verse 15 reports that for an uncertain amount of time, which will be discussed below, God has been sending messages to "their ancestors." The length of the Exile is represented in v. 21 as corresponding to seventy years of Sabbaths. This implies a 490 year period of disobedience.[5]

Verse 15 opens in strikingly ambiguous fashion. Indeed, ambiguity will characterize this entire passage. Therefore, the ambiguity of v. 15 is most appropriate. With no clear connection to the preceding verses, the "them" of v. 15 is not a readily identifiable group. There are at least three possibilities. If a connection with the preceding verses is emphasized, "them" could be the Judahites during the reign of Zedekiah. If the context of the whole chapter is considered in choosing the antecedent, "them" could be the "people of the land" in 36:1. This option would stretch the period described in vv. 15-16 from the eleven year reign of Zedekiah to the combined twenty-two and one half years of the last four kings. Finally, in the context of the Chronistic History, which runs from Adam to the Exile, "them" could be understood as Israel. The period of time described in vv. 15-16 could then be all of Israel's history. This last option seems preferable. In light of the general condemnation which Israel and its leaders, with some exceptions, receive in Chronicles, any readings of vv. 15-16 which place disproportionate blame on the final generation seem unlikely. Nevertheless, nothing in the text makes such interpretations impossible.

Verse 15 brings up the two objects of Yahweh's punishment at the beginning of the report, "his people (עַם) and his dwelling place" (מָעוֹן). Upon these Yahweh has compassion (חָמַל). The response of the people to Yahweh's compassion, however, is a three-fold rejection. In v. 16, they mock (לָעַב), despise (בָּזָה), and scoff at (תָעַע) Yahweh's acts of compassion. The people's rejection of Yahweh's three-fold, desperate attempt to reach them through messenger (מַלְאָךְ), word (דָבָר), and prophet (נָבִיא) leads to Yahweh's final abandonment. Yahweh turns against "his people" (עַם), but the text very delicately shields Yahweh

---

[4]For a discussion of the distinctive quality of 2 Chronicles 29-36 compared to the rest of Chronicles, see Stephen L. McKenzie, *The Chronicler's Use of the Deuteronomic History* (Atlanta: Scholars Press, 1984) 113.

[5]For the purpose of this analysis, the precise historical boundaries of the seventy and 490 year periods are not significant. For a survey of the many proposals, see Dillard, *2 Chronicles*, 300-302.

from direct, violent action. It is the anger (חֵמָה) of Yahweh which rises up (עלה) against the people. The extent of Yahweh's abandonment is such that there is no healing (מַרְפֵּא). This would appear to be a reference to the twice repeated phrase in Jeremiah, "The ones waiting for peace but there is no good, and for a time of healing (מַרְפֵּא) but, behold, terror!"[6]

In v. 17 the actual violence begins and, again, the direct involvement of Yahweh is shielded by the artistic use of delicate, ambiguous language. The words "Yahweh" and "God" (אֱלֹהִים) appear once each in v. 15 and once each in v. 16. In v. 17, the deity is present only in pronouns, and the extent of this presence is uncertain. Again in v. 18, Yahweh and God (אֱלֹהִים) appear once each. V. 17 begins with a causative (*hiphil*) from of the verb עלה (go up). The verse contains four carefully constructed clauses.

> (a) He brought up (עלה) against them the King of the Chaldeans
>
> (b) and he killed (הרג) their young people (בָּחוּר) by the sword in the house of their sanctuary (מִקְדָּשׁ)
>
> (c) and he did not have compassion (חמל) on young man (בָּחוּר) or virgin, old or feeble.
>
> (d) All he gave (נתן) into his hand.

The four clauses contain one verb each. The verbs in clauses (a) and (d) can only have Yahweh as the subject. The antecedent of the third person, singular pronouns must come from v. 16. The subjects of clauses (b) and (c) are ambiguous.[7] In light of the ambiguity which charac-

---

[6]See Jeremiah 8:15 and 14:19. מַרְפֵּא is a relatively rare word in the Hebrew Bible. Eight of the total sixteen occurrences are in Proverbs. Of the remaining eight, four are found in Jeremiah, two in the saying quoted here. The only other appearance of the word in Chronicles is the description of Jehoram's fatal illness in 2 Chronicles 21:18.

[7]The grammatical connections between the clauses do not clear up the problem. Clauses (a) and (b) begin with *vav* consecutives. Clause (c) begins with a *vav* conjunction and clause (d) begins with no conjunction of any kind. Most English translations (see the New Revised Standard Version, for example) avoid the ambiguity by translating the consecutive at the beginning of clause b with a relative pronoun. The King of the Chaldeans becomes the unambiguous subject of clause (b) and probably of clause (c) as well. While the Greek tradition found in LXX version of v. 17 maintains the ambiguity of clause (b) by beginning it with a simple conjunction, the later Greek tradition in the parallel 1 Esdras 1:53

terizes this entire passage, both potential readings should be allowed as possibilities. Perhaps even the narrator of the text intends for either Yahweh or the King of the Chaldeans to be taken as the subject of clauses (b) and (c).[8]

The identification of the victims in v. 17 is also the result of artful, ambiguous literary construction. At first, those killed are described as only "their young people" (בחוריהם). These persons are killed inside the temple. Yahweh has by this point disowned the temple. V. 15 described it as "his [Yahweh's] dwelling" (מעונו), on which Yahweh had compassion (חמל). In v. 17 the temple is "the house of their sanctuary" (מקדשם). In v. 17c the object of God's judgment becomes greatly amplified. Now Yahweh has no compassion (חמל). Two pairs of opposites are used in v. 17c to express the totality of the violence. Those killed are both male and female, both young and old.[9] The murders which appear to be somewhat controlled and contained in v. 17b break out of all boundaries and become complete. In v. 17d, Yahweh gives all (כל) of the people to the King of the Chaldeans. The ambiguity of subject disappears.

Once the destruction of the people is accomplished in v. 17, vv. 18-19 turn to the destruction of the temple. The second object of Yahweh's earlier compassion in v. 15 now comes under judgment. Again, pairs of opposites are used to express totality. All (כל) of the vessels (כלי) large (גדל) and small (קטן) are taken. The treasures of the house of Yahweh and the treasures of the house of the king are taken.[10] Ackroyd has argued that the taking of the temple vessels constitutes the "primary moment of judgment," because these are the implements used to

---

removes the ambiguity altogether by beginning clause (b) with a masculine plural demonstrative pronoun as the subject of a subsequent plural verb ("These killed…").

[8]Most commentators completely avoid the possibility of reading Yahweh as subject throughout v. 17. Peter R. Ackroyd acknowledges the possibility of translating God as the subject of all the verbs in the verse. See *1 and 2 Chronicles, Ezra, Nehemiah*, TBC (London: SCM, 1973) 209. Dillard allows that reading God as the subject of all the verbs in v. 17 as "a syntactic possibility" which "seems improbable." See *2 Chronicles*, 301. On the possibility and implications of such a translation of v. 17, see also Mark McEntire, *The Function of Sacrifice in Chronicles, Ezra, and Nehemiah* (Lewiston, N. Y.: Mellen Biblical Press, 1993) 44-46.

[9]Martin J. Selman, *2 Chronicles*, TOTC (Leicester: InterVarsity Press, 1994) 550.

[10]Dillard's assertion concerning the parallel fates of the temple and the Davidic dynasty is again apparent here (*2 Chronicles*, 297).

worship God. Their confiscation, therefore, puts an end to worship in the Jerusalem temple.[11]

A further connection may exist in the use of the word vessels (כְּלִי) here. In Exodus 12:35-36, when the Israelites left Egypt, they were given objects (כְּלִי) of silver and gold as symbols of their liberation. In Joshua 6:19, when the Israelites began to take control of the promised land, they took the vessels (כְּלִי) of bronze and iron from the inhabitants of Jericho to put in the treasury of Yahweh. The taking of objects (כְּלִי) tends to accompany both violent acts of liberation and destruction. Yahweh's ownership of the temple is expressed here in v. 18, as the narrator balances the sense of dispossession in v. 17. Ambiguity abounds again in v. 18. The final clause literally reads "All he caused to come to Babylon."[12] The subject of this clause could be either Yahweh or the King of the Chaldeans. V. 19 puts and end to this ambiguity of subject. The judgment of the temple is completed as they, clearly the Babylonian soldiers, burn (שָׂרַף) it. The destruction moves beyond the people and the temple to include all of Jerusalem. The devastation is total as the use of the word כֹּל (all) indicates. This word, which appeared once in v. 17 and twice in v. 18, appears twice more in v. 19. The Babylonians burn (שָׂרַף) all (כֹּל) of Jerusalem's palaces and destroy all (כֹּל) of its precious vessels (כְּלִי). In the end, vv. 17-19 present a devastating picture. The language of these verses is powerful and total. But this is the destruction of Jerusalem, the end of Yahweh's people dwelling with Yahweh in Yahweh's land, and nothing less than this type of portrayal would befit such a circumstance.[13]

In fact, the picture of total destruction in vv. 17-19 is not quite accurate, as vv. 20-21 later indicate. Some of the inhabitants of Judah actually do "escape the sword." These escapees are "taken into exile" (גָּלָה, glh). They become the Golah, the exilic community, of Hebrew tradition. The totality of vv. 17-19 and the exception revealed in v. 20 perform an important literary function. There are only two groups of Judeans in this story, those who are killed and those who are taken into

---

[11]Ackroyd, 1 and 2 Chronicles, Ezra, Nehemiah, 209.

[12]Alternative, literal translations could be "All he cased to enter into Babylon" or "All he caused to go to Babylon."

[13]There seems to be something of a consensus within the field of biblical studies that the books of Chronicles are not as artfully composed as the parallel Deuteronomistic History. I would not dispute this as a general rule, but I would contend that the devastating portrayal of violence in 2 Chronicles 36:17-19 far surpasses the more detailed account of 2 Kings 25:8-26 in literary artistry.

exile.[14] The writer tells the story as if not one person is left alive in Jerusalem.[15] This contention is expressed again in the report at the end of v. 21 that the land was not farmed, but kept sabbath, during the exile.

The harrowing story of Jerusalem's total destruction is bracketed by descriptions of two eras. The first, portrayed in vv. 15-16, is an era of total disobedience. The second, described in vv. 20-21, is one of total restoration of the land. The land keeps its sabbath for "all (כל) the days of desolation." Yahweh brings about this restoration by emptying the land. The law in Israel commanded that the land lie fallow for one year out of each seven. Proper management of food resources may have made this possible, but the seventy year period of rest in v. 21 is as total as the disobedience and the judgment earlier in the text. It would not be possible if the land were inhabited. This seventy year sabbath is a fulfillment of the word of Yahweh. The people may have been able to ignore the message of Yahweh sent "by the hand (יד) of his messengers" (v. 15), but the course of Israel's story cannot avoid fulfilling the word of Yahweh "by the mouth (פי) of Jeremiah." The pronounced judgment must take place, but it opens up new possibilities. The final clause of v. 21 reveals this in two ways. First, desolation (שמה) is balanced by sabbath. Second, though the period of seventy years is long, it does indicate an end.[16]

Theological Conclusions

According to the preceding analysis of 2 Chronicles 36:15-21, the two features which most strikingly characterize this text are brevity and ambiguity. As the last of many episodes of violence recorded in the Hebrew Bible, this story represents Israel's final word on violence. As a story of final and total destruction, it also represents the final word of violence on Israel. The end for Israel comes all too quickly and

---

[14]So convincing is the writer's portrayal that until quite recently, interpreters took this literary account quite seriously as a historical account, supposing that at least the vast majority of the Judeans still alive went to Babylon. See, for example, William F. Albright, *The Archaeology of Palestine* (Baltimore: Penguin, 1949) 130-142.

[15]H. G. M. Williamson, *1 and 2 Chronicles*, NCBC (Grand Rapids: Eerdmans, 1982) 417.

[16]Like the 490 year period of disobedience which the seventy year sabbath implies, there are numerous speculations about the precise historical period to which the seventy years refer. Again, for a survey of possibilities, see Dillard, *2 Chronicles*, 300-302.

confusingly. A sudden eruption of violence punctuates a long history of disobedience and warning.

The identity of the victims in 2 Chronicles 36:15-21 is unclear, as is the degree of their guilt. The violence in this passage is punishment for disobedience. The numerology of the text indicates that this disobedience has gone on for almost five centuries. The punishment, however, has been delayed because of Yahweh's compassion (חמל). The writer does not portray the final generation as innocent, but they do bear the collective result of many sins, the much deserved punishment of many generations. Those on whom Yahweh has compassion are clearly named and owned by Yahweh. They are "his people" (עמו) in v. 15. They are also "his people" (עמו) in v. 16 as the object of Yahweh's wrath. In vv. 17-21, however, the whole people is never referred to in any way except by pronouns. The representatives of these people who become the direct victims of murder in v. 17 are not named, but only described. Furthermore, and most troubling, the text describes them in such a way as to at least diminish their guilt. They are the young, the old, the feeble, the marginalized of society. While these descriptions perform an inclusive literary function, encompassing all within the suffering group, it is striking that these are the kinds of people the text specifically mentions. Of course, as people on the margins, they form the perfect boundaries for all inclusive expressions. They are the least capable of escape, the most easily utilized by both conqueror and author. Has the author, through the use of a literary device, inadvertently or purposely lodged the ultimate protest against punitive violence on a societal level? It is those who are least guilty, if not innocent, who suffer the most.

The connections between 2 Chronicles 36:15-21 and Joshua 6 are well worth exploring. The description of the Judeans who are killed in 2 Chronicles 36:17 is not identical to the description of the victims in Jericho in Joshua 6:21, but the similarities are noteworthy. Both verses use the same type of inclusive literary device, characterized by the naming of opposites, as described above. In both cases, young persons, old persons, male persons and female persons are explicitly mentioned. In Joshua 6:24, Jericho is burned and the objects of precious metal are taken "into the treasury of the house of Yahweh." In 2 Chronicles 36:18-19, Jerusalem is burned and objects are taken out of "the house of Yahweh. In the Joshua text, the Israelites begin their occupation of the land. In the Chronicles text, they are brutally removed from the land. The two texts would appear to be quite specific opposites of each other. What Yahweh gives to the Israelites in Joshua 6, Yahweh takes away in the same manner in 2 Chronicles 36:15-21. In describing the explicit

חרם (*herem*) texts in the Hebrew Bible, Niditch has asserted that "The very language of the texts forbids the emotions of mercy."[17] In many of these texts, including Joshua 6, those carrying out the ban are allowed to spare no one. This resonates powerfully with the language of the lack of compassion or mercy (חמל) in 2 Chronicles 36:17. The Chronicles text does not use the word חרם (*herem*),[18] which figures so prominently in Joshua, but the other connections are many, and the conclusion that Yahweh has instituted the ban upon Israel is unmistakable. The idea that the ban could be turned back upon Israel itself is present in the prophets.[19]

Along with the confusion and ambiguity concerning the victims of violence in 2 Chronicles 36:15-21, there is also confusion and ambiguity about the perpetrator of the violence. Again, literary analysis leaves open the possibility that all of this ambiguity is the deliberate creation of the biblical writer. As demonstrated in the examination of the text above, the difficulty in identifying the perpetrator is the result of the complex and enigmatic v.17. Niditch has identified a tradition within the books of Chronicles which treats the subject of war quite differently than much of the rest of the Hebrew Bible. The writer of Chronicles tones down the violent activities of David, emphasizes the peaceful character of Solomon's reign, and stresses the divine role in war to an extent that human participation is absent.[20] Niditch may have pushed too far in concluding that the books of Chronicles "reveal a late biblical tradition groping toward peace,"[21] but the view of war in Chronicles is undeniably different than that found in the Deuteronomistic History.

How does 2 Chronicles 36:15-21 fit with this proposal? If the tendency of the Chronicler is to attribute war and its outcome entirely to God's control, then it is even more difficult to diminish Yahweh's involvement in the acts described in v. 17. If it is significant that Chronicles contains texts such as 2 Chronicles 20, in which Israel is not even required to fight in order to be victorious in war,[22] then it is not surprising that

---

[17]Niditch, *War in the Hebrew Bible*, 28. Niditch also points to Deuteronomy 7:2-5 as a text where mercy and ban are placed in opposition (p. 76).

[18]This is not surprising, since the Chronicler has virtually removed this term from this account of Israel's history. While the root, חרם, appears some forty times in the Deuteronomistic history, there are only four occurrences in the books of Chronicles.

[19]See the discussion of Niditch. Ibid., 76.

[20]Ibid., 139-149.

[21]Ibid., 149.

[22]See Niditch's discussion of this text and others like it. Ibid., 144-146.

when Yahweh brings the Babylonians upon Jerusalem in 36:17 the Israelites put up no defense. If victory is completely in the hands of Yahweh, so is defeat. Yahweh is the ultimate perpetrator, the one who utterly destroys Israel itself. Is this the horrifying conclusion with which the author of 36:15-21 is trying so hard to come to grips, the statement which he can not quite bring himself to say unambiguously? If Trible, following Muilenburg, is correct that "form and content are inseparable"[23] then no form could match this content better. This most dramatic, confusing, and troubling understanding of what has happened between Yahweh and Israel must be communicated by a text that is equally dramatic, confused, and troubled.

The story of the Hebrew Bible is the convergence of a divine presence, a chosen people, and a sacred place. Second Chronicles 36:15-21 is a final, brief narrative which tells of the rupture of all three relationships which exists among this triad.[24] Yahweh disowns the chosen people. Yahweh brings about the destruction of the holy city. The chosen people are all either killed or carried off to a foreign land. While this study is concerned with a literary construction and not with history, it is important to note the extent to which the two diverge here. It is now clear, historically, that a significant number of Judeans remained alive, existing in their partially destroyed homeland after the Babylonian invasion.[25] Those responsible for the narrative in Chronicles could hardly have been unaware of this fact. This serves to accentuate the degree to which the portrayal of total destruction found at the end of Chronicles is a carefully crafted literary construction intended to communicate a theological message.

The marriage of deity, nation, and land has ended in complete divorce. It is only after the author has communicated this message that a word of hope is allowed. The end of v. 21 and all of v. 22 finally let the reader in on the secret, only after all hope has been destroyed by the preceding verses. After all the killing and burning, the reader is led step by step to a view of the future. The initial glimpse comes with the report that all were not killed, but some were also taken into captivity as slaves.[26] The end of v. 21, along with v. 22 open the view to the

---

[23]Trible, *Rhetorical Criticism*, 91.

[24]The final chapter of this study sill elaborate this theme more fully.

[25]The discussion of this issue is extensive. For a concise summary, see Bustenay Oded, "Judah and the Exile," in *Israelite and Judean History*, ed. John H. Hayes and J. Maxwell Miller (Philadelphia: Westminster, 1977) 435-488.

[26]The report of the sparing of some lives only after the full report of the destruction stands in marked contrast the literary construction in Joshua 6. In

future a bit further by indicating that this condition will not last forever. An end is in sight. The placement of the Decree of Cyrus at the very end of Chronicles declares that this hope has been brought to fruition.

In summary, the books of Chronicles, and thus the Hebrew Bible, prove to have been brought to a very careful conclusion in the story discussed above. Violence performs its now familiar role. It alters the identity of the victims. They move from being a chosen people which is the object of God's compassion to a nameless, disowned collection of individuals. Those among the group who are described, but not named, are revealed as the marginal and the helpless. Violence also changes the identity of the perpetrator. Yahweh begins the story as the compassionate, patient God of a disobedient people. As the story progresses, Yahweh becomes a wrathful avenger whose actions are confused with and indistinguishable from those of an earthly tyrant. The words of hope at the very end are gradual and muted and do not allow the reader to forget the horror which has preceeded them.

---

the description of the destruction of Jericho, the opposing fates of Rahab's family and all of the other inhabitants of the city are reported in alternating fashion (see the discussion in chapter five of this study) in order to emphasize the contrast. There is no similar attempt in v.20 to portray those who had "escaped from the sword" as the fortunate or blessed ones in comparison to those were killed in v. 17.

8

FROM BEGINNING TO END

Therefore also the Wisdom of God said, "I will send them prophets and apostles, some of whom they will kill and persecute," so that this generation may be charged with the blood of all the prophets shed since the foundation of the world, from the blood of Abel to the blood of Zechariah, who perished between the altar and the sanctuary. (Jesus of Nazareth in *The Gospel According to Luke* 11:49-51, NRSV).[1]

As a work of theology that attempts to embrace the entire Hebrew canon, from beginning to end, this study has more than one problem. First, the texts I have chosen are representative of only about half of the Hebrew Bible. The remaining half, that made up by the books of the prophets and the other poetic books, talk about violence in a very different way and await a separate analysis.[2] Second, even amongst the narrative histories contained in the Hebrew Bible, the texts I have chosen for close analysis might not all be considered the highlights. How, for example, could there be no texts about David included in such a study?

On this second point, I would not begin to argue that this is the only textual scheme about which a study of violence in biblical narrative might be organized. Most often, the story of the Hebrew Bible has been described as a movement from one great leader to the next.[3] The narrative history in the Hebrew Bible does seem to be a story about great men,[4] and they all commit acts of violence. And while Moses and

---

[1] A parallel statement also appears in Matthew 23:34-35.

[2] Part two of this book is an examination of three prophetic texts and how violence is understood and presented within them.

[3] For a succinct example of this kind of scheme, see Clines, *What Does Eve Do to Help?*, 93.

[4] I have chosen a gender exclusive term here deliberately, because it best reflects the patriarchal bias of the Bible.

Joshua figure prominently in the preceding pages, Joseph, Samuel, Saul, David, and Solomon make only minor appearances. In addition, Abraham, Isaac, Jacob, the collective Judges, Ezra, and Nehemiah are completely absent. On the other hand, Cain, Eli, Jereboam, and Rehoboam play major roles. This is not necessarily a story of the heroes of Israel. In fact, it is often a story of human beings at their worst. Walter Brueggemann has constructed a powerful theology of Israel's story around the changing relationship between the people and the land.[5] While Brueggemann's scheme and that used here might appear to be thematically linked in a text such as Joshua 6, one will find virtually no other points of contact between the collections of texts utilized by them. The most important connection between the two studies is the internal struggle in each over whether to read Israel's story as a tragedy.[6] I am in no way committed to avoiding a tragic reading, and the outcome of this struggle will be the central issue for this conclusion.

Before entering into the conclusion proper, a word about the epigraph at the beginning of this chapter is in order. This is one of the more enigmatic statements made by Jesus in the Gospels. Girard has gone so far as to say that Jesus here refers to the first and last murders in the Hebrew Bible.[7] Obviously, it does refer to the first, but the second reference is very difficult to locate.[8] Genesis 4:8 and 2 Chronicles 36:17, the central verses of the first and last texts treated in this study, do definitely record the first and last murders in the Hebrew Bible. Despite this questionable reading on Girard's part, he has seen correctly that the murder of Abel forms a "prototype" for all the murders in human history. Thus, it is at Genesis 4 that this study had to begin.

---

[5]See Brueggemann, *The Land: Place as Gift, Promise, and Challenge in Biblical Faith* (Philadelphia: Fortress, 1977).

[6]This question is, of course, influenced heavily by two other factors. First, the different arrangements of the books of the Septuagint (and subsequently the Christian Canon) and the Hebrew canon may lead to very different readings. Second, on a related note, if one reads the Hebrew Bible as the first part of the Christian canon then neither Malachi nor 2 Chronicles is the end of the story. I have attempted, as much as is possible for a Christian, to read the Hebrew Bible in isolation from the New Testament. In fact, the epigraph at the beginning of this chapter is the only reference to the New Testament in this entire study.

[7]Girard, *Things Hidden Since the Foundation of the Earth*, 159.

[8]For a thorough discussion of the problem of Jesus' reference to Zechariah in Luke 11:51 and Zechariah son of Barachiah in Matthew 23:35, see any critical commentary on Luke or Matthew. The discussion of Eduard Schweitzer is particularly to the point. See *The Gospel According to Matthew*, trans. David E. Green (Atlanta: John Knox, 1975), 444.

Unfortunately, Girard's reading has kept him from recognizing the possibility that the biblical tradition in Israel offers the killing of the young people in the temple in 2 Chronicles 36:17 as the culmination of all murders. The victims in the last murder are, of course, nameless, and this is a fact which must be taken into consideration here. Once human beings exit the garden of Eden, their subsequent story is framed by murder. It is also filled with murder. How are we to understand humanity, the world, and God in light of the realization that God's own people chose to frame and fill its own story in such a way?[9]

Humanity and Violence

The preceding interpretations of biblical texts have produced a number of revelations about violence within the human community. The most important is the way in which violence affects the identity of the human beings involved. Abel, the first murder victim, has only the most tenuous identity to begin with and loses even that once he is murdered. Even Yahweh seems to have forgotten his name by Genesis 4:10. The text remembers him once more in 4:25, only to assert that he is a replaceable unit within the first family. Cain, the first murderer, remains alive and keeps his name throughout the story, but he has broken all of his other connections, to family, land, and God.

The first group in the Bible to suffer as victims of violence is changed by oppression from the people of Israel (Exodus 1:8) to enslaved Hebrews (1:15-22). The perpetrator of this violence is converted from a neutral king (1:8) to the dreaded Pharaoh (1:11). This people enslaved by violence can only be freed by violence. The victims of the violence in Exodus 12:29 are every bit as innocent as those in 1:22, and both are as innocent as Abel. In the book of Exodus, kings, gods, and prophets wage battle and little boys die. Yahweh is either directly or indirectly implicated in the violence of Exodus 12, and the role played by Yahweh awaits further examination below, but by the end of the story the once enslaved people become willing, plundering accomplices (12:36).

---

[9]While I promised in an earlier footnote to refrain from further references to the New Testament, I cannot help but observe here that while the murder of Jesus, and the early church's struggle to understand it, fills the New Testament, the "Slaughter of the Innocents" in Matthew 2:16-18 and the killing of the "The Great Whore of Babylon" in Revelation 19 frame it. This final murder avenges all which have come before it (19:24).

Exodus 12 does contain a primary example of a people whose identity is elevated by violence. The text even makes the bold move of having the former oppressor pronounce the liberating rise in status. Thus, it is Pharaoh who pronounces the Hebrews to be "children of Israel" in 12:31. But along with the joy of liberation, one must acknowledge that this pronouncement is made not only by a wicked tyrant, but also by a grieving father whose son has just died. The chaos of mass, reciprocal violence confuses the categories of victim and perpetrator.

These categories become further confused in Joshua 6. The inhabitants of Jericho, and Canaan in general, are never accused of anything other than two dubious transgressions. They happen to live in the land Yahweh promised to Abraham and they do not exclusively worship a god, Yahweh, who has never been revealed to them. As punishment for these transgressions, they become victims of destructive violence. At the same time, the plunderers of Exodus 12:36 become conquerors in Joshua 6. As conquerors, the Israelites are also transformed into landed people. Once again, however, the improving identity of one people requires the decline, or even destruction, of another. But this time it is not oppressors becoming mourners so that slaves can become free people. Instead, it is people minding their own business becoming dead so that nomads can become farmers. The precise identity of the Israelites involved in the occupation of Jericho is also confused. At different points in the story the personnel seem to be military, religious, civilian, or a combination of these. Rampant violence breaks down the internal distinctions within a group as well.

The status and identity of the Israelites rises and falls in cycles, but generally rises until 1 Samuel 4. Here the Philistines threaten to undo everything that the Israelites have accomplished in their history as a free people. This threat is highlighted by a potential change of identity. After the Philistines have defeated the Israelites in the first battle at Aphek and are back in their camp talking amongst themselves, they refer to the Israelites as Hebrews. The status of slavery threatens once again to overwhelm the people of God. As in Joshua 6 internal identity is again confused. The identity of those gathered to fight against the Philistines changes with almost every mention in 1 Samuel 4. Violence threatens to break down both internal and external identity.

When the kingdom of Israel divides in 1 Kings 12, categories of victim and oppressor are confused still further. At the beginning of this text, it seems that Rehoboam has become another Pharaoh who has enslaved the Northern tribes. Their deliverer, Jereboam, may even be deliberately portrayed as a new Moses. This tidy casting of the story falls apart, however, when later in the text the action of the Northern

tribes is described as rebellion. Still later, the erecting of the golden
bulls by Jereboam places him in closer connection to the idolatrous
Aaron of Exodus 32-34 than to the righteous Moses. The biblical narrator
refuses to take a firm position in identifying perpetrator and victim. In
this story, the slave status of the northern tribes is improved by two
factors. First, by deciding not to go north and fight, Rehoboam and the
Southern leadership tacitly agree that Adoram's murder will end the
conflict. Second, freedom from slavery is bought with the acceptance of
a political division which lowers the status of all of Israel among the
nations of the ancient Near East.

In the final episode of violence in the Hebrew Bible, the identities of
both victim and perpetrator are clouded by ambiguity. The perpetrator
on 2 Chronicles 36:17 can be understood as either Yahweh or the King
of the Chaldeans, or both. The victims at first are only young people,
but eventually the slaughter becomes more complete, encompassing
both young and old, male and female. Throughout the description of
the violence, the victims are nameless. The people on whom Yahweh
had compassion in 36:15 are described in 36:17 using only adjectives.
These inhabitants of Judah are killed and dispossessed in a scene shock-
ingly reminiscent of Joshua 6:21. The victims who became conquerors
have become victims again.

Of all the texts examined in this study, it is only the first, Genesis
4:1-16, in which the victim, Abel, is portrayed as entirely innocent. It is
also only the first killer, Cain, who is presented as totally opposed to the
purpose of God. The portrayal of those persons involved in violence in
the Hebrew canon reveals a profound confusion about the meaning of
violence in this sacred story. Could this be the central question with
which the canon is struggling, from beginning to end?

These texts also reveal much about the nature of human violence.
From the very beginning, violent action is presented as an overwhelming force. In the first story of violence, Cain is pictured as having
a choice in Genesis 4:6-7. With frightening suddenness, however,
murder erupts from the situation and Abel is dead. Violence is portrayed as an explosive force which overcomes the coaxing of Yahweh.
While Yahweh, in his questioning, ponders carefully the choices which
lie before Cain, the murderous impulse seems to rise up and overtake
Cain with the same sudden ferocity with which Cain rises up and kills
Abel.

The violent intention of Pharaoh moves through a shocking
progression in Exodus 1:8-22. He begins with the enslavement of the
Hebrews, moves on to a secret plot to kill their male infants, and fini-
shes with a highly public declaration calling for his entire nation to

participate in the mass murder of Hebrew baby boys. Violence grows out of control in this story. When the avenger comes in Exodus 12, obviously in retaliation for Pharaoh's action in Exodus 1, it comes so quickly that Moses must hurry through the Passover instructions given him by Yahweh so that the Israelites can prepare their houses. The movement of the passage is stunning and frantic. Twenty verses are required for Yahweh to instruct Moses, seven verses for Moses to instruct the people, and one verse for the people to carry out the action. The reader must wonder why Yahweh cannot send a selective avenger, one who knows Israelites from Egyptians, one who can tell the house of a slave-owner from that of a slave. But this is not the nature of violence. Murder is rampant and overwhelming. In this case, it can only be controlled by ritual performance. In fact, the performance must appease the avenger, providing it the blood it would seek from the first born son of the house. Violence is not contained at all. The victim is merely substituted.

The end of the Passover account in 12:36 is a harbinger of what is to come in Israel's story. The liberated ones cannot avoid becoming plunderers. The impulse to violence is irresistible for humans. This plundering, however, pales in comparison to the future conquering of Canaan. In Joshua 6, the Israelites succumb to the compulsion of absolute destruction in commencing their conquest of the Promised Land. Again, the overpowering force of the violent impulse takes over as the story moves from orderly, ritual behavior to uncontrolled murder and mayhem. The tendency of interpreters to accentuate the former and diminish the latter may only serve to reveal the horror of the episode.

The reader may protest that the Israelites were only doing what Yahweh commanded them to do. A fuller discussion of God's role in the destruction of Jericho awaits the next section, but it must be stated here that God's presence in the story is ambiguous. In 6:1-5, Yahweh talks to Joshua. In 6:12-13, Yahweh is present in the form of the ark. But 6:15-19, contains only Joshua's speech about Yahweh, and in 6:20-25, Yahweh disappears from the story, except for one mention of "the house of Yahweh" in 6:24. It may be overly simplistic to point out that the Joshua's *herem* (חרם) command in 6:17-19 is absent from Yahweh's earlier directives, but this absence is a literary feature of the story which cannot be ignored. The analysis of Niditch, in which she argues that the *herem* (חרם) in this case is a form of sacrifice in order to assure God's assistance in battle, is certainly not contradicted by the text of Joshua 6, but neither is it fully confirmed.[10] It remains more a question for the

---

[10]Niditch, *War in the Hebrew Bible*, 34-35.

field of history of religions, for which this one text gives no conclusive answer. Violence takes full control of the situation, but the degree of responsibility held by the human beings involved is uncertain.

In spite of the devastating victory at Jericho, violence continues to be an inevitable part of Israel's story. This reality of human existence reaches a new level in Israel's consciousness in 1 Samuel 4, with the crushing victory of the Philistines over the Israelites at Aphek. The status of Israel as a people is judged by its success, or failure, in war. The defeat signals the need for a change and begins Israel's move toward the nation-state model. In order to compete in the violent world of the ancient Near East, Israel needs a king and a standing army. The monarchy is characterized by violence on two levels. First, Israel and its king are judged by success or failure in war against human enemies. Second, internecine strife, intrigue, and assassination become the means by which the monarchy is gained and maintained. The most troubling example of internal violence in Israel is the enslavement of the Northern tribes by Solomon, which precipitates the crisis in 1 Kings 12.[11] Despite the sound advice of elder statesmen, the urge toward violent control overwhelms Rehoboam. Even Yahweh, in 12:15, seems to have accepted the inevitability of human conflict.

The invasion of the Babylonians is the final wave of violence which washes over Israel. Again, the destructive event comes with an overwhelming sense of suddenness and completeness. The biblical story of humanity in the real world ends in 2 Chronicles 36 much as it begins in Genesis 4, with the shock of sudden murder. The difference is that in 2 Chronicles 36:20 the victims are driven eastward, out of the presence of Yahweh, instead of the perpetrator as in Genesis 4:16. The eastward movement of human beings, as a result of human conflict, away from God's presence is a common theme in the biblical story. Cain moves eastward away from the presence of God (Genesis 4:16), just as Adam and Eve move eastward out of the garden (3:24), just as Lot moves eastward away from Abram, God's chosen one (13:11), just as Hagar and Ishmael move eastward away from God's promise (21:14,21),

---

[11]Niditch has called appropriate attention to the differentiation of Solomon and David in Chronicles. The former is characterized as a man of war and the latter as a man of peace in 1 Chronicles 22:7-10. Niditch uses this text in her proposal that a new ideology, one uncomfortable with war, emerges in the books of Chronicles. See *War in the Hebrew Bible*, 139-140. Whether this is true with respect to the view of Chronicles on external conflict, there is no parallel evidence of discomfort with internal violence in Israel. First Kings 12 is repeated almost verbatim in 2 Chronicles 10.

just as Esau moves eastward away from Jacob, God's chosen one (33:16),[12] just as the Judeans would eventually be exiled eastward to Babylon. With all this eastward movement away from God's presence and blessing, is it any wonder that the children of Israel in the beginning had to wander all the way around to Moab so that they could enter the Promised Land moving westward.

In summary, these biblical stories reveal three important factors about violence in the human community: (1) Violence alters human identity; (2) violence is an overwhelming, overpowering force; and (3) the presence of violence in human society is inevitable.

God and Violence

This theme has already entered the discussion above because the involvement of God and the involvement of human beings in violence are not entirely separable themes in the narratives of the Hebrew Bible. Nevertheless, it may be profitable to focus on the former for a moment. God's involvement in the first episode of human violence, Genesis, 4:1-16, is relatively clear. Yahweh opposes the potential offender, Cain, offering him a choice between violence and non-violence. Once Cain makes his choice and becomes a murderer, Yahweh still approaches him with a question. Does this imply that Cain had another option besides evasion, and that the second half of the story could have ended differently if he had chosen a different response? This is the first of two points where the story lacks clarity. The murder of Abel follows Cain's failure to respond and enter into dialogue with the God who speaks to him. Is the separation between Cain and the presence of Yahweh at the end of the story the direct result of the murder or of Cain's failure to respond honestly to Yahweh afterwards?

The second area of ambiguity is the relationship between God and the victim. Yahweh "looks upon" Abel and his offering at the beginning of the story but does not speak to Abel. Yahweh enters into dialogue with the potential perpetrator but not with the potential victim. Further, Yahweh eventually ceases to call the victim by name as the story progresses. There are two ways to interpret this feature of the story. Does Yahweh participate in the devaluation of the victim's identity, or does Yahweh simply acknowledge that loss of identity is an inevitable result of human violence? What the story does proclaim

---

[12]On the eastward movement of the rejected brothers in Genesis, see Steinmetz, *From Father to Son*, 89-91.

clearly in the end is that an unrepentant murderer can not exist in the presence of God.

One of the questions left unanswered in Genesis 4:1-16 is answered, if only provisionally, in Exodus 1:8-22. In the story of the oppression of the Israelites in Egypt, Yahweh takes the side of the victim. Yahweh does not yet speak to the victim, nor does Yahweh act decisively to prevent or avenge violence. Because of Yahweh, the midwives do not kill the baby boys, but the text does not tell the reader whether Pharaoh's command to throw them in the river is enacted. We know, from the next story, only that at least one boy is saved. The decisive action of Yahweh comes later in the Exodus story, building in intensity throughout the plague narratives until the first Passover evening in Exodus 12.

It is in Exodus 12 that violence first becomes a social and theological problem. The previous section dealt with the social aspect of the problem, the reality that one group's status rises only at the expense of another group's status. Theologically, the problem is to understand how Yahweh is involved in acts of violence. The text is at odds with itself, both to declare Yahweh the liberator of the Israelites and to separate Yahweh from bloodshed. Can it really be Yahweh who murders the innocent Egyptian children in this story? The text tends to state quite directly that it is, but 12:23 subtly offers the alternative. It is the destroyer who actually enters and kills. The direct action of Yahweh is to prevent the destroyer from entering the homes marked by the blood of the Passover lamb.

The pattern of ambiguity established in Exodus 12 is confirmed and continued by Joshua 6. There are at least two theological givens in this story. Yahweh is on the side of Israel and Yahweh leads Israel in the conquest of the promised land. But these assumptions are tempered by the same theological problem as in Exodus 12. The violence of Joshua 6 intensifies as the episode moves from Yahweh's instructions to Joshua's instructions to the actual destruction of Jericho. At the same time, the intensity of the presence of the divinity diminishes from direct speech to the symbolic presence of the ark to indirect references in the speech of human beings. In Exodus 12:23, Yahweh seems to linger outside the Egyptian homes while the destroyer enters to kill. Likewise, in Joshua 6:20-21, Yahweh seems to linger outside the walls of Jericho while the Israelite army enters the city to destroy it.

1 Samuel 4 puts the problem of God's involvement in violence into a new perspective. Instead of God's presence bringing victory for Israel,

God's absence apparently brings defeat. If Joshua 6 comes close to being the ideal model for Holy War, 1 Samuel 4 is just the opposite.[13] There is no command or promise from God. The ark is brought to the battle only as a presumptive, human afterthought following the initial defeat. If Exodus 12 and Joshua 6 ask hard questions about God's presence and violence, then 1 Samuel 4 asks hard questions about violence and God's absence. How the reader is to understand the final verse, 4:22, is debatable. Are these words, spoken by the wife of Phinehas, to be accepted as a correct or an incorrect theological evaluation of the situation? If the arrival of the ark in 4:4 does not guarantee Yahweh's presence, then can the departure of the ark guarantee Yahweh's absence? The boundaries of the story are crucial. If the traditional 4:1 is read as part of this story, then the word of Samuel represents God's presence now, not the ark. Indeed, this seems to fit the general pattern of the entire biblical story in which the representational presence of prophecy gradually replaces direct presence and symbolic presence.[14] If Yahweh is still present through the word of Samuel, then one message of this text is that the experience of God's presence and the outcome of war are not always directly related.

In 1 Kings 12, the divisions within Israel itself are exposed. Here, the people of God become victims and perpetrators of violence simultaneously. This presents a confusing and difficult situation for the Bible's perspective on violence. With whom will Yahweh take sides now? In a delicate response to this dilemma, the text of 1 Kings 12 offers an ambiguous answer. At various points, the text seems to take first the side of the enslaved Northern tribes (12:13) and then the side of the Southern, Davidic dynasty (12:19). Yahweh appears only once in the text, in the enigmatic statement of 12:15. This evaluative declaration by the narrator implies that Yahweh caused the harsh reply of Rehoboam in order to split the kingdom because Yahweh had announced such a division through the prophet Abijah in 1 Kings 11:29-40. The logical question as to why Yahweh would instigate a prophetic word at one point which would confine Yahweh to a troubling act at a later point is simply not a concern of the text. The text struggles to maintain the ambiguity created by the conflict between a primary theological assumption, that God is in control of history, and a horrifying reality, that God's people enslave and murder one another. The problem is not settled.

---

[13]Von Rad, *Holy War in Ancient Israel*, 41-51.
[14]See Terrien, *The Elusive Presence*, 227-268.

The Babylonian invasion of Jerusalem in 2 Chronicles 36:15-21 brings the theological crisis to its climax. Through the biblical story Israel moves from being victim to being perpetrator to being both at the same time. God's role in this story and the violent events it contains becomes increasingly ambiguous. In the crisis of 2 Chronicles 36:15-21, the delicate ambiguity explodes into profound literary confusion. The text struggles to ask the questions which it must, but can not ask. Is the Babylonian king the agent of Yahweh? Does Yahweh destroy Yahweh's own people? This may be divine punishment, but why do the innocent and marginal of society receive an undue portion of violent suffering? Of course, the text does not answer these questions, but the response at the end of 2 Chronicles points to one more subject where conclusions must be proposed.

The Bible and Violence

This study began with the observation that violence dominates the biblical story, and with the assertion that biblical theology must not deny or avoid the prevalence of this theme. To this point, I have summarized what the texts examined here reveal about the relationships between human beings and violence and between God and violence. I will finish with a more speculative attempt to understand why the Hebrew Bible takes the form that it does. Why does the Hebrew Bible tell a story so permeated with violence, and why does it tell the story in this particular way? Could it be that this is the very issue the Hebrew canon is designed to confront? The community which produced the final form of the Hebrew Bible must have been confronted by the profound sense of conflict between their "chosen people" status and the harsh reality of their marginal existence.[15] In her study of war in the Hebrew Bible, Susan Niditch concluded that "The war traditions of the Hebrew Scriptures genuinely grapple with issues of compassion and enmity. The many war texts...reveal human beings' attempt to make sense of war and killing in war."[16] By adapting this statement to speak of violence in general, not just of war, my own conclusion is that violence is the issue with which the whole of the Hebrew canon, not just certain traditions within it, grapples. The written story of Israel begins and ends with violence. This violence enters the human community the

---

[15]The contemporary term for this kind of experience is "cognitive dissonance." It might not be entirely anachronistic to apply this term to an ancient people like the Israelites.

[16]Niditch, *War in the Hebrew Bible*, 151.

moment human beings leave Eden and enter the real world. The final chapter of the Hebrew canon brings Israel's story to a close with a question and a challenge. The totality of the destruction wrought by the Babylonian invasion asks the question, "Can the people of God continue to exist in such a violent world?" The mention of the exilic community and the Decree of Cyrus challenge the community of faith, whether it be in 538 B.C.E., 70 C.E., or any other time, to answer that question, in spite of all the evidence to the contrary, with a determined "yes." Yet even this hopeful challenge still lies in the shadow of the violence which so troubles the biblical story from beginning to end.

The Hebrew Bible does contain a response to the violent story of the people of Israel. It is contained in the prophetic books in the middle of the canon. Part II of this study is an exploration of the nature and adequacy of this response by examining representative texts from the prophetic literature.

PART II

PROPHETIC RESPONSES TO

THE BIBLICAL STORY

9

THE COMPASSION OF GOD

HOSEA 11:1-11

In the preceding exegesis of 2 Chronicles 36:15-21, one of the most startling features of the text is the change in God's attitude toward God's people from "compassion" in v. 15 to "no compassion" in v. 19. This passage in which God's violence turns on God's own people raises painful questions about how God feels about these people. Perhaps no text in the Hebrew Bible attempts to answer such questions as powerfully as the prophetic oracle in Hosea 11:1-11. The word "compassion" (רחם) may or may not appear in this oracle. The textual problem which gives rise to this uncertainty will be discussed below. Nevertheless, the feelings of God for the people of Israel erupt here, making this passage an important response to Israel's story.

The Text

Hosea 11:1-11 is rife with textual problems. Indeed, these problems are so severe and complex that the interpreter may initially be tempted to search for another text that addresses similar issues. Is it possible that the turmoil of the text somehow reflects the turmoil in Yahweh's heart which is the theme of the passage? At least one pair of commentators has hinted at this possibility.[1]

Aside from the constant textual difficulties, the other factor which will dominate the exegetical discussion of Hosea 11 is that it is poetry and, thus, differs significantly from the texts examined in Part I in terms of literary form.[2] Hebrew poetry is not, however, entirely unlike

---

[1]See Francis I. Andersen and David Noel Freedman, *Hosea: A New Translation with Introduction and Commentary*, AB (Garden City: Doubleday, 1980) 57.

[2]A significant body of rhetorical criticism of poetry has been developed. Recall that the most extensive example of Muilenburg's application of his

Hebrew narrative. The lines of distinction between the two have been significantly blurred by the work of James L. Kugel, among others. While an emphasis on parallelism has tended to dominate the study of Hebrew poetry, Kugel has demonstrated that narrative texts sometimes contain this feature, and that biblical poetry sometimes lacks it.[3] Indeed, if biblical texts were graded according to the intensity of parallelism, and other features typically associated with poetry, that is found within them, they would probably fall more along a continuum than into two distinct groups. Kugel is reluctant then to label texts as poetry or prose according to the degree of presence of such features.[4]

An entirely different method of distinguishing prose and poetry is to examine the frequency of certain Hebrew particles (the definite article, the direct object marker, and the relative pronoun) in a text. Andersen and Freedman have applied this method to the entire book of Hosea. Though a few passages in Hosea, such as 2:15-26, show a high frequency of these particles associated with Hebrew prose, the frequency for the book as a whole is in the range generally accepted for poetry. Most notably, Hosea 11:1-11 contains not one occurrence of any of these three particles.[5]

Hosea 11:1-11 has narrative qualities. Certainly, it tells a story that has a beginning (an idyllic childhood), a middle (apostasy and disaster), and an end (compassionate deliverance). Both Israel/Ephraim and Yahweh become highly developed characters as the text progresses. Nevertheless, it would be difficult to not to read Hosea 11 as poetry. Once this is accepted, however, the variation of intensity of poetic features even within the unit must be recognized. For example, parallelism is more distinct in vv. 8-9 than in the rest of the poem, and the clear references

---

method is his commentary on Isaiah 40-66. Even a commentary on Hosea so forthrightly socio-historical in its focus as that of Andersen and Freedman makes an abundance of rhetorical observations. These works and many others which will be mentioned below may serve as models for the interpretation presented here.

[3]See James L. Kugel, *The Idea of Biblical Poetry: Parallelism and Its History* (New Haven: Yale University Press, 1981) 59-68. Kugel's work has received primarily positive evaluation in less technical introductions to Hebrew poetry such as David L. Petersen and Kent Harold Richards, *Interpreting Hebrew Poetry* (Minneapolis: Fortress, 1992) 27-28 and S. E. Gillingham, *The Poems and Psalms of the Hebrew Bible* (Oxford: Oxford University Press, 1994) 75-78.

[4]Ibid., 85-87.

[5]Andersen and Freedman, *Hosea*, 59-65. Of course, this method is open to the charge that it employs circular reasoning. Its results should be treated with some caution.

to past and present events in vv. 1-2 and vv. 5-7 are certainly more literal than the language of vv. 10-11 which is filled with animal imagery. Such observations which take account of the identification of poetry, even if this is a tentative identification, must receive attention in the interpretation of this passage.[6]

Hosea 11 stands apart from the preceding unit in several ways. All of Hosea 10 is a message of violent condemnation. The final four verses form a particularly harsh second person address from Yahweh. Both the change in theme and the switch to third person statements by Yahweh at 11:1 signal the beginning of a distinct unit.[7] Because of the difficulties of the text mentioned above, I will break with the pattern established in earlier chapters and produce here the entire translation from which I will proceed to interpret.

(1) When Israel was a child, I loved him;
    and from Egypt I called my son.
(2) They called to them, thus they went from before them;[8]
    to the Baals they sacrificed, and to the images they
       burned incense.
(3) But I made Ephraim walk, he seized them upon his arms;[9]
    but they did not know that I healed them.
(4) With human bonds I led them, with ropes of love;
    and I was to them like those lifting a small child[10]

---

[6]Another pattern for rhetorical criticism of Hebrew poetry was established by Kenneth R. Kuntz. See "Psalm 18: A Rhetorical-Critical Analysis," *JSOT* 26 (1983): 3-31. Kuntz identifies five primary, rhetorical concerns in his study of Psalm 18 (p. 4). These are strophic structure, style and vocabulary, sense of unity or integration, use of names, and use of spatial imagery. Some of these may be of peculiar interest to Psalm 18 alone, but particularly the first, second, and fourth seem important to an examination of Hosea 11.

[7]The discontinuity between 11:1-11 and the preceding oracle may not be as great as some contend. One may wonder how Wolff can say with such certainty that "Not a single catchword connects it with 10:9-15." See Hans Walter Wolff, *Hosea*, trans. Gary Stansell (Philadelphia: Fortress, 1974) 193. I count at least ten different words, not including particles, which appear in both sections.

[8]Most commentators and English versions follow LXX, reading a first person singular subject in the first clause and first person singular object in the second. For example, NRSV reads, "The more I called them, the more they went from me."

[9]In parallel fashion to v. 2a, LXX reads, "I took them in my arms."

> unto their cheeks;
> and I bent down unto him and I fed him.[11]
> (5)He will not return unto the land of Egypt, but Assyria
>   will be his king;
>   for they refuse to return (repent).
> (6)The sword whirls[12] in his cities and finishes his idle-talkers;[13]
>   and devours because of their schemings.
> (7)But my people are hung on my return (repentance);[14]
>   to the Most High[15] they call, but he certainly does
>   not raise them up.
> (8)How can I give you up Ephraim, hand you over Israel;
>   How can I give you up like Admah, make you like Zeboim?
>   My heart turns against me, surely my sorrow[16] burns.
> (9)I will not execute the burning of my anger, I will not
>   return to destroy Ephraim;

---

[10]For the arguments in favor of this reading, using עוּל, see Wolff, *Hosea*, 191. For the arguments favoring the reading "yoke" (עֹל), see Andersen and Freedman, 581.

[11]LXX seems to read לֹא (not) of v. 5 in MT as לוֹ (to him) and to move it to the end of v. 4, which ends with αυτο. MT does place לֹא on the same line as the final colon of v. 4. This reading would require a consonantal change in MT, but one that could easily have been caused by faulty hearing of the text. The translation here reads the negative particle with v. 5 and produces the third person singular object from the preceding parallel. The difficulty of the text at this point make statements of certainty about the reading impossible. Both readings will be considered in the interpretation below.

[12]This rendering is based on the root הוּל. See Wolff, *Hosea*, 192.

[13]Ibid.

[14]This clause is generally considered corrupt. BHS makes three separate proposed emendations. The reading, "My people are bent on turning from me," based on the tradition of the Authorized Version, carries significant weight. It requires an unusual understanding of the first person singular suffix on מְשׁוּב. Anderson and Freedman argued that the suffix has a "dative or ablative force." See *Hosea*, 586. The rendering here follows MT, and an attempt will be made below to make sense of it.

[15]Wolff and others emend עַל to read Baal. See *Hosea*, 192. The translation here follows NRSV and Andersen and Freedman in reading a short form of *Elyon*. See *Hosea*, 587.

[16]This is the point where the compassion (רחם) of God may enter into the story. BHS suggests such an emendation, following a number of commentators. The Syriac and the Targum offer some support for this. The reading of נחם in MT makes good sense, however, so the emendation seems unnecessary. Nevertheless, the ideas of "burning sorrow" and "burning compassion" are not far apart.

for I am a God and not a man;
a holy one in your midst, and I will not come with agitation.[17]
(10)After Yahweh they will go, like a lion he will roar;
for he will roar, and sons will come trembling from the sea.
(11)They will come trembling like a bird from Egypt, and like a
dove from the land of Assyria;
and I will return them to their houses, saying of Yahweh.

The end of the oracle is clearly marked in typical prophetic fashion. These boundaries are supported by the major commentaries of Mays, Wolff, and Andersen and Freedman, among others.[18]

The internal structure of Hosea 11:1-11 is somewhat difficult to establish. A detailed application of the language shifts and movement of the text mentioned above offer a possibility for strophic division. Verses 1-4 contain the memory of Yahweh about Israel's younger days. The language of this section is dominated by first person verbs with Yahweh as subject. There are between six and eight of these, depending on textual and translation decisions. Verses 5-7 describe Israel's present condition, using all third person verbs. Verses 8-9 report Yahweh's inner turmoil and consideration of what to do, and are dominated by first person singular verbs. Verses 10-11 conclude with a vision of the future and third person verbs reappear.[19] National names serve to interlock all of the sections.[20] The list below illustrates the appearances of these names section by section:

---

[17]The meaning of בעיר is difficult to establish with certainty. See the discussion of options by James Barr in *Comparative Philology and the Text of the Old Testament* (Winona Lake, Indiana: Eisenbrauns, 1987) 125-126.

[18]For a significantly different alternative, see Loren F. Bliese, "Symmetry and Prominence in Hebrew Poetry: With Examples from Hosea," in *Discourse Perspectives on Hebrew Poetry in the Scriptures*, ed. Ernst R. Wendland (New York: United Bible Societies, 1994) 67. Bliese has divided Hosea into five major sections and established the division between Parts IV and V after 11:7. This structure is dependent upon a division of the book into a large number of short poems with a complex web of numerical patterns.

[19]Douglas Stuart has grouped vv. 8-9 along with vv. 10-11 under the heading "The Eschatological Future." See *Hosea-Jonah*, WBC (Waco: Word, 1987) 174-176. This may resolve the tension between vv. 6-7 and vv. 8-9, but such a resolution may miss the point of the text. This problem will be discussed further a below.

[20]See the discussion of strophic structure in Kuntz, "Psalm 18: A Rhetorical-Critical Analysis," 9-19.

v. 1 Israel
v. 1 Egypt
v. 3 Ephraim

v. 5 Egypt, Assyria

v. 8 Ephraim, Israel
v. 9 Ephraim

v. 11 Egypt, Assyria

A number of other words appear repeatedly, offering a sense of cohesion to the passage. These will be discussed in the more detailed interpretation below.[21] The emotional reflection of the present in vv. 8-9 is connected to the warm remembrance of the past in vv. 1-4 by the appearance of "Israel" and "Ephraim." The oppression of the present (vv. 5-7) is linked to the past (vv. 1-4) by the mention of "Egypt" and connected to future deliverance (vv. 10-11) by the repetition of "Egypt" and "Assyria."[22]

Along with the grammar of first person verbs, the first section of the poem is also dominated by the imagery of childhood. The childhood of Israel is not one of perfect innocence. Verse 1 recalls the period in the wilderness. This theme appears with some frequency in Hosea. Most remarkable is the frequency with which the themes of wilderness, disobedience (worship of Baal), familial relations, and feeding appear together, as in 11:1-4 (See 2:3-8[Hebrew 2:5-10], 2:14-17[Hebrew 2:16-19], 9:10-15, and 13:4-8). Incidences of disobedience in the wilderness, such as the golden calf episode in Exodus 32-34 and the Baal Peor incident in Numbers 25 are easily recalled by these passages.[23] Hosea 11:2 takes up this theme of disobedience, specifically mentioning the baals (בעלים) as the object of Israel's false worship.

---

[21]See the list in Stuart, *Hosea-Jonah*, 177.

[22]The Egypt/Assyria "envelope construction" proposed by Andersen and Freedman is not necessarily in conflict with the interlocking process I have outlined here. See Andersen and Freedman, *Hosea*, 575-576. Their attempt to find a similar envelope for vv. 1-4 is forced. A key question is whether the use of these words serves to bound and separate sections of the passage or to tie them together.

[23]For a detailed discussion of the connections with these and other passages, see Andersen and Freedman, *Hosea*, 577-578.

In v. 1 Yahweh had called Israel from Egypt, now Yahweh makes
Ephraim walk. As in v. 8, Israel and Ephraim should be understood in
parallel fashion, to refer to the same collective character. The structure of
lines in the poem continues to be uneven. The two long cola in v. 1 are
smooth and parallel each other closely. Verse 2 is composed of two short
bicola. The first bicolon is vague because of four third person plural
pronouns without clear antecedents, but the synonymous parallelism of
the second bicolon is clear and simple, perhaps clarifying the first.[24]
Verse 3 returns the emphasis to first person action of Yahweh, but the
parallelism of the components of this tricolon is uncertain.

The middle colon creates the most problems. By altering the
pronouns, the LXX reading makes the second colon a close synthetic
parallel to the first. This reading seems unlikely however. The plural
form זרועת (arms) appears approximately twenty times in the Hebrew
Bible, but none of these make direct reference to Yahweh. Direct references to Yahweh's arm are always singular. Most of these plural
references fall into two basic categories. They are either arms
strengthened by God (Genesis 49:24, 1 Samuel 22:35, Psalm 18:35) or
the arms of powerful foreign rulers and armies (Ezekiel 30:20-25 [five
times], Daniel 11: 15,22). The second category seems most likely here in
Hosea 11:3. Particularly in light of the repeated references in Ezekiel 30,
the Hebrew text of Hosea 11:3b is best understood as a reference to
Pharaoh. In opposition to Yahweh's tender caring for Israel, Pharaoh
seized (לקח) them. The confusion of Israel in the third colon reflects the
confusion of the murmuring tradition in the wilderness. V. 4 concludes
the section by reemphasizing the caring action of Yahweh in a string of
first person statements.[25] Again, there are strong synonymous elements
among the lines, but the parallel structure is not clear. The tension
between loving parenthood and divine judgment may begin to surface
here in a possible wordplay. אהבה is best translated here as "love,"
especially in light of the appearance of the same root in v. 1. That אהבה
may also mean "leather" raises the possibility that love may also
include a period of captivity.[26]

---

[24]For a detailed discussion of the wide variations in parallelism in Hosea, see
Martin J. Buss, *The Prophetic Word of Hosea: A Morphological Study* (Berlin:
Alfred Töpelmann, 1969) 43-45.

[25]Stuart has demonstrated that even if different text-critical choices are made
in v. 4, shifting the imagery to an "animal metaphor," the sense of loving care
need not be lost. See *Hosea-Jonah*, 179.

[26]On the possibility of paronomasia here, see Barr, *Comparative Philology and
the Text of the Old Testament*, 154.

Verse 5 begins a new section, but the mention of Egypt connects it back to v. 1. The story is brought suddenly to the present situation. Egypt is no longer literally relevant to the situation, but enslavement to Assyria is really no different. The oppression of the present is linked to the past. The reading of MT, reflected in the translation above, emphasizes this link through the adversative relationship between the first two parts of the tricolon in v. 5. The third and final clause is unclear. NRSV follows Andersen and Freedman by adding "to me." This may be an essentially correct interpretation of the verse, but adding words to the text seems unwarranted. A better solution to two of the major problems in vv. 5-7 would be to understand שׁוּב (return) in both v. 5c and v.7a in the sense of "repent."[27] This both takes the Hebrew text seriously and produces a coherent understanding of the passage. This meaning of the root places emphasis on the relationship between Yahweh and Israel.[28] Israel refuses to repent (v.5), but waits for Yahweh to repent (v.7). The inappropriate attempts to bring about Yahweh's repentance are described in v. 7b as calling to a different divine name, עֹל. Verse 7c reemphasizes the futility of this request. Surrounded by these wrong understandings of repentance is a violent description of their results. The three verbs in the tricolon of v. 6 grow in their intensity.

Likewise, the intensity of the entire poem grows as this strophe ushers it toward its climax. Within the desperation of these verses, a note of hope is maintained by Yahweh's claim on Israel as "my people (עַמִּי)" in v. 7.[29] This designation is crucial, perhaps even surprising in light of Yahweh's disowning of Israel at the beginning of the book of Hosea in 1:8. Verses 5-7 are very carefully structured in three successive tricola.[30] The carefully woven message, as interpreted above, is consistent with such intricate structure.

Verses 8-9 form the heart of the poem as the reader enters the anguished heart of Yahweh who considers the fate of Israel. Verse 8 is

---

[27]This verb appears three times in vv. 5-7. The interpretation here requires reading it with two different meanings. The first use in v. 5a is different from the subsequent two because it has an indirect object with an appropriate preposition. Buss argued for two different meanings of a slightly different sort, "return" in v. 5a and "turn" in v. 5c and v. 7a. See *The Prophetic Word of Hosea*, 40.

[28]The most extensive study of this root is that of William L. Holladay, who argues for such a covenant-oriented meaning of שׁוּב in cases where it means "repent" (*The Root Sûbh in the Old Testament* [Leiden: Brill, 1958]).

[29]James L. Mays, *Hosea*, 156.

[30]Buss, *The Prophetic Word of Hosea*, 42.

composed of three bicola. The first two begin the strophe in a breathless quality. Four of the first five words and seven of the first ten begin with the Hebrew letter א making their initial sounds vowel sounds.[31] Verses 8-9a are composed of a rapid series of short, parallel thoughts. The first two pairs are cast as questions. They are followed by an expression of intense emotional pain. The pain expressed over "Ephraim" and "Israel" here recall the tender memories of childhood expressed in vv. 1-4.

Verse 9a resolves the internal crisis, and the building tension of the text is relieved. The mixture of emotions is genuine. Yahweh does not decide not to have these emotions, but not to "execute (עשׂה)" them. Acting on these emotions would be a human thing to do, according to v. 9b-c. The reappearance in v. 9a of the verb שׁוב, so prominent in vv. 5-7, is tantalizing. The grammatical construction is different from any of the cases in the previous section, where this word was translated as "return" when it had an indirect, locative object and as "repent" when it had no indirect object. Here it is a finite verb followed by an infinitive. When combined with another verb form in this way, שׁוב can carry a sense of repeated action. In this case the meaning may be "I will not again destroy Ephraim."[32] Just as the hopeful designation "my people" occurred amidst words of violence and destruction in vv. 5-7, thus the reminder of past violence may appear among words of hope and compassion in vv. 8-9. As mentioned earlier, it is possible that the Hebrew word "רחם (compassion)" appears here, but it seems unlikely. The existence of a textual uncertainty may itself be the expression of a desire to find such feeling in Yahweh's words.

Verses 10-11 have a very different character from the preceding sections. A vision of the future, or oracle of deliverance, is stated here in intensely poetic language. The lines are carefully linked by repeated words שׁאג (roar) and חרד (tremble). Images of the first Exodus are evoked by the mention of Egypt and sea (ים). Yahweh is portrayed in power as a lion and the people in weakness as birds or doves. At least three features of the language in this section serve to link this vision to the earlier portions of the poem: The mention of Assyria and Egypt, the

---

[31]Buss, *The Prophetic Word of Hosea*, 38-39.

[32]Mays, *Hosea*, 51. Wolff also translates v. 9a in this way, but argues at length against the above interpretation. His argument is dependent upon a completely non-theistic understanding of the political situation described in vv. 5-7. It seems highly unlikely that the worldview of a Hebrew prophet like Hosea would have allowed him to see the destruction in v. 6 as simply "the consequences of Israel's own intentional actions." See *Hosea*, 202.

designation of the people as "sons" (as in v.1), and the possible recurrence of שׁוּב in v. 11.[33] Reading "return" here further supports the idea of a hope for restoration after a period of judgment. The vision, and the poem as a whole, are punctuated by the brief but unequivocal oracular conclusion, "saying of Yahweh."

Theological Conclusions

Hosea 11 embraces all of Israel's collective experience, from deliverance to destruction to hope of restoration. In light of historical understanding, the modern reader is tempted to reject the note of hope in this passage, knowing that ultimately Israel was completely destroyed. But the inclusion of this and other passages of hope in the Hebrew canon must be taken seriously. H. D. Beeby, and others, have correctly seen that this chapter stands in the breech between Israel's past in chapters 8-10 and its future in chapters 12-14. Beeby has incorrectly concluded that the division of the text is "arbitrary and not of crucial importance."[34] Hosea 11 strains to hold together the deliverance of the past and the reality of Israel's destruction. That some interpreters would divide the book of Hosea between 11:7 and 11:8 is testimony to the strength of the tension exerted on this text by the reality of destruction and abandonment. Wolff argues that the accusations preceding and following chapter eleven raise the question of whether Israel's disobedience or Yahweh's love will determine Israel's fate. The answer, in Wolff's words, is that "God demonstrates that he is the Holy One in that his remorse overcomes his wrath, and thus creates a new life of security for Israel."[35] The tension, however, is not so easily resolved. One is forced to ask when this new life will come.

The text of 11:1-11 shows awareness of the tension. The four subsections are easily distinguishable, but closely linked together. The interlocking patterns of language both within and among the sections attempt to hold together a multitude of opposing themes.[36] The most important of these oppositions is that between punishment and grace. Law and covenant require punishment for the one who is disobedient

---

[33]Reading the root שׁוּב rather יָשַׁב (dwell) requires a slight emendation of MT, but the Hebrew preposition עַל, which follows, and the rendering in LXX both support such an emendation. See Wolff, *Hosea*, 193.

[34]H. D. Beeby, *Grace Abounding: A Commentary on the Book of Hosea*, ITC (Grand Rapids: Eerdmans, 1989) 140-141.

[35]Wolff, *Hosea*, 203.

[36]Beeby, *Grace Abounding*, 140.

and refuses to repent (v. 5). But the disobedient one is also a child and the heart of the parent turns against itself (v. 8).[37] Fretheim has focused attention on the parental suffering God endures because of Israel's disobedience. For Fretheim, the resolution of the tension comes in God's choice to continue suffering rather than to execute judgment.[38] Yet, too much emphasis on this choice threatens to miss half of the point.[39] God would also suffer by choosing to punish. The covenant is no simple contractual agreement. Love is involved (v.1). Stuart's association of vv. 8-9 with vv. 10-11 in the "eschatological future" dissolves the tension by separating compassion and punishment chronologically. Divine love can then be emphasized over judgment by making the future more important than the present or the past.[40]

Some interpreters risk moving too far in the other direction. Andersen and Freedman concluded that God's decision in v. 8-9 is for punishment and judgment. Being God—not human—requires righteous consistency, not favoritism.[41] They resolve the internal conflict in the other direction. The elasticity of this text, created by linguistic linkages and textual uncertainties belies such easy resolutions. The tension of the passage must be maintained.

It is when the emphasis falls on judgment that the problem of victimization most clearly arises. Hosea 11 tends to go the way of all prophetic literature by laying the blame for violence on the victim. Questions and problems abound. Surely, those nations which inflict the punishment are not innocent in the eyes of God. Surely, the generations which actually suffer destruction are no more guilty than those which have gone before them. Will those generations in the future be any more deserving of deliverance? Such difficulties are not fully settled by an expression of Yahweh's compassionate feelings, whether their effect is past or future.

---

[37]Fretheim, *The Suffering of God: An Old Testament Perspective*, 119-120.

[38]Ibid., 143-144.

[39]Fretheim's statement that "It is going too far to speak of conflict in God here, for judgement is never the will of God for the people..." seems to be an overstatement. Ibid., 144.

[40]Stuart, *Hosea-Jonah*, 183.

[41]Of course this requires some creative grammatical gymnastics. Andersen and Freedman translate לא in v. 9a as an "asseverative." Thus, these lines read, "I will certainly act out my burning anger. I will certainly come back to destroy Ephraim." See *Hosea*, 588-589. Stuart's suggestion that what separates God from humans is the divine, sovereign freedom to choose either path seems more to the point. See *Hosea-Jonah*, 183.

Despite the unresolvable conflict in the heart of the prophet, the heart of God, and the heart of the canon, the reader of this text knows that judgment will become the choice. Israel will be destroyed, the northern kingdom in the days of Hosea and the southern kingdom a little more than a century later. Yet, this vision of Yahweh's compassion remains in the heart of the canon. The only way to keep this from becoming a promise unfulfilled is to cast it into the future. Somehow, violent destruction in the present, as described in v. 6, does not contradict the love of God. Nevertheless, the presence of both obviously creates tremendous pain.[42] It is this pain, in fact which holds together the contradictions. Milazzo describes the divine-human relationship in terms of these kinds of contradictions: "Permanence in transience; brokenness in the midst of continuity; restoration in the midst of abandonment."[43] Hosea 11:1-11 stands, like the prophetic corpus as a whole, on the brink between past deliverance and future restoration. The problem with which it struggles is the violent destruction of the present. The compassion of Yahweh for the people of Israel is in question, and only a future of restoration offers any hope of resolution. It is to the possibility and meaning of such restoration that we must turn next.

---

[42]Hanson, *The People Called: The Growth of Community in the Bible*, 164.

[43]Milazzo, *The Protest and the Silence: Suffering, Death, and Biblical Theology*, 50.

10

THE RESTORATION OF
GOD'S PEOPLE

EZEKIEL 37:1-14

The book of Ezekiel contains four visions. The first vision, reported in 1:1-3:15, constitutes Ezekiel's call. The second, in 8-11, portrays Israel's cultic disobedience and Yahweh's departure from the temple. The fourth and final vision, in 40-48, describes the reconstructed temple and the return of Yahweh's glory. The third vision, described in 37:1-14 is the briefest and most well known. Bracketed by the visions of Yahweh's departure and return, this vision of restoration acts as a turning point in the Book of Ezekiel. What does the vision of the valley of dry bones say as a response to Israel's violent story?

The Text

Beginning in chapter thirty-three, the book of Ezekiel focuses upon redemption, consolation, and restoration. Ezekiel 36 contains prophecies about the restoration of Israel. These prophecies are punctuated by a stunning vision in 37:1-14. The boundaries of this text are easy to establish. The initial phrase, "the hand of Yahweh was upon me," is typically, though not exclusively, associated with visions in the book of Ezekiel. The first vision in Ezekiel is bracketed by the report of "the hand of Yahweh" being upon the prophet in 1:3 and 3:14. Likewise, the second vision begins with the same note in 8:1. The onset of the third vision is clearly established with the same phrase in 37:1. The use of this phrase in connection with visions has drawn significant attention. Bernard Duhm proposed a fairly specific psychological state.[1] J. J. M.

---

[1]Bernard Duhm, *Das Buch Jesaja* (Göttingen: Vandenhoeck and Ruprecht, 1914) 59.

Roberts has presented a more carefully balanced case that "the hand of Yahweh" refers to ecstatic experience, while the precise nature of the prophet's mental and physical state can not be precisely described.[2] In this case, the expression provides a sharp distinction between the dry bones experience and the prophetic activity of Ezekiel which immediately precedes it. The section comes to a clear ending with a double prophetic formula in 37:14[3]

What makes this text significantly unique is the combination of visionary and prophetic elements.[4] Zimmerli correctly distinguishes this vision from those in 3:12-15 and 11:23-25. These earlier visions depict reality, ether present or future. Zimmerli labels the vision in 37:1-10 a "sign." This provides at least a partial explanation of why the vision does not come to a distinct end like the earlier ones, but blends into a command for the prophet to preach.[5] The passage can be divided first into two basic sections, vv. 1-10 and vv. 11-14. There is a strong sense of tension between these two sections. Michael Fishbane has argued persuasively for the unity of vv. 1-14 based on elements of literary structure. He noted the repetition of a pair of words, רוּחַ (spirit) and נוּחַ (literally, "cause to rest" in the *hiphil* found in this text) in v. 1 and v. 14 as reflected elements at the beginning and end of the passage. Further, Fishbane argued for a relationship between vv. 3-10 and vv. 12-13, the latter being "divine explication" of the "divine instruction" in the former. These chiastic elements stand around v. 11 as the center of the text. Fishbane calls the statement, "Our bones are dried up, our hope has perished, and we have been cut off," in v. 11 a "popular adage." This adage is the central point of the text, both interpreting the dry bones vision which comes before and pointing ahead to the divine

---

[2]Roberts argued on the basis of both biblical and extra-biblical texts describing illness or plague as "the hand of Yahweh." See "The Hand of Yahweh," *VT* 21 (1971): 244-251. While the prophetic vision formula is significantly different from such occurrences, it seems unlikely that it is completely unrelated. The attribution of Ezekiel's muteness in 33:22 to "the hand of Yahweh" lends weight to the argument for such a connection, and mitigates against a precise definition of the experience.

[3]For a thorough guide to prophetic formulae from a form-critical perspective, see Ronald M. Hals, *Ezekiel*, FOTL (Grand Rapids: Eerdmans, 1989) 359-363.

[4]John W. Wevers, *Ezekiel*, NCBC (Grand Rapids: Eerdmans, 1969) 194. Despite this tension, form critics generally resist splitting vv. 1-10 and vv. 11-14 into individual units. See Hals, *Ezekiel*, 266-270.

[5]Walther Zimmerli, *Ezekiel 1: A Commentary on the Book of the Prophet Ezekiel, chs. 1-24*, trans. Ronald E. Clements (Philadelphia: Fortress, 1979) 27-28.

message to Israel which follows.[6] This understanding of the structure and meaning of the text is fairly convincing. The tension between the unburied bones of vv. 1-10 and the graves of vv. 12-14 is unresolved, however, and will be addressed further below.

The first major section of this text, vv. 1-10, displays a clear pattern of movement in two cycles from the instructions of Yahweh to the work of the prophet to the response of the vision. This can be demonstrated in the outline below.

> 1-2 Vision
> 3 Dialogue
> 4-6 Command to prophesy and prophecy to bones
> 7-8 Bones respond
> 9 Command to prophesy and prophecy to breath
> 10 Breath responds

The nature of the vision connects it with scenes of violence. That the setting is a field of battle becomes increasingly clear throughout the text. Ezekiel's initial description in vv. 1-2 tells of a field of bones which can only have resulted from a large number of dead bodies being left unburied and exposed to the elements.[7] The identification of the victims in v. 9 as "murdered ones" (הרג) completes the description.

Prophetic literature typically avoids repeating a prophecy word for word. Either the speech of God to the prophet or the prophet's words to the recipients are recorded, but not both. In this case it is the former. Nevertheless, a certain amount of repetition is created in vv. 1-10 when the prophet reports seeing the prophecies fulfilled (vv. 7-8 and v. 10) in words that reflect the quotations of the prophecies themselves.[8] It is typical for commentators to note the thematic and lexical connections

---

[6]Michael Fishbane, *Biblical Interpretation in Ancient Israel* (Oxford: Clarendon, 1985) 451-452. Fishbane discusses Ezekiel 37 under the heading of "mantological exegesis." His placement of both visions and oracles under the rubric of mantology provides a further basis for his argument in favor of the unity of 37:1-14.

[7]The allusion to Jeremiah 8:1-3 is fairly certain. See Keith W. Carley, *Ezekiel among the Prophets: A Study of Ezekiel's Place in Prophetic Tradition* (London: SCM, 1975) 55-56.

[8]The contention by Fox that the duplication of language makes the image more memorable is also possible. See "The Rhetoric of Ezekiel's Vision of the Valley of the Bones," 10. The repetition in Genesis 1 may also serve this purpose, among others.

between this passage and the creation story in Genesis 2.[9] The two stage creation of human life, forming of bodies and entering of breath along with the other similarities, certainly warrants such comparisons.[10] The pattern of creative speech by God followed by a report of the creative event in similar words, however, is also reminiscent of Genesis 1. The resulting creative power behind this text is formidable.

A number of words are repeated frequently in vv. 1-10. Among the most noticeable are "spirit" or "breath" or "winds," all three of which are translations of the Hebrew word רוּחַ, and various forms of the word for "bone" (עצם). The former appears nine times in vv. 1-10 and the latter eight times.[11] These two elements which must be joined to recreate life are the focus of the passage, but breath overshadows bone in ways more significant than the comparative number of times each is mentioned. In v. 4 Ezekiel is first commanded to "prophesy concerning" (על) the bones. In v. 9, he is first commanded to "prophesy unto" (אל) the winds or breath. Though the repeated command in these two verses to "say unto" (אל) the bones and the breath is identical, the bones are more passive participants onto which sinews and skin must be put and into which breath must be put. The only active verb of which they are the subject is "come near" (קרב) in v. 7. The winds are commanded to "come" (בוא) and "breathe" (פוה) in v. 9. רוּה is the creative force.

Two other important words are repeated in this text, but are often completely obscured by English translation. The Hebrew word הנה, most commonly translated as "behold" or "lo," appears twice in v. 2, once in v. 5, and twice in vv. 7-8. The double uses of this word thus bracket the bone portion of the vision. The repeated appearances of הנה serve to heighten the startling nature of the vision Ezekiel sees. The Hebrew adverb "מאד," often translated as "very" or "exceedingly,"

---

[9]See, for example, Walther Eichrodt, *Ezekiel: A Commentary*, trans. Coslett Quinn (London: SCM, 1970) 509 or Charles R. Biggs, *The Book of Ezekiel* (London: Epworth, 1996) 109.

[10]Within the context of historical-critical interpretation, it is somewhat ironic that interpreters would focus on connections between the Book of Ezekiel, which is commonly thought to exhibit strong priestly influence, and the Yahwistic creation story in Genesis 2. The differences have received less attention. In Ezekiel 37, God does not touch the bones or breathe into the bodies. In fact, God does not even speak to the bones and the breath directly. Eichrodt gives some attention to the blending of traditions here (*Theology of the Old Testament, vol. II*, 47-48).

[11]The fourth occurrence of רוּה, in v. 9, is not reflected in LXX, making the total appearances of *pneuma* in its different forms add up to eight.

appears twice in v. 2 and twice in v. 10. The two uses of מְאֹד at the beginning magnify the quantity and intensity of the vision of death. The bones are "very many" and "very dry." The two uses at the end emphasize the grandness of the vision of new life. There is a "very, very great multitude." The term חַיִל (multitude) often connotes an army.[12] This may increase the power of the image, but it also renews questions about the role of violence in the passage.

It is quite unusual, of course, that the prophet should prophesy to the vision. Verse 11 provides a transition to a more common prophetic event. The structure of the second section of the text can be depicted as follows:

11 Explanation of vision
12-14 Command to prophesy and prophecy to people

This division immediately reveals the tension created in all of vv. 1-14. There are three cycles of command to prophesy followed by the prophecy itself, but the final prophecy is not enacted immediately here in the text, as were the prophecies to the bones and breath in the vision. The role of the vision may be to provide assurance to the prophet and subsequent readers of the entire story that this actual prophecy will be fulfilled, but what of the people within the prophet's audience in the story, who are apparently not prior to the vision?

This second main section has an internal structure that also focuses on triplets. The lament of the people in v. 11b is three-fold. The prophecy in v. 12 is a threefold response. The three components of the prophecy—opening of graves, bringing up from graves, and returning to land—are repeated in vv. 13-14. Once again, this heightens the tension inherent in the delivery of prophetic oracles. The text compensates for the inability of the actual oracle to be fulfilled by repeating its elements in what Hals has appropriately called an "elaborated recognition formula" in vv. 13-14.[13] The piling up of prophetic sayings attempts to make the fulfillment of this prophecy as certain as those within the earlier vision.[14] The actual effectiveness of this device on a real audience is impossible to measure.

---

[12]Fox, "The Rhetoric of Ezekiel's Vision of the Valley of the Bones," 11.

[13]Hals, *Ezekiel*, 268.

[14]The attempts of historical-critical interpreters to identify some of these repetitive elements as later accretions may be correct. See, for example, Wevers, *Ezekiel*, 194 and Walter Zimmerli, *Ezekiel 2: A Commentary on the Book of the Prophet Ezekiel, Chs. 25-48*, trans. J. D. Martin (Philadelphia: Fortress, 1983) 256.

One problematic feature of the last three verses is the appearance of the Hebrew form עמי (my people) in v. 12 and v. 13. עמי appears at the end of two identical Hebrew phrases.[15] The phrases can be translated as "I will cause you to come up from your graves, my people." The presence of עמי is more likely, based on the external evidence of the versions, at the end of v. 13.[16] Its appearance there and its absence in v. 12 in the original Hebrew text at the end of an identical phrase could explain both the addition in v. 12 of MT and the deletion in v. 13 of the Syriac. Leslie C. Allen argues for a two stage gloss from 34:30 to 37:13 and then to 37:12.[17] Zimmerli was likewise inclined to omit both occurrences from the original text, because its addition is far easier to explain than its omission. Nevertheless, Zimmerli did note the tremendous theological significance of the inclusion of עמי in MT.[18] Hals did not reach a firm text-critical conclusion, but strongly seconded Zimmerli's theological evaluation.[19] The use of "my people" here is of critical importance, and makes the text-critical arguments worthy of attention. The status of Israel as Yahweh's people is perhaps the primary issue in understanding Israel's story. Israel's loss of this status directly in Hosea 1:9 and indirectly in 2 Chronicles 36:15-21[20] is in need of reversal. This reversal occurs in Ezekiel 37:12-13, regardless of whether it occurs once or twice or whether it occurred in the original text. The text-critical dispute in the versions may even further reveal the importance of this theme.

There is additional thematic tension between vv. 1-10 and vv. 11-14. In the first section, the scene of the miracle is a field of battle, as noted above. In the second, the scene is a graveyard. In the first, the failure of the bodies to be buried is essential to the understanding of the pro-

---

Nevertheless, such elements in the final form of the text serve a significant rhetorical function.

[15] The first occurrence is absent from both LXX and the Syriac versions. Therefore, it is typically rejected as a gloss in MT. The second does not appear in the Syriac, but is reflected in LXX.

[16]BHS labels the occurrence in v. 12 an addition, but not the one in v. 13.

[17]Allen's textual scenario is feasible. His additional argument concerning the movement of לעם from 37:27 seems overly speculative and further clouds the issue. See Leslie C. Allen, *Ezekiel 20-48*, WBC (Waco: Word,. 1990) 183. Eichrodt's contention that the addition of עמי first entered the text at v. 12 and was then repeated in v. 13 ignores the evidence from the Syriac version, which he did not mention. See Eichrodt, *Ezekiel*, 506.

[18]Zimmerli, *Ezekiel* 2, 256.

[19]Hals, *Ezekiel*, 269-270.

[20]See the argument in chapter seven of this work.

phetic message. In the second, the burial of the bodies is essential. The identification of the two restoration scenes is apparent. The bones represent those killed during the destruction of Israel by the Babylonians. Return to the land is not a necessary component of this restoration. The buried bodies of vv. 12-13 are those dying in exile in Babylon. An alternative to viewing the text as a clumsy combination of two very different images[21] is to take the two images together as a statement of completeness. The whole of the exilic experience, from invasion to deportation to death in a foreign land, would be reversed by the experience of restoration.

Theological Conclusions

This is clearly a text which fights to hold itself together. How does it succeed as a response to Israel's experience? This is a message to Israelites in exile in Babylon. The second portion of the text, vv. 1-14, would seem to be most relevant for their situation. The visionary experience in vv. 1-10 is a stark reminder of the violent event which placed them in their present condition of exile. The completeness of Israel's destruction is an issue with which the prophets in general struggle.[22] Such a vision of death and the abomination of exposed bodies expresses the full horror of Israel's story of destruction.

Lest it be forgotten that the exiled Israelites were victims of violence, this text brings together the destruction of Israel that began the Exile and the continuing experience of the Israelites in Babylon. As the preceding analysis of the text reveals, this juxtaposition creates considerable tension. A full restoration of Israel requires that defeats both past and present be overcome. The prophetic message here proclaims just that. Not only will Yahweh's action take account of those wasting away in Babylon, but it will somehow remember those who were killed so many years ago.

It is at exactly this point where prophetic proclamation risks collapse. Can it somehow atone for the suffering of the past? The terrible difference between the two halves of this text emerges here. Those in vv. 11-14 may truly be delivered and restored. The "killed ones" in vv. 1-10 receive only a symbolic, visionary restoration. One could argue, as the first half of the Book of Ezekiel does, that the punishment of des-

---

[21]Biggs (*The Book of Ezekiel*, 119) identifies vv. 12-14 as a later interpretation of the vision in vv. 1-10.

[22]See von Rad's discussion of this theme in *Old Testament Theology, Volume II*, 270-272.

truction and exile was deserved because of Israel's disobedience.[23] The problem still remains, however, that the punishment was not equally received by all. Second Chronicles 36:15-21 made this clear. The punishment deserved by many generations was delayed and accumulated. It then fell full force on a single generation, many of whom died young and innocent. Others were spared death but deported. Ezekiel 37:1-14 holds these two groups uneasily together.

Human identity in the face of violent destruction is still an open question. This text struggles with the restoration of identity. Will Israel again be the people of God? The witness of Hebrew Text is a double affirmative answer to this question, but the textual difficulties can not be avoided for the sake of an easy, comfortable theological answer. Further, no regained identity as "my people" occurs in vv. 1-10. To what extent, if any, are the "killed ones" able to regain their lost identity? The only possible positive answer to this question lies in the holding together of the vision and the prophetic word.

Israel's perception of its experience of exile may be further understood by exploring the concepts of honor and shame in ancient Near Eastern cultures. These concepts have only recently begun to receive attention from biblical scholars.[24] In Ezekiel 5:15, Yahweh is aware of the shame that his abandonment will cause Israel.[25] They will become "a mockery and a taunt...to the nations around." Loss of identity which is provided by covenant relationship is a devastating blow to Israel. The regaining of the designation "my people" is critical to the regaining of identity.

Finally, the theological tension inherent in prophetic oracles may be subtly acknowledged in this text. How are people who have suffered such utter destruction supposed to gain hope from the oracle of restoration in vv. 12-14?[26] Indeed, how is the prophet himself supposed to

---

[23]Hanson, *The People Called: The Growth of Community in the Bible*, 219-220.

[24]See Saul M. Olyan, "Honor, Shame, and Covenant Relations in Ancient Israel and its Environment," *JBL* 115 (1997): 201-218. The concept of honor and shame in "patron-client" relationships and the relevance of these concepts for understanding the breakdown of relationship between Israel and Yahweh in the Exile receive brief mention from T. Raymond Hobbs in his addition to Olyan's article. See T. Raymond Hobbs, "Reflections on Honor, Shame, and Covenant Relations," *JBL* 116 (1997): 501-503.

[25]Hobbs, "Reflections on Honor, Shame, and Covenant Relations," 503.

[26]For a powerful example of how such visions of restoration can fail, see the two distortions of the dry bones vision in Charles Frazier's novel *Cold Mountain* (New York: Atlantic Monthly Press, 1997) 9-10, 47-48.

believe? Again, the uneasy pairing of vision and oracle attempts a solution. The fulfillment of the two prophecies within vv. 1-10 creates a momentum. Of course, the prophecy in v. 12 is not yet fulfilled, but a sense of expectation builds in the repeated cycles. Further, though the language of the third prophecy is not repeated in a statement of fulfillment, it is repeated in the expanded recognition formula of vv. 13-14. The intensity of rhetorical effort to hold vision and oracle together through the inclusio of "spirit" (רוח) and "to live" (נוח) and the linking effect of the lament in v. 11 reflect the struggle of faith in the face of destruction.

11

PEACE ON EARTH

ISAIAH 11:1-10

The preceding two chapters have examined prophetic responses to the
violent narrative framework of Israel's story presented in Part I. Isaiah
11:1-10 continues the theme of restoration, particularly in reference to
the Israelite monarchy. Once again, Israel's new world is portrayed in a
vision, as in Ezekiel 37:7-10 and Hosea 11:10-11. The vision in Isaiah
11:6-10 takes the theme of restoration to a higher pitch, however, por-
traying a world at peace with Israel at its center. Such a vision of perfect
peace is perhaps the ultimate response to the violent condition of humanity. The attention this text has received throughout the history of
biblical interpretation reveals its significance as a response to the world
in which people live.

The Text

The boundaries of this text are disputed at both ends. Most commentators begin the unit with 11:1. One exception is Otto Kaiser, who
includes 10:33-34 as part of this unit as a statement of judgment which
11:1-10 is the corresponding promise of deliverance.[1] BHS, following
the Leningrad Codex, marks the end of 10:34 with the sign of a closed
paragraph. In addition, 11:1 is marked as the beginning of a new liturgical lesson. Clearly, there is a sense of separation between 10:34 and
11:1. Judgment and salvation are opposite themes. Isaiah 11:1-10 may
be seen as a response to 10:33-34, but the best choice seems to be to treat
11:1-10 as a distinct unit, even if it is related to what precedes it.[2]

---

[1]Otto Kaiser, *Isaiah 1-12*, OTL, trans. R. A. Wilson (London: SCM, 1972) 156-
157.

[2]See the arguments against Kaiser in Hans Wilderberger, *Isaiah 1-12*, trans.
Thomas H. Trapp (Minneapolis: Fortress, 1991) 462-463.

The endpoint of the unit has created a greater range of opinion. At least two issues are of importance, literary style and thematic continuity. 11:1-9 is unanimously understood as poetry, but some commentators and some versions present v. 10 as prose.[3] Oswalt seems to make the identification of vv. 10-11 as prose the basis for considering 11:1-9 a unit.[4] BHS (the Hebrew text) presents all of Isaiah 11 as poetry. This poetic pattern was followed by Watts, who divides the chapter after v. 10[5] and by Kaiser who divides it after v. 9.[6] Motyer, emphasizing both the "root of Jesse" inclusio (v. 1 and v. 10) and the "on that day" linkage (v. 10 and v. 11) treated 11:1-16 as a unit. He did, however, divide into subunits between v. 10 and v. 11.

Because attention to form and structure lead to an impasse, as indicated in the discussion above, thematic connections gain importance. The key question remaining in the establishment of boundaries is whether to include v. 10. Isaiah 11 treats two related, but distinct, subjects. The first part of the chapter addresses the future role of the king and the second half addresses the people of Israel, both Ephraim and Judah. Ultimately, this forces the decision that v. 10, which still speaks of the Davidic king stands with vv. 1-9 and apart from vv. 11-16.[7] There remain significant linkages between vv. 1-10 and vv. 11-16, most notably the appearance of נס (signal) in v. 10 and v. 12 and the repetition of "on that day" in v. 10 and v. 11.

The text of this passage is in relatively good condition. A handful of textual issues will require discussion as they arise, but the various translations are in close agreement. Throughout the interpretation below, attention is given to the poetic aspects of 11:1-10.[8] Like Hosea

---

[3]NRSV and Wilderberger, for example, print v. 10 as prose. See Wilderberger, *Isaiah 1-12*, 461. NRSV also prints 11:11 as prose, but Wilderberger treats it as poetry (p. 486).

[4]John N. Oswalt, *The Book of Isaiah: Chapters 1-39* (Grand Rapids: Eerdmans, 1986) 284-288.

[5]John D. W. Watts, *Isaiah 1-33*, WBC (Waco: Word, 1985) 168.

[6]Kaiser, *Isaiah 1-12*, 157,163.

[7]Wilderberger, *Isaiah 1-12*, 463.

[8]Chris Franke outlined a methodological approach using rhetorical criticism for his own study of passages from Deutero-Isaiah. See *Isaiah 46, 47, and 48: A New Literary-Critical Reading* (Winona Lake, Indiana: Eisenbrauns, 1994) 12-19. Franke's attention to poetic imagery and the structure of the passage on many levels provides a good parallel to the approach I will take below. On the other hand, his use of stress and syllable counts rests on a foundation which is less firm. Disagreements and divergences concerning methodology in this area provide reason for great caution in its use. Wilderberger has also made use of

11:1-11, however, this poem progresses like narrative and tells a story. In vv. 1-5 a new king arises, his character develops, and he takes control. In vv. 6-10 his reign brings about peace and the world takes notice. Isaiah 11:1-10 falls into two fairly obvious subsections, based on theme and the nature of the language. Verses 1-5 introduce the new king and detail his attributes; vv. 6-10 announce the resulting conditions of his reign. Both of these subsections are filled with poetic imagery. Though the anthropomorphic imagery of vv. 2-5 and the dominant animal imagery of vv. 6-8 present a sense of contrast, these two sets of images are brought together by v. 8 and the final line of v. 6. The plant imagery and references to Jesse in v. 1 and v. 10 provide an additional sense of unity to the passage. Some may regard the shift from "stump (גזע) of Jesse" in v. 1 to "root (שרש of Jesse" in v. 10 as a sign of the "clumsy" later addition of v. 10.[9] It is hard to imagine a redactor this clumsy, however. The historical development of the text is not of concern here. What is important is to note the possibility that this is an artistic literary device of the final author. The "root of Jesse" in v.10 may then be seen as a more complete reference back to the full image created in v. 1a and v. 1b, where "his root (שרש)" appears in parallel to "stump of Jesse."

The "branch" from Jesse's root in v. 1 is obviously a reference to a new king arising out of the Davidic line. One significant textual dispute arises at this point. Many commentators emend "יפרה (bear fruit)" of MT to "יפרח (grow out).[10] The emendation is apparently supported by the ancient versions and would make v. 1a and v. 1b more precise synonymous parallels. On the other hand, the reading in MT presents a sensible development from one line of the bicolon to the next, and the emendation is not necessary.[11] Further, the "fruit" which this branch will produce is exactly what the text goes on to describe in vv. 2-5. Thus, v.1 introduces the new king whose character and accomplishments are the subject of the verses to follow. The interpretation of

---

stress counts (*Isaiah 1-12*, 465). His contention that longer lines are of greater importance than shorter ones is difficult to accept. In fact, Wilderberger seems to make little, if any, use of this contention in his exegesis of the text.

[9]See, for example, Ronald E. Clements, *Isaiah 1-39*, NCBC (Grand Rapids: Eerdmans, 1980) 125.

[10]See the arguments of Kaiser, *Isaiah 1-12*, 156; and Clements, *Isaiah 1-39*, 122.

[11]In agreement with Watts, *Isaiah 1-33*, 168. On the other hand, Barr, following I. Eitan, has offered a reading of "come out" in v. 1b without emending יפרה, based on an Egyptian root. See *Comparative Philology and the Text of the Old Testament*, 333.

Motyer raises some additional questions about the understanding of the parallelism in v. 1. Motyer read "his root" of v. 1b as "the root support and origin of the Messianic family," instead of seeing the root as simply Jesse himself.[12] The latter seems to fit better with v. 1a. The question may be whether "stump" and "root" are synonymous parallels. Of course, they are not botanical synonyms, but the plant morphology of the verse is not scientifically precise in any case. Branches do not come from roots. On the whole, Motyer's messianic emphasis seems misplaced. It does seem significant that Jesse is used here rather than David. This new king will be David's equal, not simply the equal of his failed descendants.

No literary analysis of v. 2 and what follows can ignore the shadow cast by "messianic" interpretations of this passage. Some commentators allow an understanding of this passage as a prediction of the coming of Jesus to dominate their reading.[13] Others use the term "Messiah" in a more reserved manner, which could also refer to an ideal king occupying the throne of David.[14] Still others avoid the term "Messiah" altogether, though the issue still seems to influence their interpretation.[15]

For the spirit of Yahweh to be upon a person is nothing new in the Hebrew Bible at this point. Yahweh's spirit had been upon judges, kings, and prophets before. More important here are the definitions which pile up in the last three cola of v. 2. The three pairs of traits listed here describe what it means to have the spirit of Yahweh.[16] These are the qualities shared by the great kings of the past, David and Solomon. David is described in similar terms in 2 Samuel 14:17 and Solomon in 1 Kings 3:10-14.[17] When the qualities of this ideal leader are connected to kings of the past, tension arises between the military aspects of their leadership and the message of peace contained in the text. Most troubling are the inclusion of "planning (עצה)" and "might (גברה)." Wilderberger has attempted to use Proverbs 8:14 to establish that such qualities have a civil application. "Thus, Isaiah makes use of images

[12]Alec Motyer, *The Prophecy of Isaiah* (Leicester: IVP, 1993) 121.

[13]For example, see Oswalt, *Isaiah 1-39*, 276-284.

[14]This seems to be the path followed by Wilderberger, for example (*Isaiah 1-12*, 463-485). Wilderberger's discussion of Ancient Near Eastern parallels establishes that the type of expectations expressed in this passage were not unheard of for human kings in that environment (pp. 463-464).

[15]For example, see Watts, *Isaiah 1-33*, 169-176.

[16]Kaiser, *Isaiah 1-12*, 158.

[17]Wilderberger, *Isaiah 1-12*, 471-472.

commonly used when describing the ideology of kingship, but radically reshapes them to convey his expectation of peace."[18] The inability of the text to sustain this contention will become clear below.

Verse 3a repeats the phrase "fear of Yahweh" from the end of v. 2. This second occurrence is often omitted as the result of dittography.[19] The repetition forms a link, however, between the inner qualities of character developed in v. 2 and the outward manifestations of these qualities in vv. 3-4. V. 4 signals something of a shift as the actions described become more specific. The verb roots in v. 3b-c, שׁפט (judge) and יכח (decide) are repeated in v. 4a-b. The imperfect forms in v. 3 become perfect forms in v. 4 as the actions take on greater force and effect. The force of the text continues to build in v. 4c-d as images of violence break. loose from the ordered, civil affairs of the first half of the verse. The illusion that this text might only be about peace is shattered by verbs of "striking (נכה) and causing death (מות). While "the rod of his mouth" and "the breath of his lips" are the subjects of these verbs, leading to the potential counter-argument that the violence is only metaphorical, the reader must remember that the peaceful images of the text are only metaphorical too. Verse 4 speaks of reversal, of winners becoming losers and losers becoming winners. The images that bring about this reversal are violent ones.

One may understand the violence of v. 4 to be targeted at those who deserve it, but the text reveals that the results are not so well ordered. The "meek of the earth (ארץ)," who are helped in the first half of the verse, are threatened by the striking of the earth (ארץ) in the second half. Indeed, some have proposed a textual emendation because of the supposed awkwardness of the repetition of ארץ in this verse. If one consonant is changed so that the word becomes ערץ, then v. 4c may read "And he shall strike a violent one with the rod of his mouth."[20] This is a more comfortable image, created by a clever, but unwarranted, change in the text.

In defense of such a desire to contain and channel the violence of the text, we should recall the change made within the text of Exodus from 11:5 to 12:29, where the victim of the Destroyer is altered from a female slave to a prisoner. The retaining of ארץ in v. 4c creates a potential difficulty in relation to the close parallel line in v. 4d. How is "earth" to

---

[18]Ibid., 472.

[19]See BHS, Clements, *Isaiah 1-39*, 123; and Wilderberger, *Isaiah 1-12*, 473.

[20]BHS proposes this emendation and it is followed by some commentators. See Clements, *Isaiah 1-39*, 123. The ancient versions all support the reading of MT.

be understood as parallel to "wicked (רשע)." Again, the emendation to "violent one" is appealing. Oswalt proposed that v. 4d develops v. 4c. The second line defines more precisely who will be attacked.[21] This understanding may diminish the problem that the emendation attempts to address, but ambiguity concerning the intended targets of attack remains.

This text does not make clear whether "the wicked" are Israelites who have oppressed their own people or wicked nations which have oppressed Israel.[22] Perhaps it is both, but in the final analysis, v. 4 talks about two groups, one which will be helped and one which will be killed. While the goals stated in the first half of the verse are cause for hope, the nagging problem that the identity or status of one group can not be improved without destroying the identity of another remains.[23]

Verse 5 is a smooth synonymous bicolon, which rounds off the section begun in similar fashion by v. 1. The generalities of v. 5 form a fitting summary statement of the character whose deeds are described in increasing detail in vv. 3-4. "Righteousness (צדק, as in v. 4b)" and "faithfulness" are named as the undergarment (אזור), the foundational qualities of an ideal ruler.[24] One final question raised in relationship to violence in this section is whether the אזור carries military connotations. One other use of the same word in Isaiah 5:27 clearly points in this direction, while another in 8:9 does not. It is difficult to hold to the notion that the king is being described in vv. 1-5 in primarily civil, non-military, terms.[25] The grand vision of peace lies ahead in vv. 6-10,

---

[21]Oswalt, *Isaiah 1-39*, 281.

[22]Given the context of the entire unit, an internal designation seems more likely, but an external reference has been suggested. See, for example, Christoph Barth, *God With Us: A Theological Introduction to the Old Testament*, ed. Geoffrey W. Bromiley (Grand Rapids: Eerdmans, 1991) 344.

[23]On the "interplay of masculine and feminine nouns" in this verse, see Gillingham, *The Poems and Psalms of the Hebrew Bible*, 25.

[24]There has been some textual dispute of the second appearance of אזור. Wilderberger proposed changing the second to הגר (belt). See *Isaiah 1-12*, 478-479. This proposal is appealing. "Faithfulness" could then be understood as the quality which binds the others together. On this understanding, see Oswalt, *Isaiah 1-39*, 282. Nevertheless, the emendation has little textual support. See the discussion of Watts, *Isaiah 1-33*, 169. BHS proposes אסור, which, in light of Jeremiah 37:15 and Ecclesiastes 7:26, seems very unlikely.

[25]Wilderberger continued to make this argument, even in v. 5. Ibid., 472-479. His proposed reading of הגר in place of אזור creates greater difficulty, in light of 2 Samuel 20:8 where a הגר clearly has a military purpose.

but a close examination of vv. 1-5 reveals that it is not achieved by entirely peaceful means.

Verse 6 begins with a startling image portrayed in three successive pairings of animals, each a predator matched with potential prey. Following the enigmatic final line of v. 6, these images of peace within the animal world are continued. Kaiser has drawn the connection between this vision and the Priestly view that prior to Genesis 9:2 animals did not eat each other.[26] Several key questions arise in any attempt to understand the role of these images. How literally should they be understood? If this is mythological imagery, what is its background? How are vv. 6-8 related to the more realistic v. 9?

Regardless of the textual history of the various parts of Isaiah 11:1-10, the mythical vision now stands within the context of a salvation oracle. The repetitive nature of vv. 6-8 creates an overwhelming image. In the final form of the text, the mythical vision and the more realistic description of the ideal king must be understood in relation to each other. The results of the righteous rule described in vv. 1-5 are such that ordinary language may fail to express its beauty and grandeur. In the final form, the "little child" of v. 6 can only be the ruler described in vv. 1-5. He will lead a world of beings at peace with one another. Natural enemies will not only exist peacefully together (v. 6), but will also share resources and become like one another (vv. 7-8). Some commentators have attempted to explicate details of this vision, such as the precise types of snakes mentioned in v. 8. These attempts actually seem to rob the vision of some of its power, separating the various parallel elements rather than allowing them to accumulate and overwhelm the reader. More important is the sense of movement from being together in v. 6 to eating and rearing offspring together in v. 7 to the specific inclusion humanity in v. 8. This last development allows for smoother movement into v. 9. Oswalt has outlined the various modes in which the elements of vv. 6-8 may be read, arguing that a "figurative" understanding of the animal images allows for a less specific understanding of the third person plural, pronominal subject at the beginning of v. 9. "They" can be human beings if the animals are not understood literally.[27] The movement toward human involvement in vv. 6-8 supports this understanding.

Childs has commented extensively on the relationship between vv. 6-8 and the surrounding framework. He is correct that "we are in another atmosphere" in vv. 6-8, but his contention that there is "a

---

[26]Kaiser, *Isaiah 1-12*, 160.
[27]Oswalt, *Isaiah 1-39*, 284.

complete lack of tension" in the passage ignores much of the character of vv. 1-5.[28] In fact, the appearance in vv. 1-5 of military apparel, actions, and leadership roles creates a tremendous sense of tension in the text. In v. 9 "they will not destroy," but in v. 5 the righteous king has acted destructively. How shall "a wolf live with a lamb" when all of the wolves ("the wicked" in v. 4) have been killed?

Wilderberger states that "Isaiah indicates in v. 9 that he is reinterpreting the ancient mythological imagery." The idea that the text now seeks to apply the vision seems appropriate. Verse 9 continues to expand the vision as well. The "holy mountain" becomes the "earth."[29] The "knowledge" (דעת) possessed by the king in v. 2 now fills this earth. The fantastical vision of vv. 6-8 is thus brought together with the political vision of vv. 1-5, and a picture of the future is imagined.

This process continues in v. 10. Again, there is expansion of the political vision. The ideal king, as "root of Jesse," is now not only a perfect ruler for Israel, but for all "peoples" and "nations." This verse also serves to create a connection with what follows in vv. 11-16. The beauty of the vision of peace is again shattered by the images of warfare between Israel and its traditional enemies.

Theological Conclusions

An attempt to understand Isaiah 11:1-10 as a response to Israel's story creates some desire to place it within a context. This has been extremely difficult to do. Much of Isaiah 1-39 is typically assigned to the Assyrian crisis of the late eighth century. It is also generally accepted that the book of Isaiah received many revisions and additions during or after the Babylonian Exile of the sixth century. Conclusions about the textual history of 11:1-10 cannot be reached with any certainty.[30] This text, 11:1-10, does not contain any internal, chronological markers. Childs was reluctant to include this text among the Assyrian passages for this

---

[28]B. S. Childs, *Myth and Reality in the Old Testament* (London: SCM, 1960) 64-65. Childs's discussion is form-critical in nature. He assumes that vv. 1-5, 9 are an Isaianic framework into which a preexisting mythical vision has been inserted. He attributes the "lack of tension" he described to the assumption that this is only a fragment of a myth. All elements which might be in conflict with a biblical understanding of the world have been removed (pp. 65-67).

[29]Clements, *Isaiah 1-39*, 124. Clements also noted the connections between v. 9 and Isaiah 65:25 and Habakkuk 2:14.

[30]Wilderberger has argued for a connection to the Assyrian crisis, though not with great conviction. See *Isaiah 1-12*, 468. Gillingham assumes significant Exilic influence. See *The Poems and Psalms of the Hebrew Bible*, 162.

reason.[31] More important for this study is to recognize this passage within the Hebrew Bible as a response to all of Israel's story. It expresses a hope that the best part of that story, the Davidic monarchy, will repeat itself in an idealized fashion.

The reflection on Israel's story found here agrees that restoration requires violent destruction as a first step. The nation of Israel must be pruned back to the original root from which it grew. The Israel ruled by the descendants of David must be obliterated and the slate wiped clean.[32] Thus, even such an idyllic vision as Isaiah 11 must be proceeded by the horror of Isaiah 10.

Whether 10:33-34 is considered part of this unit or an element of its literary context, Isaiah 10-11 creates an image of destruction and restoration. Isaiah 11:1-10 tells the full story of this transformation from a "stump" in the ground to a "glorious dwelling."[33] The transformation takes place in three phases. First, Yahweh raises up a new ruler and endows him with the necessary gifts. The text enumerates these gifts in a powerful poetic progression in v. 2. Second, the new king establishes his authority. This process is described in a confusing mixture of language and images. Some of the statements, such as v. 4c-d, are overtly violent in nature. Some, such as v. 4a-b, do not contain any elements of violence. Still others, such as v. 5, are ambiguous about the role of violence in the process. The need for enforcement has already been subtly blended into the text in the list of v. 2 which contains "the spirit of power and might." Third, the results of the new king's reign come to fruition. This new state of being for Israel is described in striking images of peace and harmony. Within this description, the text moves the process slightly farther as the vision becomes international in scope in vv. 9-10.

---

[31]Childs, *Isaiah and the Assyrian Crisis* (London: SCM, 1967) 63-64.

[32]Childs, *Biblical Theology of the Old and New Testaments: Theological Reflection on the Christian Bible*, 177.

[33]Von Rad noticed and identified this progression, but failed to see the inherent contradictions in the punishment of the guilty in the second stage and the resolution of conflicts in the third (*Old Testament Theology Volume II: The Theology of Israel's Prophetic Traditions*, trans. D. M. G. Stalker [Philadelphia: Westminster, 1965] 169-170). Similarly, Hanson's notion of a "divinely given triad" ignores the incompatibility of the kind of "שׁלום" described in 11:6-9 and the violent enforcement of "righteousness" in 11:3-5. See *The People Called*, 182-183. Christoph Barth noticed that this text considers violent destruction as a necessary step in the path to peace, particularly the destruction of the corrupt monarchy. He failed to question, however, what kind of peace could be established in such a contradictory manner (*God With Us*, 224).

It is not surprising that the beginning and end of Isaiah 11:1-10 have received tremendous attention throughout the history of interpretation and use of the Bible. Indeed, phrases like "stump of Jesse" and "a wolf shall dwell with a lamb" have become familiar expressions in the English language apart from the role they play in this text. It is also no surprise that the middle of the unit has been largely ignored. The vision of restoration and peace in vv. 6-9 eclipses the preceding verses with its overwhelming beauty. Perhaps the text is even structured to create this effect. The reality is, however, that Israel knows only too well how the prosperity of nations comes about. The great empires of the ancient Near East regularly trampled the inhabitants of Palestine in order to extend the peace and prosperity of their own lands. If peaceful existence is to be realized in Israel, then the army raised up from bones in Ezekiel 37 will have to be lead by the king who grows from a stump in Isaiah 11 to carve out an environment for this existence through battle against enemies both internal and external.

The "poor" and the "meek" may gain a just existence, but this restoration of identity, as always, must be accompanied by the reduced identity of others. The "wicked" may have earned their punishment, but even deserved punishment calls the grand vision into question. The image of the wolf and the lamb living peacefully together is tarnished by the realization that those designated as the predators of society have all been killed two verses earlier. I used the term "transformation" earlier, but careful reading of this text reveals that the only possibility of transformation Israel knows is one brought about by destruction and a new beginning.[34] Peace on earth is gained only by violence and maintained only by force. Despite political and textual attempts to hide the iron hand in the velvet glove, the hardness of human existence remains.

---

[34]In Terrien's terms, "ideological continuity" requires "historical discontinuity" (*The Elusive Presence*, 303).

12

CONCLUSION

THE HEART OF
THE HEBREW BIBLE?

The reader will notice that in the preceding three chapters I have not attempted to establish or maintain consistent connections between prophetic oracles and specific events in Israel's story. First of all, such identifications are often difficult to establish with precision. It is commonly accepted that prophetic oracles written or spoken in response to one particular situation were often reshaped in response to later events. Second, and more important, when the prophetic books found their place in the canon, it was as a response to Israel's entire story. This understanding is born out by the entire history of interpretation of the prophets, as communities of faith—both Jewish and Christian—have continued to apply the prophetic message to their own situations.

Humanity and Violence

This study began with the observation that human violence is the primary factor which shapes the biblical story. Often it is assumed that the prophets offer an alternative vision as a response to Israel's story. The real world that Israel experienced was one determined by conflict and death. The progress of one group of people always depended on the destruction of another. Human violence as a mechanism of determining identity always escaped boundaries and ran out of control. Is the world imagined by the prophets of Israel any different? This is the critical question that must be used to evaluate the prophetic traditions as an alternative vision. The preceding interpretations of three representative prophetic texts offer a disturbing answer to this question. Human beings are still actors in the prophets' stories, even though the activity of God is often more overt than in the narratives that tell Israel's story.

In Hosea 11, Israel suffers from the violent oppression of other nations. It is destruction which stirs up Yahweh's compassion. This poem essentially retells Israel's story. It boldly asks whether there can be a different world in which Israel can live. Human violence is still understood as the tool of God's punishment. The vision at the end of the poem offers a future hope that the compassion of God can generate a world in which Israel does not suffer at the hands of other peoples. Such a world is held out as a possibility in 11:10-11, but it is dependent on a future restoration.

The "valley of bones" vision of Ezekiel 37 offers a picture of this restoration. It is quite clearly a response to total destruction. The Exile left Israel not only dead and destroyed, but also exposed and defiled. The forces of empire building had left the Israelites dead in their violent wake. Even those still alive in Babylon understood that the Exile was becoming their grave. Perhaps Israel had deserved punishment as 2 Chronicles 36:15-21 claims, but the experience of the Exile was out of proportion with the sin. The human violence of the Babylonian empire was not a carefully measured dose of retribution. How can restoration be envisioned in this context? What Ezekiel sees in the valley may be a vision, but it acknowledges the reality of the ebb and flow of human existence. The powerful get what they want. When the bones come to life and stand, it is as an army. The precursor to the regaining of identity, land, and homes is battle. Ezekiel 37 retains a certain ambiguity about this issue, but when Yahweh says in 37:12, "I will bring you unto the land of Israel," the conquest language of Joshua 1 is easily recalled.

More than any other text, Isaiah 11 holds out the hope that the violent ways of humanity and the world might come to an end. Here the end of the restoration process is envisioned. Nevertheless, reality can not be fully pushed away. Violent destruction is necessary to pave the way for peace, and in order to establish it. The visionary experience of 11:6-8 creates a kind of amnesia about the process which precedes it, but careful attention to the text disrupts this effect. Peace on earth is established by military skill and might. Those who might disturb the peace are killed, their destruction justified as punishment. The experience of peace is described in unreal terms which force the imagination into another time and place. The real world contains only steps toward peace which include violent enforcement, and raise troubling questions about the realization of the future vision in this world.

The prophetic visions of compassion, restoration, and peace all exhibit a tension between hope for the future and the reality of the present. The restoration of the nation of Israel is the central element. This points back to the story of Israel outlined in Part I. The story of Israel is dominated by human violence. Is it possible for the prophets to conceive and sustain a vision of a restored Israel which exists by some other means? The visions struggle to break free of this reality, but ultimately do not.

God and Violence

Readers may notice a surface similarity between this book and others, such as Christoph Barth's *God With Us: A Theological Introduction to the Old Testament*. The narrative pattern used by Barth is somewhat similar to that which I used in Part I. He also ends his work with a discussion of the prophets. What is the difference? It is important to note that in all of Barth's chapter titles God is the subject. He acknowledged his indebtedness to G. Ernest Wright's *God Who Acts*.[1] Most of my chapter titles in Part I have God's People as subject, often in passive voice. The "God of Mighty Acts" stands above the fray and it seems to me that too much focus on this God causes us to ignore the realities of life on earth. Israel knew these realities, and they are included in its story. It may be argued that Barth and others read the Bible in a way closer to the way the Bible intends itself to be read. The Bible is recital, and Israel's confession of how God is at work in the story is important.[2] But underneath this acting God there is a human story happening, and the Bible does not ignore this story. The contrast between these two approaches once more raises the question of the relationship between the two spheres of action. Creeds speak of a God at work, ordering the world. The biblical stories I focus on in Part I of this study tell of a people in the world, killing and being killed.

Hosea 11 may be an attempt to recast the vengeful, violent God of Israel's story as a compassionate God. There is a struggle portrayed within God's own personality in 11:8-9. As recital theology points out, there is an assumption that events on earth are in some way under

---

[1]Barth, *God With Us*, 5.

[2]Ibid. I am not singling out Barth here because he is alone in this tendency. He followed in a great tradition of Old Testament Theology developed by Wright, von Rad, and others. The organization of Barth's work simply makes it a convenient example for comparison. In fact, he does not completely ignore the tension between the "mighty acts" emphasis and the tragedy of Israel's story (see pp. 292-295 and pp. 319-339). If, however, God is at work in these tragic events, then should they be understood as "mighty acts?" Why are they not elements of the recital?

God's control. Because of this element of Israelite faith, two crucial questions become one. "Can God refrain from vengeance and act compassionately?" is the same as asking "Can there be a world free from the ravages of violence?" Whether the people of Israel are killed and their nation destroyed is God's choice. If only God's acts were controlled by compassion, then there would be hope for a new future, that which is portrayed in 11:10-11. But even this future vision can not break free from the violent ways of the world. If Israel is to have a new existence, then Yahweh must roar like a lion.

Ezekiel 37 confirms this prophetic understanding of God's participation in the violent ways of the world. Before the prophecy of restoration in 37:11-14, God must resurrect Israel's army in 37:1-10. The restoration of the nation requires a new conquest. Those whom God calls "my people" are those whom God leads in battle and makes victorious. Isaiah 11:6-9 may paint a picture of the world as God would have it be, but the process of getting it there is the same. God will have to work through the violent ways of humanity, raising up and endowing a king with the power to destroy and reshape the world.

God participates in the violence of the world through the representative king. This reveals a problem with the way much biblical theology is done, including attempts that begin with recital. The recital is an idealized portrait. Its elements are rehearsed and biblical texts are amassed to support them. A text like Isaiah 11:6-9 can be used to support the argument that Israel and its prophets envisioned a future of perfect peace, a future radically different from the past. Attention to all of 11:1-10 reveals, however, that this future is not so different. It is a vision dependent upon the hope that God will help Israel be the winner, as it was in the days of Joshua and David, instead of the loser, as it was in the latter days of the monarchy.

The Bible and Violence

The reshaping of the canon in the Greek and Christian traditions is testimony to the temporal failure of such visions. No longer are the visions able to reside at the heart of the canon, because they are so tragically unrealized. They must be pushed forward to the end of the canon and projected into the distant future. New theological movements such as messianism and apocalypticism, which rose to prominence in post-biblical Judaism, constitute parallel responses to the unrealized visions of restoration and peace. The movement of the prophetic literature to the end of the canon also transferred the end of the narrative framework of the Hebrew Bible to the middle of the Greek canon. At the same time, the reordering of Chronicles and Ezra-Nehemiah buried Israel's violent end even deeper. The Hebrew canon, with its more troubling order, still emerged as authoritative within Judaism. But additional authoritative writings, Mishnah and Talmud, developed to add a new ending. In spite of all this maneuvering, the violence of the biblical story still seeps through to raise critical and painful questions about the meaning of human existence. Such questions appear to be growing in their importance and urgency in our own day.[3] The violent story of Israel refuses to be quiet, however we try to overcome it, because this story of destruction, loss, and suffering is our own.

---

[3] I had already conceived of and written most of this book before the publication of Regina M. Schwartz's *The Curse of Cain: The Violent Legacy of Monotheism* (Chicago: University of Chicago Press, 1997). Schwartz has attempted to find the root cause of violence in the "principle of scarcity" which is reflected in the scarce god of particularistic monotheism. Note that she has offered a newly revised canon as a solution to violence. "My re-vision would produce an alternative Bible which subverts the dominant vision of violence and scarcity with an ideal of plenitude and its corollary ethical imperative of generosity" (p. 176).

BIBLIOGRAPHY

Ackroyd, Peter R. *I and 2 Chronicles, Ezra, Nehemiah*, TBC. London: SCM, 1973.

Albright, William F. *The Archaeology of Palestine*. Baltimore: Penguin, 1949.

_____. "Northwest-Semitic Names in a List of Egyptian Slaves from the Eighteenth Century B. C.," *JAOS* 74 (1954): 222-233.

Allen, Leslie C. *Ezekiel 20-48*, WBC. Waco: Word, 1990.

Alter, Robert. *The Art of Biblical Narrative*. New York: Basic, 1981.

Andersen, Francis I. and David Noel Freedman. *Hosea: A New Translation with Introduction and Commentary*. AB. Garden City: Doubleday, 1980

Andersen, Francis I. *The Sentence in Biblical Hebrew*. The Hague: Mouton, 1974.

Bar-Efrat, Shimon. *Narrative Art in the Bible*. Sheffield: Almond Press, 1984.

_____. "Some Observations on the Analysis of Structure in Biblical Narrative," *VT* 30 (1980): 154-173.

Barr, James. *Comparative Philology and the Text of the Old Testament*. Winona Lake, Indiana: Eisenbrauns, 1987.

_____. *Semantics of Biblical Language*. Oxford: Oxford University Press, 1961.

Barth, Christoph. *God With Us: A Theological Introduction to the Old Testament*. Ed. Geoffrey W. Bromiley. Grand Rapids: Eerdmans, 1991.

Beeby, H. D. *Grace Abounding: A Commentary on the Book of Hosea*, ITC. Grand Rapids: Eerdmans, 1989.

Berlin, Adele. *Poetics and Interpretation of Biblical Narrative* Winona Lake, Ind.: Eisenbrauns, 1983.

Biggs, Charles R. *The Book of Ezekiel*. London: Epworth, 1996.

Blenkinsopp, Joseph. *The Pentateuch: An Introduction to the First Five Books of the Bible*. New York: Doubleday, 1992.

Bliese, Loren F. "Symmetry and Prominence in Hebrew Poetry: With

Examples from Hosea." In *Discourse Perspectives on Hebrew Poetry in the Scriptures,* ed. Ernst R. Wendland. New York: United Bible Societies, 1994, pp. 67-94.

Boesak, Alan A. *Black and Reformed: Apartheid, Liberation and the Calvinist Tradition.* Johannesberg: Skotaville, 1984.

Boling, R. and G. E. Wright. *Joshua.* AB. Garden City, N.J.: Doubleday, 1983.

Brown, Robert McAfee. *Unexpected News: Reading the Bible with Third World Eyes.* Philadelphia: Westminster, 1984.

Brueggemann, Walter. *First and Second Samuel,* Interpretation. Louisville: John Knox, 1990.

_____. *1 Kings.* Atlanta: John Knox, 1982.

_____. *Genesis,* Interpretation. Atlanta: John Knox, 1982.

_____. *The Land: Place as Gift, Promise, and Challenge in Biblical Faith.* Philadelphia: Fortress, 1977.

_____. *Old Testament Theology: Essays on Structure, Theme, and Text.* Minneapolis: Fortress, 1992.

Burkert, Walter. *Homo Necans: The Anthropology of Ancient Greek Sacrificial Ritual and Myth.* Trans. Peter Bing. Berkeley: University of California Press, 1983.

Buss, Martin J. *The Prophetic Word of Hosea: A Morphological Study.* Berlin: Alfred Töpelmann, 1969.

Butler, Trent C. *Joshua.* WBC. Waco: Word, 1983.

Campbell, Anthony F. *The Ark Narrative.* Missoula, Montana: Scholars Press, 1975.

Carley, Keith W. *Ezekiel among the Prophets: A Study of Ezekiel's Place in Prophetic Tradition.* London: SCM, 1975.

Cassuto, Umberto. *A Commentary on the Book of Exodus.* Trans. Israel Abrahams. Jerusalem: Magnes, 1974.

Childs, Brevard. *The Book of Exodus: A Critical, Theological Commentary,* OTL. Philadelphia: Westminster, 1974.

____. *Isaiah and the Assyrian Crisis.* London: SCM, 1967.

____. *Myth and Reality in the Old Testament.* London: SCM, 1960.

Clements, Ronald E. *Isaiah 1-39,* NCBC. Grand Rapids: Eerdmans 1980.

Clines, David J. A. *What Does Eve Do to Help? And Other Readerly Questions to the Old Testament.* Sheffield: JSOT, 1990.

Coats, George W. *Genesis: With an Introduction to Narrative Literature,* FOTL. Grand Rapids: Eerdmans, 1983.

_____. "The Traditio-historical Character of the Reed Sea Motif," *VT* 17 (1967): 253-265.

_____. *Moses: Heroic Man, Man of God*, JSOTS, 57. Sheffield: Sheffield, 1988.

_____. "Despoiling the Egyptians," *VT* 18 (1968): 452-457.

Cross, Frank Moore. *Canaanite Myth and Hebrew Epic: Essays in the History of the Religion of Israel.* Cambridge: Harvard University Press, 1973.

Davies, G. Henton. "Glory." In *The Interpreter's Dictionary of the Bible*, vol. 2. Ed. G. A. Buttrick et al. Nashville: Abingdon, 1962, pp. 401-403.

DeVries, Simon J. *1 Kings*, WBC. Waco: Word, 1985.

Dillard, Raymond. *2 Chronicles*, WBC. Waco: Word, 1987.

Duhm, Bernard. *Das Buch Jesaja.* Göttingen: Vandenhoeck and Ruprecht, 1914.

Durham, John I. *Exodus.* WBC. Waco: Word, 1987.

Exum, Cheryl J. "You Shall Let Every Daughter Live: A Study of Exodus 1:8-2:10," *Semeia* 28(1983): 63-82.

Eichrodt, Walther. *Ezekiel: A Commentary.* Trans. Coslett Quinn. London: SCM, 1970.

Farley, Margaret. "Feminist Consciousness and the Interpretation of Scripture." In *Feminist Interpretation of the Bible*. Letty Russell, ed. Philadelphia: Westminster, 1985, pp. 40-55.

Fewell, Danna Nolan. "Joshua." In *The Women's Bible Commentary*. Ed. Carol Newsom and Sharon Ringe. Louisville: Westminster, 1992, pp. 63-66.

Fishbane, Michael. *Biblical Interpretation in Ancient Israel.* Oxford: Clarendon, 1985.

Fokkelman, J. P. *Narrative Art in Genesis.* Amsterdam: VanGorcum, 1975.

Franke, Chris. *Isaiah 46, 47, and 48: A New Literary-Critical Reading.* Winona Lake, Indiana: Eisenbrauns, 1994.

Frei, Hans W. *The Eclipse of Biblical Narrative: A Study in Eighteenth and Nineteenth Century Hermeneutics.* New Haven: Yale University Press, 1974.

Fretheim, Terrence. *The Suffering of God: An Old Testament Perspective.* Minneapolis: Fortress, 1984.

Gillingham, S. E. *The Poems and Psalms of the Hebrew Bible* Oxford:

Oxford University Press, 1994.

Girard, René. *Job: The Victim of His People*. Trans. Yvonne Freccero. Stanford: Stanford University Press, 1987.

_____. *The Scapegoat*. Trans. Yvonne Freccero. Baltimore: Johns Hopkins University Press, 1986.

_____. *Things Hidden Since the Foundation of the Earth*. Trans. Stephen Bann and Michael Metteer. Stanford: Stanford University Press, 1987.

_____. *Violence and the Sacred*. Trans. Patrick Gregory. Baltimore: Johns Hopkins University Press, 1977.

Gitay, Yehoshua. "Reflections of the Poetics of the Samuel Narrative: The Question of the Ark Narrative," *CBQ* 54 (1992): 221-230.

Gottwald, Norman K. *The Tribes of Yahweh: A Sociology of the Religion of Liberated Israel, 1250-1050 B.C.E.* Maryknoll, N. Y.: Orbis, 1979.

Gowan, Donald E. *Genesis 1-11: From Eden to Babel*. ITC. Grand Rapids: Eerdmans, 1988.

Gray, John. *I & II Kings: A Commentary*. 2nd ed., OTL. London: SCM, 1970.

_____. *Joshua, Judges, Ruth*. NCBC. Grand Rapids: Eerdmans, 1986.

Greenberg, Moshe. "The Thematic Unity of Exodus iii-xi." In *Fourth World Congress of Jewish Studies*. Jerusalem: World Union of Jewish Studies, 1967, pp. 151-154.

Gruber, Mayer I. "The Many Faces of Hebrew µynp acn >lift up the face<," *ZAW* 95(1983), pp. 252-260.

Gunn, David M. *The Story of King David: Genre and Interpretation*. Sheffield: JSOT, 1978.

Gutierrez, Gustavo. *On Job: God-Talk and the Suffering of the Innocent*. Maryknoll, N. Y.: Orbis, 1989.

Hals, Ronald M. *Ezekiel*, FOTL. Grand Rapids: Eerdmans, 1989.

Hamerton-Kelly, Robert. *Sacred Violence: Paul's Hermeneutic of the Cross*. Minneapolis: Fortress, 1992.

Hamlin, E. John. *Joshua: Inheriting the Land*, ITC. Grand Rapids: Eerdmans, 1983.

Hanson, Paul D. *The Diversity of Scripture: A Theological Approach*. Philadelphia: Fortress, 1984.

_____. *The People Called: The Growth of Community in the Bible*. San Francisco: Harper & Row, 1986.

Haran, Menahem. "Explaining the Identical Lines at the End of Chronicles and the Beginning of Ezra," *BRev*, 2 (1986), 18-20.

Hauser, Alan J. "Linguistic and Thematic Links Between Genesis 4:1-16 and Genesis 2-3," *JETS* 23 (1980): 297-303.

Hertzberg, S. *I & II Samuel: A Commentary*, OTL. Philadelphia: Westminster, 1964.

Hobbs, T. Raymond. "Reflections on Honor, Shame, and Covenant Relations," *JBL* 116 (1997): 501-503.

Holladay, William L. *The Root Sûbh in the Old Testament* (Leiden: Brill, 1958.

Hyatt, J. P. *Exodus*, NCBC. Grand Rapids: Eerdmans, 1980.

Jones, G. H. *1 and 2 Kings, vol I*. NCBC. Grand Rapids: Eerdmans, 1984.

Kaiser, Otto. *Isaiah 1-12*, OTL, trans. R. A. Wilson. London: SCM, 1972

E. Kautzsch and A. E. Cowley. *Gesenius' Hebrew Grammar*. Oxford: Clarendon, 1910.

Klein, Ralph. *1 Samuel*, WBC. Waco: Word, 1983.

Knight, George A. F. *Theology as Narration: A Commentary on the Book of Exodus*. Grand Rapids: Eerdmans, 1976.

Kugel, James L. *The Idea of Biblical Poetry: Parallelism and Its History*. New Haven: Yale University Press, 1981.

Kuntz, Kenneth R. "Psalm 18: A Rhetorical-Critical Analysis," *JSOT* 26 (1983): 3-31.

Labuschange, Casper J. "The Pattern of Divine Speech Formulas in the Pentateuch," *VT* 32 (1982): 268-296.

Levenson, Jon D. *Creation and the Persistence of Evil: The Jewish Drama of Divine Omnipotence*. San Francisco: Harper & Row, 1988.

Licht, Jacob. *Storytelling in the Bible*. Jerusalem: Magnes, 1978.

Lohfink, Norbert. *Theology of the Pentateuch: Themes of the Priestly Narrative and Deuteronomy*. Edinburgh: T&T Clark, 1994.

Mack, Burton. "Introduction: Religion and Ritual." In *Violent Origins: Walter Burkert, René Girard, and Jonathan Z. Smith on Ritual Killing and Cultural Formation*. Ed. Robert G. Hamerton-Kelly. Stanford: Stanford University Press, 1987.

Mauchline, John. *1 and 2 Samuel*, NCBC. Oliphants: London, 1971.

Mays, James L. *Hosea*, OTL. Philadelphia: Westminster, 1969.

McCarter, Kyle P. *Textual Criticism: Recovering the Text of the Hebrew Bible*. Philadelphia: Fortress, 1986.

_____. *1 Samuel: A New Translation with Introduction and Commentary*, AB. Garden City, N. Y.: Doubleday, 1980.

McCarthy, Dennis J. "Moses' Dealings with Pharaoh: Ex. 7, 8-10, 27,"

CBQ 27 (1965): 336-347.

McEntire, Mark. *The Function of Sacrifice in Chronicles, Ezra, and Nehemiah.* Lewiston, N. Y.: Mellen Biblical Press, 1993.

McKenzie, Stephen L. *The Chronicler's Use of the Deuteronomic History.* Atlanta: Scholars Press, 1984.

Milazzo, G. Tom. *The Protest and the Silence: Suffering, Death, and Biblical Theology.* Minneapolis: Fortress, 1992.

Miller, Patrick D. "Introduction." In *Old Testament Theology: Essays on Structure, Theme, and Text.* Minneapolis: Fortress, 1993, pp. xiii-xviii.

Miscall, Peter D. "Moses and David: Myth and Monarchy." In *The New Literary Criticism and the Hebrew Bible.* Ed. J. Cheryl Exum and David J. A. Clines. Valley Forge: TPI, 1993, pp. 184-200.

Moberly, R. W. L. *At the Mountain of God: Story and Theology in Exodus 32-34,* JSOTS 22. Sheffield: Sheffield, 1983.

_____. *The Old Testament of the Old Testament: Patriarchal Narratives and Mosaic Yahwism.* Minneapolis: Fortress, 1992.

Mosala, Itumaleng J. *Biblical Hermeneutics and Black Theology in South Africa.* Grand Rapids, Eerdmans, 1989.

Motyer, Alec. *The Prophecy of Isaiah.* Leicester: IVP, 1993.

Muilenburg, James. "Form Criticism and Beyond," JBL 88 (1969): 1-18.

_____. *The Way of Israel: Biblical Faith and Ethics.* New York: Harper, 1961.

Na'aman, N. "Habiru and the Hebrews: The Transfer of a Social Term to the Literary Sphere," *JNES* 45 (1986): 271-88.

Niditch, Susan. *War in the Hebrew Bible: A Study in the Ethics of Violence.* Oxford: Oxford University Press, 1993.

Noth, Martin. *Exodus,* OTL. Philadelphia: Westminster, 1962.

_____. *Konige,* BKAT. Neukirchen-Vluyn: Neukirchen Verlag, 1968.

Oduyoye, Modupe. *The Sons of the Gods and the Daughters of Men: An Afro-Asiatic Interpretation of Genesis 1-11.* Maryknoll, N.Y.: Orbis, 1984.

Olyan, Saul M. "Honor, Shame, and Covenant Relations in Ancient Israel and its Environment," *JBL* 115 (1997): 201-218.

Oswalt, John N. *The Book of Isaiah: Chapters 1-39.* Grand Rapids: Eerdmans, 1986

Patrick, Dale. *The Rendering of God in the Old Testament.* Philadelphia: Fortress, 1981.

Perdue, Leo G. *The Collapse of History: Reconstructing Old Testament Theology.* Minneapolis: Fortress, 1994.

Petersen, David L. and Kent Harold Richards. *Interpreting Hebrew Poetry*. Minneapolis: Fortress, 1992.

Polzin, Robert. *Samuel and the Deuteronomist: A Literary Study of the Deuteronomic History, Part 2: 1 Samuel*. San Francisco: Harper & Row, 1989.

von Rad, Gerhard. *Genesis*, OTL. Philadelphia: Westminster, 1972.

____. *Holy War in Ancient Israel*. Trans. Marva J. Dawn and John Howard Yoder. Grand Rapids: Eerdmans, 1991.

____. *Old Testament Theology Volume II: The Theology of Israel's Prophetic Traditions*. Trans. D. M. G. Stalker Philadelphia: Westminster, 1965.

Rice, Gene. *1 Kings: Nations Under God*. Grand Rapids: Eerdmans, 1990.

Ricoeur, Paul. *Essays on Biblical Interpretation*. Ed Lewis S. Mudge. Philadelphia: Fortress, 1980.

____. *The Symbolism of Evil*. Trans. Emerson Buchanan. Boston: Beacon, 1969.

Roberts, J. J. M. "The Hand of Yahweh." *VT* 21 (1971): 244-251.

Robinson, J. *The First Book of Kings*, CBC. Cambridge: Cambridge University Press, 1972.

Rost, L. *The Succession to the Throne of David*. Trans M. D. Rutter and D. M. Gunn. Sheffield: Almond, 1982.

Schwager, Raymond. *Must There Be Scapegoats: Violence and Redemption in the Bible*. Trans. Maria L. Assad. New York: Harper & Row, 1987.

Schwartz, Regina M. *The Curse of Cain: The Violent Legacy of Monotheism*. Chicago: University of Chicago Press, 1997.

Schweizer, Eduard. *The Gospel According to Matthew*. Trans. David E. Green. Atlanta: John Knox, 1975.

Selman, Martin J. *2 Chronicles*, TOTC. Leicester: InterVarsity Press, 1994.

Setel, Drorah O'Donnell. "Exodus." In *The Women's Bible Commentary*. Ed. Carol A. Newsom and Sharon H. Ringe London: SPCK, 1992, pp. 26-35.

Soggin, Albert. *Joshua*, OTL. London: SCM, 1972.

Spina, Frank Anthony. "The "Ground for Cain's Rejection (Gen 4): "*ᵃdamah* in the context of Gen 1-11," *ZAW* 104 (1992): 319-332.

Steinmetz, Devora. *From Father to Son: Kinship, Conflict, and Continuity in Genesis*. Louisville: Westminster/John Knox, 1991.

Sternberg, Meir. *The Poetics of Biblical Narrative: Ideological Literature and the Drama of Reading*. Bloomington: Indiana University Press, 1985.

Stuart, Douglas. *Hosea-Jonah*, WBC. Waco: Word, 1987.

Terrien, Samuel. *The Elusive Presence: Toward a New Biblical Theology*. San Francisco: Harper & Row, 1978.

Thiselton, Anthony C. *New Horizons in Hermeneutics*. Grand Rapids: Zondervan, 1992.

Trible, Phyllis. *Rhetorical Criticism: Context, Method, and the Book of Jonah*. Minneapolis: Fortress, 1994.

____. *Texts of Terror: Literary-Feminist Readings of Biblical Narratives*. Philadelphia: Fortress, 1984.

Vawter, Bruce. *On Genesis: A New Reading*. London: Geoffrey Chapman, 1977.

Villa-Vicencio, Charles. *Theology and Violence: The South African Debate*. Grand Rapids: Eerdmans, 1988.

Watts, John D. W. *Isaiah 1-33*. WBC. Waco: Word, 1985.

Wenham, Gordon. *Genesis 1-15*. WBC. Waco: Word, 1987.

West, Gerald. *Biblical Hermeneutics of Liberation: Modes of Reading the Bible in the South African Context*, 2nd ed. Maryknoll, N. Y.: Orbis, 1995.

Westermann, Claus. *Genesis 1-11: A Commentary*. Trans. John J. Scullion. Minneapolis: Augsburg, 1984.

____. *Genesis: A Practical Commentary*. Grand Rapids: Eerdmans, 1987.

Wevers, John W. *Ezekiel*, NCBC. Grand Rapids: Eerdmans, 1969.

Wicke, Donald W. "The Literary Structure of Exodus 1:2-2:10," *JOTS* 24(1982): 99-107.

Wilder, Amos N. *The Bible and the Literary Critic*. Minneapolis: Fortress, 1991.

Wilderberger, Hans. *Isaiah 1-12*. Trans. Thomas H. Trapp. Minneapolis: Fortress, 1991.

Williams, James G. *The Bible, Violence, and the Sacred Liberation from the Myth of Sanctioned Violence*. San Francisco: Harper Collins, 1991.

Williamson, H. G. M. "Did the Author of Chronicles also Write the Books of Ezra and Nehemiah?," *BRev*, 3 (1987): 56-59.

____. *I and 2 Chronicles*, NCBC. Grand Rapids: Eerdmans, 1982.

Wink, Walter. *Engaging the Powers: Discernment and Resistance in a World of Domination*. Minneapolis: Fortress, 1992.

van Wolde, Ellen. "The Story of Cain and Able: A Narrative Study," *JSOT* 52 (1991): 25-41.

Wolff, Hans Walter. *Hosea*, trans. Gary Stansell (Philadelphia: Fortress,

1974.

Woudstra, M. H. *The Book of Joshua*, NICOT. Grand Rapids: Eerdmans, 1981.

Wuellner, Wilhelm. "Where Is Rhetorical Criticism Taking Us?" *CBQ* 49 (1987): 448-463.

Zakovitch, Yair. "Humor and Theology or the Successful Failure of Israelite Intelligence." In *Text and Tradition: The Hebrew Bible and Folklore*. Ed. Susan Niditch. Atlanta: Scholars Press, 1990, pp. 75-98.

Zimmerli, Walter. *Ezekiel 1: A Commentary on the Book of the Prophet Ezekiel, chs. 1-24*. Trans. Ronald E. Clements. Philadelphia: Fortress, 1979.

Zimmerli, Walter. *Ezekiel 2: A Commentary on the Book of the Prophet Ezekiel, Chs. 25-48*. Trans. J. D. Martin Philadelphia: Fortress, 1983.

INDEX

Author Index

Scripture Index

References to verses within the primary text interpreted in each chapter are not included in this index. Citations in square brackets, [ ], are verse references in MT when they differ from the English verse reference.

Book design: Marc A. Jolley
Jacket Design: Jim Burt
Jacket Art: *Cain Slaying Abel*, by Peter Paul Rubens
Text font: Book Antiqua
Printer: Edwards Brothers